# Autism

# COGNITIVE DEVELOPMENT

This series presents the work of an outstanding group of scientists working together at the Medical Research Council's Cognitive Development Unit who, in spite of diverse backgrounds, have evolved a common approach to the fundamental issues of cognitive developmental psychology. This is nativist rather than empiricist, focusing on the dynamics of change rather than on stages. Covering a range of topics from early infancy onwards, the series will collectively make up a major, new, coherent position.

# Autism

*Explaining the Enigma*

Uta Frith

Basil Blackwell

Copyright © Uta Frith 1989

Illustrations on pages 59, 75, 87, 88, 121, 133, 134, 137, 152, 153, 160, 162, 164, copyright © Axel Scheffler 1989

First published 1989
Reprinted 1990

Basil Blackwell Ltd
108 Cowley Road, Oxford, OX4 1JF, UK

Basil Blackwell, Inc.
3 Cambridge Center
Cambridge, MA 02142, USA

*British Library Cataloguing in Publication Data*
A CIP catalogue record for this book is available from the British Library.

*Library of Congress Cataloging in Publication Data*
Frith, Uta.
Autism: explaining the enigma.
(Cognitive development)
Bibliography: p.
Includes index.
1. Autism.   I. Title.   II. Series: Cognitive development
(Oxford, England)
RJ506.A9F695 1989      618.92′8982      88–28021
ISBN 0–631–15833–2

Typeset in 10 on 12 pt Plantin
by Columns of Reading

Printed in Great Britain by
Billing & Sons Ltd, Worcester

For Chris, Martin and Alex

# Contents

# Notes on Style

Throughout this book I use a capital A for Autism. This is because I use the word as a shorthand label for the distinctive developmental disorder that is often called early infantile autism, or early childhood autism.

When the pronoun 'he' is used in a general sense then it always includes 'she'. Sometimes I have used the pronoun 'it' to include both 'he' and 'she'.

# Acknowledgements

When I began as a student at the Institute of Psychiatry in London, Chris Frith was my first tutor. He not only taught me psychology but also English. Chris is my first and constant collaborator because he has discussed and transformed all the ideas that surface in this book, well before some of them were tried out in experiments, and well before any of them were written down.

Beate Hermelin and Neil O'Connor started me on the quest for an explanation of Autism. They taught me that it is possible to apply methods of general cognitive psychology to problems of abnormal development. In this and many other things they have always guided me by their example.

John Morton is responsible for the book being written at all. He taught me not to be afraid of theory, and not to be taken in by the illusion of truth conjured up by data. Alan Leslie provided step-by-step discussions of the theoretical framework and continuous refinements of the ideas behind the words. Both John and Alan have read repeated drafts of each chapter. Each time their critical comments resulted in dramatic changes of form and content. These drafts were then typed and retyped with great forbearance by many secretaries under the direction of Amy Davies and Doris Long.

Many other friends have read and commented on portions of the book. Without their expert help it would have been much poorer and less accurate. I would particularly like to thank my colleagues at the Cognitive Development Unit, Mike Anderson, Rick Cromer, Mark Johnson and Annette Karmiloff-Smith. I would also like to thank Christopher Gillberg, Josef Perner, Ros Ridley, Mike Rutter and Deirdre Wilson for the invaluable feedback on chapters they read.

Lorna Wing has given me painstaking help with my understanding of population studies and of the long-term development of autistic children.

My friend Heide Grieve has advised me on historical and literary matters. Philip Carpenter made helpful suggestions concerning the structure of various chapters of the book. Perhaps the most enjoyable aspect of producing the book was having the opportunity to work with Axel Scheffler. I remember the many sketches he discarded before he was satisfied that his wonderfully unconventional illustrations conveyed exactly what was intended. During the long time it took to write the book, my sons, Martin and Alex, have given me much cheerful encouragement, not to mention some spirited but constructive criticism of style!

I owe a huge debt of gratitude to Anthony Attwood, Simon Baron-Cohen, Amitta Shah, Digby Tantam and Rita Jordan. By their creative and diligent work on their doctoral theses, they all gave me a better understanding of Autism and hence helped me to write the book in the first place. I thank them for their critical reading of chapters of the book, but even more I thank them for their crucial contribution to the substance of the book. Siné McDougall, Fran Siddons and Francesca Happé only joined me at the proofreading stages but their help and enthusiasm has been invaluable.

There are other friends who have had a large share in teaching me about Autism and who are also my models of ideal teachers of autistic children. In particular, Wendy Brown, Mick Connelly, Sibyl Elgar and Elizabeth Graves have provided essential support and facilities for research over many years.

If this book is readable, then it is largely due to one single person, namely Margaret Dewey. With her deep knowledge of Autism and her exquisite gift for communication, she has commented in detail on all the sections of this book. More than that, through recasting and rephrasing, she often clarified my thoughts and smoothed out rough edges in the writing. Without her sensitive editing and her insightful questioning, many more problems would have remained unsolved than there undoubtedly still are.

The author and publishers are grateful for permission to quote from J. R. Bemporad, 'Adult recollections of a formerly autistic child', *Journal of Autism and Developmental Disorders*; H. Lane, *The Wild Boy of Aveyron*, published by Unwin Hyman Limited; and from *The Little Flowers of St Francis of Assisi*, translated by Dom Roger Hudleston, published by Burns & Oates Limited.

# 1

# What is Autism?

'She was so pretty – hazel eyes with long curling eyelashes and finely tapered eyebrows, flaxen coloured curls and such a sweet, far-away expression; I hoped against hope that all would eventually go well, and that she was just a slow starter.' This extract from a mother's letter shows us the first of many puzzles of the disorder called 'childhood autism'. The typical image of the child suffering from 'Autism' is most surprising. Those familiar with images of children who suffer from other serious developmental disorders know that these children *look* handicapped. In contrast, more often than not, the young autistic child strikes the observer with a haunting and somehow other-worldly beauty. It is hard to imagine that behind the doll-like image lies a subtle yet devastating defect, a defect as cruel on the child as it is on his family.

What is this defect? How can one explain its many paradoxical features? These are the questions we shall try to understand in the course of this book. To answer these questions we must remove a number of misunderstandings right from the start. The first of these is the belief that Autism is merely a disorder of childhood. We hear a great deal about autistic children, but not much about adults. In fact, Autism starts to be noticed in childhood, but it is not a disorder of childhood. Instead it is a disorder of *development*.

Autism has to be seen not just as a snapshot. Since it is a disorder that affects all of mental development, symptoms will, necessarily, look very different at different ages. Certain features will not become apparent until later; others disappear with time. In fact there is enormous change. To illustrate this, I will sketch an unembellished picture of the life of a prototypical autistic child. Peter is a fictitious case for this purpose. I have put together true observations from many different cases but in such a way that they could well occur together.

When making up the case of Peter I had to choose a particular socio-cultural background. This does not affect the basic nature of the symptoms, only their content. It does not affect the basic course of the disorder, only minor details. This insight is not new. Indeed, many people have expressed their astonishment at how recognizably similar autistic children are, even if they come from different countries and communities. Here we can dispel another misunderstanding about Autism: autistic children are not made autistic by parents who do not love them enough. Autism is a rare and tragic event that can hit anyone, any family, without warning. Its biological origin is likely to be well before birth.

## Peter

Peter is the much-wanted and much-loved son of a well-adjusted and well-to-do family in London. He has a sister who is two years older. In the first year of life Peter did not seem different from any other baby. He cried and laughed at much the same things as his sister had done. In photographs he looks a handsome, healthy and happy baby. If there were any subtle signs of later problems, nobody was aware of them. It was only when he was a toddler that Peter's parents started to worry. He seemed to become more and more different from other children of his age. Unlike his sister, who had started to talk at 12 months, he did not say a word until he was much older. Even more upsetting was that he did not seem to understand anything that was said to him. He did not look up when his name was called. He did not show any interest in listening to or looking at people speaking to him. Instead, he could be totally absorbed in minute examination of a building block. Peter sat on anybody's lap who would hold him as if he was sitting on a soft piece of furniture, and was just as happy if he could sit by himself in another part of the room. When his mother came to pick him up he never stretched out his arms, unlike his little cousin of the same age.

Nobody at first considered that Peter was anything but a very independent, self-sufficient child who was late in talking. It was the grandmother who insisted that Peter's hearing be tested. Was Peter deaf? Perhaps deafness would explain not only why he did not speak, but why he seemed to be so much in a world of his own and took so little part in the world of others. However, this line of explanation was cut short when Peter's hearing was found to be normal and when it became more and more apparent that he was in fact unusually responsive to sounds. He was badly frightened by the noise of the vacuum cleaner. He screamed and screamed and would not calm down, nor did he ever get used to it. Eventually cleaning was done only when Peter was out of the house. On the other hand, Peter was fascinated by the noise of the buses that passed by on the street. He never failed to rush to the window when he heard the familiar engine noise. When he did this he never pointed to the bus, or shouted excitedly, in order to attract somebody's attention. This is what his sister had invariably done when she saw a picture of Mickey Mouse.

Peter's sister, from when she was 18 months, had delighted in playing 'going to the shops', 'having tea', 'putting dollies to bed', but Peter never did anything of the kind. He had a large collection of toy cars, but instead of playing with them in the way his little cousin did, he was interested only in placing them in long straight lines and in closely observing the spinning of the wheels. He never responded to other children coming to play with him. Some time in Peter's third year his parents knew that something must be very wrong. He still did not show any sign of language and in so many respects seemed to be left behind by other children his age. However, he loved music and endlessly listened to Vivaldi's 'Four Seasons'. His parents had heard of Autism, but dismissed the idea because they thought to be autistic meant avoiding people and not showing any emotional responses. Peter, they had noticed, liked to be in the company of people, in fact, preferred to be near his mother and sister, and was happiest when his father played rough-and-tumble games with him. Peter had outbursts of hilarity, and occasionally violent tantrums, although it was very hard to understand why he had them.

When Peter was three years old he was diagnosed as autistic after lengthy interviews, observations and tests. On psychological tests involving language Peter performed very poorly indeed for his age, but on a test where he had to fit geometric shapes together he performed exceedingly well. At home he soon became a wizard at jig-saw puzzles and could even do them picture-side down. This skill in particular gave Peter's mother hope that eventually he would surprise them all and turn out to be an unusually gifted child.

During the time when language and social skills normally develop rapidly, that is, between the ages of three and five, Peter learned these skills extremely slowly and he and his family had to undergo their most difficult period. He was very hard to manage – especially out of the home and out of his routine. Strangers openly commented that the child must be hopelessly spoiled. However, Peter was allowed to do what he liked only because it seemed quite impossible to make him fit in with others' wishes or to interrupt his own routines. Severe tantrums were still common.

At last, Peter started to speak. But language did not open the doors to communication as everyone had hoped would surely happen. Strangely, he often echoed what other people said. Peter was quite indifferent to make-believe play or simple group activities. Cuddly toy animals gave him no particular pleasure. He treated them just like his cars, that is, as things to put in a row. Often the family felt as if there were an invisible wall preventing them from making proper contact with Peter. However much they tried, he never quite became part of any group, whether children or adults. Most of the time it seemed as if he was looking through people not at them.

Peter was very set in his ways and it was extremely tricky to cut his hair which had to be done when he was asleep. He was often seen flapping his hands and looking at them from the corner of his eyes. Sometimes, on the street or in a shop, he made a high-pitched noise and jumped wildly up and down for no accountable reason. It was difficult to travel with him anywhere. The family more and more adapted to him and his rigid ways. They tolerated what could not be changed, but teaching little Peter the mundane living skills such as dressing, eating, washing was a long and tiring struggle. Eventually, with much perseverance, progress was made.

Peter became much easier to manage after his fifth birthday. His language showed marked improvement, though he continued to echo phrases and to use them inappropriately. He spoke in a strange sing-song voice when he was not parroting what other people said. His understanding of language seemed strangely limited. He knew some quite rare words and their meaning, and was able to name all shades of colours. He knew what a dodecahedron was, but he did not seem to know the meaning of such a common word as 'think'.

Peter made excellent progress at a special school. He learned to master many skills, including reading, writing and arithmetic. He learned to swim and enjoyed doing crafts. His drawings were remarkably skilful. Peter's sister was the first to realize that he had memorized all London bus routes by number and destination. Nobody quite knew how he had managed to do this or why. He began to collect anything to do with buses – much to the delight of relatives searching for presents for him. Consequently, his room was soon full of miniature models, posters and maps. Strangely, Peter never actually showed much interest in travelling on buses. A visit to a transport museum left him indifferent.

At age ten Peter was tested by a psychologist and was said to score in the normal range of intelligence on non-verbal tests. On verbal tests he scored in the range of mild retardation.

Given his abilities and his educational achievements, the family was optimistic about Peter's further progress. Other people often commented now on how 'sociable' Peter had become. He was not at all shy and often approached visitors to the house or the school, asking their names and addresses. 'Dulwich,' he would say, 'that is number 12.' Next time they came, the same kind of interchange would take place. Although often he was rather too talkative, in a repetitive sort of way ('today is Monday, yesterday was Sunday, tomorrow is Tuesday'), it was often strangely difficult to get important information from him. For instance, when he was quite badly injured after a fall, he never told anyone about it, and his mother was horrified when she discovered the blood on the clothes as she put them in the washing machine.

In his teens, when his normal peers became independent and more self-conscious, especially about their appearance and the effect they might have on others, Peter seemed markedly ignorant of the effect he made. Yet he often asked, 'Am I right? Am I a good boy?', showing that he cared. Unfortunately, the very fact that he asked these questions in appropriate as well as inappropriate circumstances, and the fact that he became extremely miserable when criticized, revealed how out of touch with reality he was. He was now very tall and still quite good-looking, but he struck anyone who did not know him as extremely childish. From now on it became more obvious, just by looking at him, that he was mentally handicapped. His movements were ungainly and his voice loud and squeaky. He often grimaced and twisted his hands and fingers. He behaved just the same whether in company or alone. He was quite likely to yawn prodigiously and pick his nose when somebody tried to talk to him. It is not surprising that he was never invited to join other teenagers in after-school activities. His mother saw to it that Peter went swimming, which he much enjoyed.

Peter considered a girl at a supermarket check-out his friend because she smiled as she was paid by him. He clearly had no proper understanding of what a friend was, even though every effort was made to explain. Sometimes he had severe bouts of frustration and unhappiness. He realized that he was different, but he could not understand how and why. Peter's understanding was extremely literal. Once, when his mother remarked that his sister was crying her eyes out, he anxiously looked on the floor to see if the eyes were there. Peter did not appreciate teasing. It just made him cross.

Having left school, Peter lived at home. Although he could read very well, he did not read for pleasure. He was often restless and he endlessly pestered others with repetitive talk. He liked to watch television, and was glad to sit in front of the set with others for company. When there was slapstick comedy, he joined in the laughter. As for soap operas, which his mother watched avidly, he could not fathom the plots. Yet he knew all the characters' names and the actors who portrayed them. He liked the goodies to be good and the baddies to be bad, but was confused if somebody was a bit of both.

Peter is now over 30 years old and still lives at home. He leads a simple life. He helps with the filing and tea-making at his mother's office, and copies labels in neat writing. He also helps with the gardening and with household chores. Every day he paces round the lawn on exactly the same track. Peter is still totally naive and does not understand the ways of the world, for instance, why people lie or cheat. Adulthood for Peter is not a stage of maturity, but rather permanent immaturity. This seems to suit his youthful appearance. His voice remains loud and peculiar, his gait is stiff and ungainly, and his posture slouched. He does not have any girlfriends and this makes him sad. The independent living that his parents had hoped for seems out of reach.

Peter's family are aware that there are other autistic individuals who have few practical skills, who are difficult to cope with, and who have remained mute forever. They appreciate that Peter has come a long way from the days when he looked 'through people' and would not speak at all. But they are worried what will happen to him when they can no longer look after him. They fear that in an indifferent environment he could fall into neglect or become prey to exploitation.


What does Peter's story tell us? Perhaps the most obvious point is that the clinical picture of childhood Autism is very different at different ages. There is inexorable change: there are ups and downs, there are setbacks and there is progress. The story also tells us that a relatively able individual who had the benefit of an excellent upbringing can become reasonably well adapted. All the same, there is still a handicap. This is both sad and strangely puzzling. Mental development is not only distorted and delayed but, if its aim is maturity, then this aim is never reached. On the other hand, physical maturity is reached, and there are considerable achievements in isolated areas. There is accumulation of knowledge and there is mastery of various skills. Despite many prerequisites for leading a normal adult life, existence for somebody like Peter remains curiously restricted and abnormal.

What is this extraordinarily puzzling disorder that is at once so subtle and so vicious in its effects? That allows so much developmental progress to happen and yet cruelly prevents full integration into the adult community? From the very beginning of awareness of such strange developmental patterns, people have attempted to answer this question. In the two following chapters, we shall consider some of the debates and the colourful as well as sober answers that are to be found in story and history. What we shall turn to next, however, are the beginnings of the scientific recognition of Autism.

## How Autism was First Recognized

Any treatment of the topic of childhood Autism must start with the pioneers Leo Kanner and Hans Asperger who, independently of each other, first published accounts of this disorder. These publications, Kanner's in 1943[1] and Asperger's in 1944[2], contained detailed case descriptions and also offered the first theoretical attempts to explain the disorder. Both authorities believed that there was present from birth a fundamental disturbance which gave rise to highly characteristic problems.

It seems a remarkable coincidence that both chose the word 'autistic' in order to characterize the nature of the underlying disturbance. In fact, it is not really a coincidence, since the label had already been introduced by the eminent psychiatrist Eugen Bleuler in 1911. It originally referred to a basic disturbance in schizophrenia (another term coined by Bleuler), namely the narrowing of relationships to people and to the outside world, a narrowing so extreme that it seemed to exclude everything except the person's own self. This narrowing could be described as a withdrawal from the fabric of social life into the self. Hence the words 'autistic' and 'autism', from the Greek word *autos* meaning 'self'. Today they are applied almost exclusively to the developmental disorder that we here call Autism, with a capital A. I prefer to use Autism rather than 'early infantile autism' or 'childhood autism', terms which imply some contrast to 'adult autism', and may wrongly suggest that one can grow out of it.

Both Kanner, working in Baltimore, and Asperger, working in Vienna, saw cases of strange children who had in common some fascinating features. Above all the children seemed to be unable to entertain normal affective relationships with people. In contrast to Bleuler's schizophrenia the disturbance appeared to have been there from the beginning.

Kanner's paper has become the most quoted in the whole literature on Autism, Asperger's paper, written in German, and published during the Second World War, was largely ignored. The belief has grown that Asperger described quite a different type of child, not to be confused with the one Kanner described. This belief has no basis, as we see when we look at the original papers. Asperger's definition of Autism or, as he called it, 'autistic psychopathy' is far wider than Kanner's. Asperger included cases that showed severe organic damage and those that shaded into normality. Nowadays, the label 'Asperger's syndrome' tends to be reserved for the rare intelligent and highly verbal, near-normal autistic child.[3] This is clearly not what Asperger intended, but having this special category has proved clinically useful. Kanner's syndrome is nowadays often used to indicate the child with a constellation of classic, 'nuclear' features, resembling in astonishing detail the features that Kanner identified in his first, inspired description. Again, the category is clinically useful since it communicates a prototypical pattern.

In this book we shall not use these labels nor argue about possible subgroups of Autism. Instead, we shall be concerned with identifying the common denominator in all cases of Autism. This, of course, does not preclude the existence of subgroups. Indeed it is an essential step towards further refinement in diagnostic categorization.

### How Kanner and Asperger Described Autism

Kanner published his paper entitled 'Autistic Disturbances of Affective Contact' in the now extinct journal *Nervous Child*: 'Since 1938, there have come to our attention a number of children whose condition differs so markedly and uniquely from anything reported so far, that each case merits – and, I hope, will eventually receive – a detailed consideration of its fascinating pecularities.'

He proceeds to present vivid pictures of the 11 children he considered to be suffering from this condition. The paper ends with a concise discussion and comments section. Some quotes from this part of the paper can illustrate the incisiveness of Kanner's observations. They will also serve as a reference point for the most important features of classic Autism. These features, autistic aloneness, desire for sameness and islets of ability, are discernible in all true cases, despite variation in details and despite the coexistence of additional problems.

Regarding 'autistic aloneness':

> The outstanding, 'pathognomonic', fundamental disorder is the children's inability to relate themselves in the ordinary way to people and situations from the beginning of life.
>
> There is from the start an extreme autistic aloneness that, whenever possible, disregards, ignores, shuts out anything that comes to the child from the outside.

He has a good relation to objects; he is interested in them, can play with them happily for hours . . . the child's relation to people is altogether different . . . Profound aloneness dominates all behaviour.

Regarding 'desire for sameness':

The child's noises and motions and all his performances are as monotonously repetitious as are his verbal utterances. There is a marked limitation in the variety of his spontaneous activities. The child's behaviour is governed by an anxiously obsessive desire for the maintenance of sameness . . .

Regarding 'islets of ability':

The astounding vocabulary of the speaking children, the excellent memory for events of several years before, the phenomenal rote memory for poems and names, and the precise recollection of complex patterns and sequences, bespeak good intelligence.

Kanner's main conclusion is in the form of a bold statement that he himself liked to quote in later papers.

We must, then, assume that these children have come into the world with innate inability to form the usual biologically provided affective contact with people, just as other children come into the world with innate physical or intellectual handicaps.

Asperger, who seems to avoid concise formulations, does not offer as many opportunities for quotations. His strength lies in detailed, lively and sympathetic descriptions. His attempts to relate autistic behaviour to normal variations of personality and intelligence demonstrate a unique approach to the understanding of Autism. This is how he introduced his case studies:

In what follows I will describe a type of child which is of interest in a number of ways: the children have in common a fundamental disturbance which manifests itself very characteristically in all behavioural and expressive phenomena. This disturbance results in considerable and very typical difficulties of social integration. In many cases, the failure to be integrated in a social group is the most conspicuous feature, but in other cases this failure is compensated for by particular originality of thought and experience, which may well lead to exceptional achievements in later life.

The behavioural and expressive phenomena that Asperger referred to are captured in the following observations:

The characteristic peculiarity of gaze never fails to be present . . . They do not make eye contact . . . they seem to take in things with short peripheral glances.'

There is a poverty of facial expression and gestures . . . yet there are many stereotypic movements. These do not express meaning . . .

The use of language always appears abnormal, unnatural.

The children totally follow their own impulses, regardless of the demands of the environment.

The children are simply not geared towards learning from adults or teachers.

They have isolated areas of interest.

There can be excellent ability of logical abstract thinking.

There are original word creations.

Like Kanner, Asperger suggested independently that there is a 'disturbance of contact' at some deep level of affect and/or instinct. Both stressed the peculiarities of communication and the difficulties in social adaptation of autistic children. Both paid particular attention to movement stereotypies and to the puzzling, very patchy pattern of intellectual achievements. Both were impressed by occasional feats of intellectual prowess in narrow areas.

How are these odd and diverse features to be explained and how are they related? In the course of this book we shall attempt to arrive at a theory which can make sense both of the symptoms and of the extraordinary fact that the symptoms occur together.


### Kanner's Cardinal Features

Despite all the variety of individual differences that appear in the case descriptions, Kanner was convinced that only two features were of cardinal significance. What this means is that he thought them necessary and possibly sufficient for the diagnosis of Autism. These features refer not directly to behaviour, but to psychological problems at a level deep enough to explain a large range of behaviours. We shall examine these at length when we discuss them in the light of recent empirical evidence.

The main feature, and the one that gave the name to the disorder is *autistic aloneness*. Exactly what this is cannot be identified with a specific behaviour. It can only be inferred from behaviour. In particular, it can be inferred from certain impairments of ordinary two-way communications. Asperger spoke of autistic children never being on the same wavelength as their normal peers in any group activity. This intangible difference of autistic children, pervading all sorts of behaviour, is highly conspicuous to the experienced clinician. Theirs is not just any social abnormality. In particular it is not the same as shyness, rejection or avoidance of human contact, although autistic behaviour has sometimes been interpreted in this way. *Autistic aloneness*, as we shall see, has nothing to do with being alone physically, but it does have to do with being alone mentally.

The second cardinal feature was termed *obsessive insistence on sameness*. Again Kanner identified an inferred quality at a deep level. This densely formulated concept suggests several factors at once: repetitiveness, rigidity, singlemindedness, pedantry, and inability to judge the significance of subtle differences.

Examples of behaviours which relate to obsessive insistence on sameness come from three related categories: first, there are simple repetitive movements, utterances and thoughts. Second, and unique to autistic children, are so-called elaborate routines, demonstrated in action, language or thought, without apparent purpose. Third, there is pursuit of extremely narrow topics of interest, a preoccupation to the exclusion of almost everything else. It is not surprising that diagnostic schemes have particular difficulty with the concept of elaborate routines. It is the least explored of all the features of Autism, notwithstanding its status as a cardinal symptom.

### Diagnostic Criteria Today

In international collaboration, experts have agreed to use certain behavioural criteria for the diagnosis of Autism. These have been made explicit in published reference works. The most detailed and most recent scheme is the one described in the Diagnostic and Statistical Manual (DSM-III-R) of the American Psychiatric Association.[4] A very similar diagnostic scheme is available in the International Classification of Diseases (ICD-10) issued by the World Health Organization.[5] The essential criteria are specified by concrete examples under the following headings:

Qualitative impairment in reciprocal social interaction.

Qualitative impairment in verbal and non-verbal communication, and in imaginative activity.

Markedly restricted repertoire of activities and interests.

Kanner's main symptom, 'autistic aloneness', is still the first and most important symptom for all attempts at diagnosis. It is also generally stipulated that the disorder should be of early onset, that is, before age three. Nevertheless, it is recognized that there are exceptional cases with later onset due to sudden viral disease or similar causes.

An important criterion for diagnosis today concerns impairments of language and communication. Its importance stems from the fact that it tends to be the most frequent cause for clinic referral initially. Impairments can range from no speech at all to merely delayed language acquisition and odd usage of language, including gestures and body language. It has been recognized that there can be profound impairment in the ability to engage in meaningful communication despite adequate speech. Current diagnostic schemes also pay particular attention to the abnormal lack of imaginative activity. This refers to absence of pretend play as well as lack of interest in typical fictional stories.

An enduring criterion for diagnosis concerns the various repetitive and restrictive phenomena that are implicit in Kanner's second cardinal symptom, the 'obsessive desire for sameness'. Elaborate routines, rituals, peculiar preoccupations and oddly narrow interests are unique features of more able autistic children. They are virtually never found in any other condition in early childhood. Severely mentally retarded autistic children, as a rule, show only the simplest repetitive behaviours, but show them excessively. Even bright autistic children are likely to exhibit simple stereotypic movements, such as hand flapping, in addition to more complex repetitive routines. Resistance to change in routines is a common feature, but need not be present in all cases.

Whether or not a symptom is seen as primary, secondary, or merely optional, varies according to the overall interpretation of the clinical picture. As we review the available evidence in the following chapters, we shall arrive at a reasoned view of the nature and importance of the various signs and symptoms of Autism. We shall aim to find out how all the symptoms fit together and how they are related. Could they all be surface manifestations of a single underlying abnormality? What could this abnormality be? Before we can directly tackle these questions it is necessary to prepare the way. We have to sort fact from fiction and we shall have to eliminate some long-standing confusions and misconceptions about how Autism is recognized and how it might be caused. This will be the task of chapters 2 to 6. Three frequent questions can however be dealt with immediately: Is it difficult to diagnose Autism? How early can it be recognized? What happens to the autistic child after growing up?

*Is Autism difficult to diagnose?*

The diagnosis of Autism is based on behaviour. Interpreting the significance of deviant, absent or delayed behaviour depends on a sound background of clinical knowledge.[6] Since Autism is a rare disorder, there are relatively few experts who have the experience of a large number of cases. But experience matters. Experience allows diagnosticians to sense quickly that elusive feature, autistic aloneness. At that stage, however, they will consider Autism only as an hypothesis to be checked out systematically. They will listen at length to the family and carefully observe the patient. They will administer psychological tests and construct a history of the course of the disorder from the beginning. In this way, Autism can be diagnosed reliably.

In order to evaluate autistic symptoms it is necessary to take into account the age of the child and, even more importantly, its mental age. There are behaviours which children cannot show below a certain mental age. For instance, below two years the average child cannot be expected to talk in grammatical sentences. All this should be obvious to an expert, but the well-meaning amateur often does not realize what a difference mental age makes.

Diagnosticians often differ when it comes to borderline cases. Therefore it is possible that a child may be labelled autistic at one centre and something else at another. This worries lay people who may wrongly jump to the conclusion that it is impossible to diagnose Autism, and that different authorities are talking about different conditions when they talk about autistic children. The conclusion is unwarranted. In fact there is strong consensus among experienced clinicians.

If a young child is referred on the basis of queries regarding social and intellectual development, the possibility of Autism needs to be considered. However, many other possibilities must be considered as well. Questions to be asked include: Is this a developmentally delayed child who will catch up eventually? Is there a serious neurological or sensory defect that impedes normal development? Is this child specifically impaired in language development? A glance at a textbook of child psychiatry will show that there are a great number of developmental abnormalities.[7] In addition, there are some borderline or unclassifiable disorders. Often they are designated as such to avoid the risk of inappropriate classification. In this respect Autism is no exception.

*How early can Autism be recognized?*

If Autism is a disorder that in most cases the child is born with, then one might expect that something wrong should be noticeable within the first few months. Actually, if something wrong is noticed very early, it often turns out to be a false alarm. When the child is very young the possibility of developmental delay, with the possibility of catching up at some time in the future, must always be considered. In the case of extensive brain abnormality with consequent severe mental retardation, there are clear early signs. But it is another question how early we can see specific signs of Autism. In chapter 4, we shall see that lack of social and emotional responsiveness is widespread in non-autistic mentally handicapped children. Even in otherwise normal children there can be transient problems in social development. These may be reminiscent of childhood Autism. Of course, the temporary nature of the problems will be perceived with hindsight. It would be ridiculous to speak of Autism being 'cured' in such a case. Yet such claims have been made!

We can continue in the assumption that in most cases Autism exists from birth. This does not mean that we have to assume that symptoms have to be present from birth. A clear-cut example that shows how separate the onset of a disease is from the first appearance of symptoms is Huntington's chorea. Here a genetic defect, existing from conception, does not manifest itself until late adulthood.

In the well-documented cases of Elly (Park),[8] David (Everard)[9] and Simon (Lovell),[10] the parents all reported that the first flickers of anxiety were not experienced until some time in the second year. Anne Lovell, the mother of Simon, says, 'It is to my mind one of the most exquisitely cruel aspects of Early Childhood Autism that it only becomes apparent to the parents very slowly that there is anything wrong with the child.'

Here we are back to the chilling image of the healthy and beautiful child who innocently harbours the devastating time bomb of Autism.

### What happens to the autistic child after growing up?

Kanner and especially Asperger in their earliest descriptions made the point that Autism is not a progressive disease. For this reason, Asperger chose 'psychopathy' in preference to 'psychosis' as a name for the disorder. He emphasized that, contrary to the process of deterioration which is frequently seen in adult psychoses, his patients showed increased adaptation and compensation. So convinced was he of this that he may well have presented too optimistic a picture of outcome. Possibly, emphasis on good outcome may have contributed to the misunderstanding of Asperger's syndrome as something altogether different from Autism. Asperger's rather rosy view must be seen in the light of his fervent belief in the powers of education and the possibilities of compensation for a deficiency that he himself acknowledged as persistent.

What has emerged from studies of now adult autistic individuals? The general conclusion must be that Autism, like mental retardation, does not go away, despite changes in behaviour.[11] Nevertheless, autistic people can, and often do, compensate for their handicap to a remarkable degree. They may be guided to a niche in society where their assets are put to good use. They may remain at home as helpful companions to ageing parents who understand them. There are less favourable outcomes too. However, one must remember that to predict the future of an individual autistic child is just as uncertain as it is in the case of a normal child. As far as social behaviour is concerned, the extreme aloofness of many young autistic children often subsides. Whatever type of therapy or teaching is applied, and whatever improvement occurs, in the experienced clinician's assessment there remains a persistent if subtle deficit. The persistence is another puzzle and also another clue in our search for an answer. It appears that there is something that is missing, something that cannot be corrected or substituted.

Autism is a recognizable entity, not only because of the characteristic set of clinical features, but also because it follows a characteristic time course. A most important point – and one we shall come back to again and again – is that Autism is a developmental disorder. What this means is that the whole of development will be affected from infancy onwards. If a mental disorder first manifests itself when the development of various abilities is completed, we expect breakdown, perhaps regression or progressive deterioration – but all superimposed on previously established skills. With a developmental disorder of early origin the very process of building up experience is affected. What this means for our search for explanations is that it would be wrong merely to focus on separate features, fascinating as these may be. It is easy to get sidetracked by bizarre and flamboyant detail, but we have to see details as small pieces of a larger puzzle. The pieces will have to be fitted together into a coherent picture, a picture which takes account of developmental forces.

# 2

# Lessons from the Wild Boy

Autism is not a modern phenomenon, even though it has only been recognized in modern times. In view of the short history of psychiatry, and the even shorter history of child psychiatry, we know that a disorder recently described is not necessarily a recent disorder. An increase in diagnosed cases does not necessarily mean an increase in cases. There are tantalizing hints of Autism in the medical records of history.

A case description by the apothecary of Bethlem Hospital, the London mental asylum, has often been quoted and never contested, as early evidence of Autism. The case was that of a five-year old boy who was admitted in 1799. It was particularly noted that this boy never engaged in play with other children or became attached to them, but played in an absorbed, isolated way with toy soldiers.

There are several other intriguing possibilities that provide historical evidence. There are the 'blessed fools' of Old Russia, whose relevance to Autism remained unrecognized until recently, when pointed out by the eminent scholar of Russian history Horace W. Dewey. These we shall briefly consider in the following chapter. The evidence to be discussed in this chapter has already been much quoted in relation to Autism and comes from so-called feral children. These are rare children who grew up in the wild, outside human contact of any kind, had no language, and were so different from ordinary folk that they were classified in the Linnaean system as a different species, *Homo ferus*. When these unfortunate creatures were captured into society, attitudes towards feral children were not unlike those towards rare zoo-animals. They evoked baffled incomprehension, but also kind solicitude and scientific curiosity.

There are two well-documented cases of the late eighteenth and early nineteenth century: the 'wild boy of Aveyron' and the mysterious case of Kaspar Hauser. We will look at these accounts in some detail, since they are not merely of historical interest. Amongst other things they will allow us to examine two causes of Autism that were discussed then and are still being considered today: the biological and the social-environmental.

The common background of the two cases is formed by the most heartrending and extreme circumstances of social deprivation. Could prolonged severe deprivation of human contact result in Autism? The two cases might help us to answer this question. Did they both show the elusive feature of 'autistic aloneness'? This feature, as we already saw, is not the same as total withdrawal from human contact, but something more subtle, something that can take many different forms and can manifest itself quite differently at different stages of development. Would this feature be identifiable across a vast distance of time and culture? Can we, in cases that were described 200 years ago, identify critical similarities with children diagnosed autistic today? If so, then we might be able to distil those features that are the essence of the disorder beyond our immediate time and cultural context.

### The Case of the Wild Boy of Aveyron

In the last years of the eighteenth century, the intellectual and fashionable world was enthralled by the case of a wild boy who had been found in a forest of central France. The boy, who appeared to be 12 years old, did not speak, did not respond to questions, did not even respond to noises made next to him. He had no clothes and his body was covered in scars. His whole appearance and range of behaviour seemed totally asocial.

Here, then, seemed to be a boy who provided an ideal example of what a human being would be like who grew up outside human society. Some believed that such a child would be truly savage and bereft of all moral sensibility. Others on the contrary thought that he would reveal pure human virtues unspoilt by society. A few, however, considered the possibility that brain pathology might be present in such a child. If this were true, the example would lose its point. Indeed, some eminent physicians who examined the child found him similar to other children 'of incomplete and damaged constitutions'. They believed that the boy's muteness and strangeness was due to 'constitutional imbecility'. This theory also provided a reason for the boy's living in the wild at all. Perhaps desperate, impoverished parents had abandoned the boy because he was seriously abnormal. They might even have intended to kill him, a conjecture based on a serious wound on his throat.

Public fancy was not captured by this relatively simple explanation, but instead was intrigued by a social-environmental explanation. The

# DE L'ÉDUCATION

## D'UN HOMME SAUVAGE,

OU

## DES PREMIERS DÉVELOPPEMENS PHYSIQUES ET MORAUX

DU

## JEUNE SAUVAGE DE L'AVEYRON.

Par E. M. ITARD, Médecin de l'Institution Nationale des Sourds-Muets, Membre de la Société Médicale de Paris, etc.

---

Quand on dit que cet enfant ne donnait aucun signe de raison, ce n'est pas qu'il ne raisonnât suffisamment pour veiller à sa conservation; mais c'est que sa réflexion, jusqu'alors appliquée à ce seul objet, n'avait point eu occasion de se porter sur ceux dont nous nous occupons.......................... Le plus grand fonds des idées des hommes est dans leur commerce réciproque.

CONDILLAC.

---

A PARIS,

Chez GOUJON fils, Imprimeur-Libraire, rue Taranne, No. 737.

VENDÉMIAIRE AN X. (1801).

Figure 2.1 *Title page of Itard's treatise* On the Education of a Wild Man, or The Beginnings of Physical and Moral Development of the Wild Boy of Aveyron

Reproduced by kind permission of The British Library

Figure 2.2  *Contemporary portrait of Victor (c. 1775–1828)*

Reproduced by kind permission of The British Library

idea was that the boy, who was named Victor, had been a perfectly
normal child who through an unkown fate was lost or abandoned when
still very young. By living outside human society he was stunted in his
development to the point of appearing mentally retarded. Language, of
course, would never have been acquired, through lack of opportunity.
The burning question was: Could Victor be educated? Could he be
brought back from his savage state into the civilized world? Itard, a
physician fascinated by this question, took on the challenge. By doing so
he became one of the pioneers of special education. The story of Victor's

education has become well known recently through a magnificent film by Truffaut which was closely based on Itard's own writings.

### Was Victor autistic?

In his scholarly study of the wild boy of Aveyron, Harlan Lane discusses the possibility that Victor was an autistic child.[1] Lane's account includes translations of Itard's reports on Victor's education and other relevant documents and provides a most valuable and comprehensive case history. Lane points out how similar many of Victor's behavioural oddities are to those found in autistic children, but nevertheless rejects Autism as the correct diagnosis. Curiously he considered that Autism was ruled out on the basis of the following well documented observations: (1) Victor showed rapid changes in mood, provoked by identifiable causes, usually by his transactions with people. (2) He was not profoundly withdrawn from people, but showed affection to those who were kind to him. He had a desire to please, but also often reacted with rage against people when provoked. (3) He did not show a maniacal concern for order. (4) He had no difficulty with practical manipulation. (5) He had gestural language and was, within his limits, communicative. The question is, do these observations really rule out Autism?

We have already seen in the previous chapter that any of the observations would fit older autistic children very well. Why are they thought to be incompatible with Autism? Such a belief would arise from the erroneous notion that Autism can be diagnosed at any point in the child's development by a single set of behavioural criteria. However, it is simply wrong to expect that a young autistic child's profound withdrawal and insistence on sameness will remain identifiable hallmarks throughout life. Perhaps it was necessary to wait 20 to 40 years – that is, as long as it took the first generation of psychiatrically identified autistic children to grow up into adults – before this truth could emerge. The full picture of the disorder, as I have emphasized already, is one of development. Total indifference to social contact or profound withdrawal is rarely seen after age five, and in any case is not a unique behavioural criterion of Autism. The cardinal feature of 'autistic aloneness' is evident in more subtle ways throughout the life of the autistic individual.

Therefore, evidence that Victor was responsive to people (Lane's points 1 and 2) does not rule out that he was autistic. There is ambiguous evidence that suggests that he may or may not have shown obsessive desire for order (point 3). But this is not critical in terms of current diagnostic procedure. Repetitive behaviour is frequently but not necessarily continuously present in Autism and can take very many different forms. The evidence pointing to Victor's good practical ability (point 4), as in handling objects or doing certain chores, is perfectly compatible with Autism. Indeed, an excellent ability to manipulate objects is frequently observed – often in contrast to poor ability in manipulating people. Autistic children also have considerable if limited competence with gestures, and have the ability to communicate at least to some extent (point 5). Therefore, in the light of current knowledge, none of Harlan Lane's considered objections cast doubt on the diagnosis of Autism.

### More evidence for Autism

If we can dismiss the objections so readily, what then of the evidence that can be considered directly suggestive of Autism? For this purpose, we can use the evidence from the first scientific paper written about the case, by the distinguished Abbé Pierre-Joseph Bonnaterre, Professor of Natural History at the Central School for Aveyron. This was in 1800, before Victor had received any systematic education.

*Evidence of a serious impairment in reciprocal social interactions*

His affections are as limited as his knowledge; he loves no one; he is attached to no one; He shows some preference for his caretaker, but as an expression of a need and not out of a feeling of gratitude; he follows him, because the man is concerned with satisfying his needs and appeasing his hunger . . . I led him one day to the home of Citizen Rodat . . . All had been arranged for his welcome. Beans, potatoes, chestnuts and walnuts, were prepared, the only food Victor would eat at first. The abundance of food pleased him greatly. Without paying any attention to the people around him, he grabbed the beans, placed them in a pot, added water, and put the pot on the fire . . .

This anecdote is comically reminiscent of a story I was told by Margaret Dewey. She invited an autistic young man of high academic ability to dine at her home for their first meeting. On entering the house, Sidney immediately strode to the kitchen, where he seasoned the entire dinner to his liking. Only then did he return and accept the proffered handshake and introduction. While the anecdote about Victor could conceivably be attributed to his total lack of training in manners, the same excuse cannot be made for Sidney, whose cultured family made every effort to indoctrinate him with the basic rules of politeness.

The oddness of Victor's relationship to people can be evaluated more clearly from later reports, after he had already had several years of education in Itard's house. Highly revealing is the statement that Victor had 'no sense of gratitude toward the man who feeds him, but takes the food as he would take it from the ground'. Also, he was said to be totally unaware of the fact that no one was obliged to feed him, and quite oblivious to being served by the hand of a pretty girl. These observations seem as pertinent for modern-day autistic adolescents as they apparently were for Victor. All these behavioural signs are pointers to the elusive but critical feature of 'autistic aloneness'.

*Evidence of specific intellectual impairment*

> He reflects on nothing, therefore he has no judgement, no imagination, no memory. His imbecility is evident in his gaze, as he does not fix his attention on anything. It is evident in his vocalizations, which are discordant, inarticulate, and can be heard night and day; in his gait, walking as he does always at a trot or a gallop; in his actions, which lack purpose and determination.'

The chief examples that can be taken as signs of hidden intelligence are from Victor's expert conduct in preparing a meal of beans. There he showed economy and suppleness of movement, planning and coordination of several activities, such as shelling the beans, separating the bad ones, throwing the empty pods on the fire and getting water. This sort of feat would not normally be expected from a severely retarded child. But it is exactly the kind of task that can be performed as a reliable routine by an autistic individual whose interest is engaged by it. For instance, otherwise very retarded and mute autistic adolescents can learn to wash cars, clean rooms, prepare vegetables, lay the table and so forth.

It is interesting to note that, in the first overall assessment of Victor's intellectual capacity quoted above, gaze, voice and gait are all mentioned as peculiar. These three channels of non-verbal expression are just as critically involved in social communication as is language. They are always noticeably abnormal in autistic individuals beyond the age of ten. Abnormalities of ordinary communication are also signs that point to Autism.

*Evidence of a characteristic impairment of sensory attention*

> The shrillest cries, the most harmonious sounds make no impression on his ear . . . and he shows no awareness of noises made next to him; but if a cupboard that contains his favourite foods is opened, if walnuts, to which he is very partial, are cracked behind him, . . . he will turn around to seize them.

It is a striking observation in almost all accounts of autistic children that they have been thought deaf at one time, yet that they also have unusually sensitive perception of certain sounds.

*Evidence of lack of imaginative play*  Victor was reported to be 'indifferent to all childish amusements'. 'When he is alone he is happy to sleep, for he has nothing to do after he has eaten, and he almost never plays . . . He likes to run bits of straw through his teeth and suck the juice out of them – that is his favourite amusement.'

*Evidence for stereotypies*  The first reports contain some descriptions of how Victor fills the empty hours that must be created by his lack of imagination as much as by his lack of social interaction or interest.

> He normally wakes at dawn: then he takes a sitting position, wraps his head and body in his blanket. He rocks back and forth and lies down intermittently, until it is time for breakfast. During these periods, which could be called recreation, he wants neither to get up and start the day nor leave his room . . . [later in the afternoon] when he has no beans to shell, he retires to his room, stretches out on the straw, wraps himself up in his blanket and rocks back and forth or goes to sleep.

## What became of Victor?

It was with extraordinary courage that Itard, in 1801, took on a formidable task: to educate Victor in his own home. This courage was the more remarkable as Pinel, the most eminent physician of the day, and experienced with disorders of the mind, examined Victor and declared that he was 'congenitally retarded', and that there was no hope of turning him into a normal child. Pinel was right, yet Itard showed that education did lead to dramatic improvements in the quality of Victor's life. Despite remaining mute, Victor had many accomplishments, such as a certain amount of useful sign language. The young savage from the forest of Aveyron had made incredible progress.

Most unexpected, however, even for those who had only modest hopes for him, was that he never learned the meaning of some basic social values. He never showed evidence of friendship or pity, nor embarrassment, and he retained what was described as unbounded egoism. This observation again fits extraordinarily well with modern-day autistic adults. Itard, after five years of inspired teaching, resigned and stated in his final report that the education of the young man was still incomplete, and would probably always remain so.

Ironically, while Victor was able to survive alone in the wild, he was unable to live independently in society. Mme Guérin, the woman Itard had engaged to look after Victor, was given a stipend to continue to look after him. He lived in her house until he died in his forties. Many authorities, including Édouard Séguin, one of the founders of psychology as a science, and Franz Gall, the famous promotor of phrenology, investigated Victor in his later years. They all concluded that he was 'a true idiot', meaning he was similar to other people they knew as mentally defective from birth.

### The mystery of the wild boy

There are three pertinent questions that Lane puts against the possibility that Victor was autistic: (1) How could a psychotic child have survived in the wild? (2) Are *all* feral children to be presumed psychotic? (3) What is there about Victor's deviant behaviour in society that cannot be explained by his adaptive behaviour in the forest?

The first question is as difficult to answer as it would be to explain how a young normal child could have survived alone. We do not know at what age Victor was abandoned. Lane suggests he was left at five, since before this age it would be difficult to imagine that any child, healthy or not, could have survived in the conditions that he lived in. On the other hand, to assume that he was abandoned much later would make the muteness more difficult to explain. Yet there is quite a good pointer towards Victor's age when he was abandoned. For two years prior to his capture he had been sighted on several occasions, and during a hard winter people had been readily prepared to feed him and take care of him when he appeared near a village. When he was captured, again during a severe winter, he was thought to be about 12. This would suggest that he was abandoned not much before age ten. Even at that age, it is astonishing that he was able to survive for two years. Without shelter and clothing, he had to tolerate extremes of weather and hunger, not only lack of comfort. Could an autistic child do this? Curiously, in quite independent accounts, it has often been said that autistic individuals may tolerate extremes of pain, hunger and temperature without complaint. Altogether, autistic individuals seem to be peculiarly qualified – better than normal children are – to lead the rugged, solitary life that Victor lived when roaming the forests. In the case of a normal child it would be more difficult to explain why he did not seek refuge with people. Villagers, by all accounts, were often nearby and ready to help him. If he was autistic this may not have occurred to him. Perhaps he found it impossible to differentiate well-meaning people from creatures of the wild.

This point also goes some way towards answering Lane's second question: Are all feral children autistic? From what we have just discussed it may be inferred that an unduly high proportion of feral children suffered from Autism before they were abandoned. Indeed

Autism with its often severe conduct problems may be the cause for the abandonment in the first place. On the other hand, it would be ridiculous to assume that all feral children would be autistic. There are, no doubt, different reasons for young children being lost, hidden, isolated or abandoned, and different reasons for their survival in isolation.

The third question turned on the point of parsimony of explanation. What else is needed to explain Victor's odd behaviour but his prolonged social deprivation? Let us take an example from a different handicap: we might compare somebody who is deaf with somebody of normal hearing brought up in a totally noiseless world. Would the inappropriate responses of the two people tested in a normal environment be indistinguishable? Even if they were, would we say therefore that it does not add anything to know that one of them is actually deaf? The hearing person, as long as his or her auditory system did not suffer permanent damage from disuse, could be educated to comprehend the meaning of sounds and to speak. For the deaf person, teaching sign language might be more appropriate. I think it adds much to the evaluation of Victor's limited progress to know he was autistic. He could not learn to comprehend what he was not able to perceive.

Perhaps we can answer the question in another way. In the case of the wild boy of Aveyron, it is very difficult to understand how his characteristically odd behaviour could have been considered entirely shaped by and truly adaptive to his life in the wild. He was undersized and underweight, he suffered many wounds, and he was eventually driven by extreme weather into the vicinity of villages. Once he was 'tamed', he preferred human company to the wild. His behaviour recorded in later years shows much change and a high degree of adaptation to the requirements of the Itard household. At the same time, the oddness of his newly acquired behaviour that is evident in many examples fits in so well with modern descriptions of autistic children that the resemblance seems uncanny. One last example, taken from Lane's rendering of an eyewitness description, helps to illustrate this contention.

It is a description that is heavily biased towards the idea that it is truly civilization that stands between modern man and savage. Only through an enlightened education, exerting its influence from earliest childhood, was it conceivable that moral behaviour would develop. Only by education would a child be integrated into society. This theory was part of the mainstream Enlightenment philosophy that flowered in the eighteenth century.

Itard and Victor were guests at a dinner in the house of the celebrated Mme Récamier.

> Mme Récamier seated him [Victor] at her side, thinking perhaps that the same beauty that had captivated civilised man would receive similar homage from this child of nature, who seemed not yet 15 years old . . . Too occupied with the abundant things to eat, which he devoured with startling greed as soon as his plate was filled, the young savage hardly heeded the beautiful eyes whose attention he himself attracted. When dessert was served, and he had adroitly filled his pockets with all the delicacies that he could filch, he calmly left the table . . . Suddenly a noise came from the garden, and M. Itard was led to suppose his pupil was the cause . . . We soon glimpsed [him] running across the lawn with the speed of a rabbit. To give himself more freedom of movement, he had stripped to his undershirt. Reaching the main avenue of the park . . . he tore his last garment in two, as if it were simply made of gauze; then, climbing the nearest tree with the ease of a squirrel, he perched in the middle of the branches.

The story continues with the boy not heeding Itard's entreaties to come down, leaping from tree to tree in the process. Eventually, it was the gardener who enticed him down by showing him a basket of peaches. Victor let himself be hurriedly covered and bundled off home in a carriage. The guests were left to discuss the 'perfection of civilised life and the distressing picture of nature untamed'.

What this account illustrates vividly is how 'autistic aloneness' is evident even if the autistic person is in the midst of company and enjoying himself. The aloneness is poignant because of an inability to understand states of mind. It is as if, for Victor, minds did not exist. It follows that he is unconcerned about the effect his behaviour has on other people's opinion of him. His behaviour seemed not to be influenced by intention to please, gratitude or appreciation of being a focus of interest. Mme Récamier's gardener must have known this when he offered peaches instead of entreaties.

In my view the evidence presented allows us to assume that Victor was autistic. Of course there can be no conclusive answers in a case of two centuries ago. What of other historical cases with similarly extreme social deprivation? Would we again come to the conclusion that the child in question was autistic? If so, it would be necessary to take seriously the possibility that Autism and feral existence are causally connected. If not, we can dismiss any strong claims of such a connection. There is in fact a second case where severe social deprivation occurred and where excellent documentation of behaviour exists. This case will again allow us to check whether presence or absence of 'autistic aloneness' can be gauged across a considerable distance of time and culture.

## The Case of Kaspar Hauser

On Whit Monday 1828, a very odd-looking lad appeared on the Unschlittplatz in Nuremberg (figure 2.3). He seemed to move his feet without knowing how to walk and he seemed to comprehend nothing at all. At first, he was thought to be drunk or mad, as he repeated over and over again the obviously rehearsed sentence: 'I want to be a horseman like my father was.' He had a letter on him for the Captain of Cavalry in Nuremberg. This letter asked that he be allowed to serve the King as a soldier, and named 30 April 1812 as his date of birth. According to this he was 16 years old, yet he was only 4 foot 9 inches tall. To everyone's amazement, he could write his name: Kaspar Hauser. But he could not talk, except for a few fragments of speech. It became apparent from his strange appearance and behaviour that he had lived all his life in a cellar and had never seen his keeper. It was soon deduced that he had been fed solely on bread and water – as he rejected any other food – and that a wooden horse, which he pined for constantly, had been his only companion. Kaspar was placed at first in a prison cell for tramps, but he was looked after kindly by the warder's family. He then lived with various more or less benevolent families receiving sporadic tuition and schooling. He was considered to be one of the sights of Nuremberg, and was officially adopted by that city.

The sensation that the case created induced many speculations: was he an idiot, a savage, a madman or a deceiver? That he was not an impostor was readily established. But there were persistent rumours that he was of royal blood. These speculations were fired by an attempt at murder which he survived. Kaspar was in fact ultimately assassinated by an unknown person only five years after he had appeared. This happened at the time when he was rumoured to be writing his autobiography. In 1908 the highly acclaimed novelist Jakob Wassermann wrote an epic novel based on the facts of the case, citing every shred of evidence which portrayed Kaspar as a tragic victim of court intrigue. Indeed, there is little reason to doubt such a possibility other than that it is fanciful and romantic. But then, real life is often said to be stranger than fiction. Werner Herzog's stunning film *Kaspar Hauser* vividly conveys the plight of Kaspar, who remained a stranger in the world for all of his tragically stunted life.

The justification for discussing the case in the present context is that there is a detailed first-hand account of Kaspar's physical and mental state with many precise observations. The 'account of an individual kept in a dungeon separated from all communication with the world from

Figure 2.3  *Contemporary portrait of Kaspar Hauser*
Reproduced by kind permission of The British Library

# Kaspar Hauser.

Beispiel

eines

Verbrechens

am

Seelenleben des Menschen

von

Anselm Ritter von Feuerbach.

Ansbach, bei J. M. Dollfuß.

**1832.**

Figure 2.4  *Title page of Anselm von Feuerbach's Example of a crime
on the soul of man*
Reproduced by kind permission of The British Library

early childhood to about the age of 17' was written by Anselm von Feuerbach, then President of the Bavarian Court of Appeal at Anspach near Nuremberg.[2] A famous lawyer, Feuerbach was interested in the case as a species of crime never yet treated by legislation, a 'crime on the soul of a man'.

From Feuerbach's account, which is both passionate and objective, we can piece together a clinical picture of the strangeness of Kaspar's behaviour. According to this report, when found, Kaspar could say only a few phrases, fragments jumbled together. Yet he learned language rapidly, apparently from the prison warder's children. He also received toys and drawings which he seemed to like. He was especially pleased with the gift of a toy horse to which, it was noted, he solicitously offered his own food and drink.

Initially, Kaspar preferred darkness and preferred to sit on the ground with legs stretched out before him. This gave some clues to the terrible conditions of his dungeon. His 'hearing was without understanding, his seeing without perceiving'. He showed pronounced lability of emotions and was highly excitable.

Kaspar formed personal attachments readily, first to Julius the eleven-year-old son of the prison warder, then to others. He obeyed authority without question. He was eager to learn, especially to write and to draw. His memory for names and titles of people was considered astonishingly good, and pleased people. Memory of his life in the dungeon, however, was practically absent. In a short time of tuition he soaked up a large amount of knowledge, including even Latin. Due to his improved diet – food other than bread and water was only very gradually accepted – Kaspar grew more than 2 inches in a few weeks.

Feuerbach was especially interested in Kaspar's sensory perception of the world and odd physiological reactions. There were parallels with another celebrated case, publicized by Voltaire, concerning a person who was blind from a few weeks of age and whose vision was restored by a cataract operation. In both cases scientifically controlled observations were made. Kaspar, just like the previously blind man, failed to appreciate size constancy and depth cues. For instance, objects that looked small at a distance were mistaken as toys. These observations confirmed the belief that Kaspar was kept without the opportunity of normal visual stimulation. This is consistent with Kaspar's own later reports. He claimed that men and horses in pictures at first appeared to him as if carved in wood. A landscape looked ugly to him, but walls did not. He also explained that at first when he saw the world it was like a window shutter splashed with paint that was held close before his eyes. All these new sensations were eventually sorted out by his rapidly increasing experience, and as far as we know his visual perception gradually improved.

Feuerbach was particularly interested in Kaspar's seemingly superior acuteness of sensory perceptions. Clearly, they had not been blunted by experience. His visual acuity, hearing and sense of smell were found to be highly discriminating. However, it seemed that his sensory acuteness gradually diminished. It was noted that Kaspar above all liked the smell of the bread spices then common (fennel, anise and caraway) and hated the taste of opium, which were presumed to have been familiar to him from his dungeon days.

Kaspar learned to play chess, learned to garden, learned that plants were not artefacts, and that animals were not like people. And he learned to ride, for which he showed talent. Many people came to visit him, and he was talked about all over Europe. One year after his sudden, and still mysterious, appearance he began to show sadness and indignation at having been locked up for so long.

Many people found it most surprising that Kaspar showed a pronounced love of order and cleanliness. Everything had to have its place, and Kaspar would carefully brush specks of dust from clothes. He apparently also was very careful and proud of his hundreds of little possessions. Each had its proper symmetrically arranged place. Such refinement was unexpected in someone who had been incarcerated in a dark cellar.

About a month after his appearance Kaspar began to have dreams and at first thought them to be real. This was while he was living with an important benefactor, the kindly Professor Daumer. This observation together with the hint that Kaspar later could distinguish between dreams and reality is interesting because it suggests that Kaspar became aware of his own mental states and could talk about them. This is very different from the wild boy of Aveyron, who gave no evidence of such awareness.

People were curious to know whether Kaspar had any religious understanding. However, he simply could not understand what the clergymen were talking about. He was 'astonished at the discovery of an invisible inner world of the mind'. This observation again suggests that he was becoming aware of such an inner world. How else could he have been astonished at it?

However, Kaspar remained a stranger in the world. He must indeed have stood out from ordinary people. His speech probably never became quite normal. It was awkward, simple and literal. His voice sometimes took on a harsh and foreign sound. His movements remained stiff and unpliant. Feuerbach talks of a curious mingling of childish and adult mind. He noted many contradictions in Kaspar's judgements, abilities and feelings. For example, Kaspar was mild and gentle, feeling sorry for the worm in case he trod on it, timid to the point of cowardice, but also reckless, stubborn and capable of insisting on his rights. Feuerbach considered Kaspar to be 'without a spark of fancy or sense of humour'. Significantly, however, he credited him with a 'dry downright healthy common sense'.

### Was Kaspar autistic?

The contemporary accounts of Kaspar allow us to piece together a clinical picture that is very different from that of Victor. This picture does not permit us to conclude that Kaspar was autistic. I would, for instance, be quite confident that any observer as careful as Feuerbach would not remark on common sense as a special attribute in an autistic individual. Even in very able autistic people, whose high verbal ability and abstruse knowledge may be impressive, there is a striking lack of common sense. Common sense, amongst other things, implies a set of background assumptions held by all members of a community. If autistic people were able to share in this they would be able to avoid literal misunderstandings, would appreciate in-jokes and so forth. In short, they would no longer be odd.

Some of the observations on Kaspar might be taken as evidence of Autism: oddities of sensory perception, general awkwardness, love of order, relative poverty of language, general naivety and lack of worldly wisdom. The same question that was asked for the wild boy of Aveyron should also be asked here: Can all the strange features be parsimoniously explained as effects of prolonged and severe deprivation? The sensory and motor impairments could certainly be a direct result of having been imprisoned in a dark cellar without much opportunity for seeing or moving about. So could his lack of knowledge about the world, his simplicity and his confusion. His peculiar language might be due to having learned to speak so late in life. What about Kaspar's pedantry, or insistence on order? In ordinary life it seems that most young 'uncivilized' children have to be constantly admonished to be orderly and are taught cleanliness with great difficulty. Indeed, many people may not value these notions at all. Kaspar apparently did. But this may be no more surprising than that a tendency to be pedantic can exist at all in anybody. It need not be a sign of pathology.

The main reasons for rejecting a diagnosis of Autism for Kaspar is that there is nothing that suggests 'autistic aloneness'. There are, for instance, many examples of good communication and affective contact. There is his indignation and awareness of the moral issues in his case. There is no incident of embarrassing behaviour (for instance, undressing and climbing trees at a high society gathering, as in the case of Victor). Instead, it seems Kaspar was not oblivious to other people's reactions and interests. We hear that he pleased people by remembering their names and titles and he formed trusting relationships. This social responsiveness is the more remarkable as one might have expected that Kaspar, who had been cruelly treated, who moreover had suffered an attempt at murder, would avoid and distrust people emotionally and physically.

Another important feature of Autism is absent if we believe that Kaspar whiled away much of his lonely time in symbolic play with his toy horse. We are told of his eagerness to learn to speak, and to communicate. It is evident that he was most particular about his possessions and about his rights, both of which are sophisticated social concepts, often beyond the grasp of autistic people. All of these points are in sharp contrast to the case of the wild boy of Aveyron, and all are critical points, as their presence seems to argue against Autism. On the other hand, some of the features which show similarities between the two boys are not critical for the diagnosis of Autism, and can be explained by long-term isolation in childhood.

Kaspar's story of recovery, as we can see, is rather different from that of Victor's. Kaspar received only haphazard education, not nearly as expert and committed as that of Victor. Nevertheless, he seemed to make enormous progress. There is little doubt, however, that Kaspar had suffered physical and mental deprivation to the extent that possibly irreversible organic damage occurred. Some strangeness clearly persisted.

Here, then, we have a contrast between two cases of severe social deprivation, only one of which clearly shows the typical features of Autism. Such evidence works against any social-environmental theory of the origin of Autism. In Victor's case, Autism may have been the cause of abandonment, rather than the other way round. It is deeply mysterious why Kaspar was treated as he was. It is not unthinkable that as a young child he did show some backwardness which prompted his removal from an important family. Whatever the truth of the matter, which we may never know, one must agree with Feuerbach's judgement that a horrible crime was committed on the soul of a man.

### The Case of Genie

It is exceedingly difficult to try and look through the veil of time at cases of strange children who may or may not have shown evidence of Autism. If we could have seen Kaspar and Victor before and after their isolation we could draw unequivocal conclusions. As it is, we can only use the evidence available and speculate. However, this does not apply to the case of Genie. Astonishingly, Genie presents a close modern parallel to Kaspar Hauser. Genie was a girl who was found in 1970 after 13 years of extreme physical and social deprivation. She had been strapped to a potty chair in a small closed room for most of her life and was only minimally cared for. When she was discovered she showed many similarities to Kaspar. She was only 4 feet 6 inches tall, she was completely unsocialized, could not speak and was unable to stand erect. In the case of Genie, there is medical evidence from her early childhood to prove that she was a normally developing baby except for a congenital hip dislocation. The terrible fate that befell her and stunted her development from about the age of two was due, partly at least, to a psychotic father and to an intimidated, blind mother who were both sure she was destined to die young.

The interest in their case is so great that it has received comprehensive documentation and discussion and has been written up in a book by Susan Curtiss.[3] There is no need to go into detail here, except for pointing out the similarities between Genie and Kaspar. Both were eager to communicate with others and able to form attachments. As far as Genie's language development is concerned, we have excellent information which unfortunately is not available for Kaspar. It seems, however, that in both cases speech at first was learned rapidly, yet retained abnormalities, a finding which throws important light on the existence of a critical period in development for language learning.

Autism was specifically ruled out as a diagnosis for Genie. After only four weeks of being released from her modern day dungeon 'she had become alert, bright-eyed, engaged readily in simple social play with balloons, flashlight and toys, with familiar and unfamiliar adults. She exhibited a lively curiosity, good eye–hand coordination, adequate hearing and vision, and emotional responsiveness. She had ample latent affect and responses.'

This case then, strengthens our conclusions that the developmental abnormalities that are induced by severe deprivation are not very similar to the abnormalities seen in autistic children. In particular, they do not include autistic aloneness.

The preliminary concept of Autism that we gained in chapter 1 enabled us to make sense of the material available on some of the most enigmatic cases in the history of child psychology. Victor and Kaspar have provided an unusual opportunity to explore the nature of Autism beyond the boundaries of recent scientific accounts.

These cases show that the devastating effects of social deprivation on development could be ameliorated, but not entirely reversed. The case of Victor, where improvement was more limited, shows that Autism is much more resistant to treatment than severe deprivation. Genie, who was normal in early childhood and could not be considered autistic even when seen at her worst soon after discovery, improved dramatically. If these cases represent extreme states of emotional rejection and social deprivation without causing Autism, then it is unlikely that milder states would. David Skuse reviewed the evidence from recent cases of children who were found in conditions of varying degrees of social and physical neglect and isolation.[4] In none of these cases has Autism been a result. Instead it seems that there is an excellent prognosis for the victims of early deprivation provided that there is no organic damage.

By delving into history we can discover how different minds have tried to solve problems that have remained problems today. In the next chapter, we shall delve even deeper, namely into the realms of myth. Here too we shall find evidence of the existence of Autism long ago and a rich source of ideas about the nature of Autism.

# 3

# Beyond Enchantment

## Sleeping Beauty

The classic fairy tales 'Snow White' and 'The Sleeping Beauty', popularized by the brothers Grimm in the early years of the nineteenth century, contain a number of different themes. One of these is the theme of death-like sleep or, rather, life-like death. This strangely paradoxical image conveys a quality of experience that is familar to those who are closely involved with an autistic child; the beautiful child is tantalizingly near, yet so far. The hedge of thorns or the glass coffin are perfect for representing the impossibility of reaching the child. In the case of Autism, however much the child's appearance seems to indicate that it is normal and healthy ('awake'), the child's social isolation shows after all that it is not ('asleep').

It is interesting that in the two stories two different causes of the death/sleep are proposed: in Snow White it is a simple physical one – a poisoned piece of apple; in Sleeping Beauty it is a curse. Although differing in their explanation, in either case the cure is simple and related to the cause; remove the poisoned piece of apple, and remove the curse. When we consider causes of Autism, we come across precisely these extremes of biological and psychogenic explanations. The fairy tales remind us that neither precludes the possibility of cure, and both offer equal odds as regards the probability of finding it ('the prince'). Of course, one should not be taken in by the happy ending. This is, after all, only a thematic device of fairy tales for the purpose of stressing the moral argument.

People in the past must have encountered Autism and must have attempted to come to terms with it. The chilling and fascinating combination of childhood innocence and madness cries out for symbolic elaboration. No wonder there are many stories and myths that evoke images of autistic children. It is my contention that these myths have not

Figure 3.1  *St Francis and a disciple*. Fresco by Giotto, Chiesa Superiore, Assisi
Reproduced by kind permission of The Mansell Collection/Alinari

come out of the blue. They partially owe their existence and their survival to the real experience of Autism. As Wilhelm Grimm said in his introduction to the fairy-tale collection which he published with Jakob Grimm in 1812, 'the states of life portrayed here are so basic that many people will have found them in their own lives. But, because they are true, they remain new and moving.'

The phenomenon of Autism with its many puzzles has deep significance for individuals who experience it at first hand. But over and above this, it has a wider cultural significance. It is no exaggeration that through understanding Autism we will gain a better understanding of ourselves. It will be evident that this process was begun long ago.

Myths can enrich and inform our experiences, but they can also inhibit the development of scientific theories. It is for two reasons then that it is important to look at myths of Autism: we can gain insights from earlier attempts at understanding Autism, and, by seeing myths for what they are, we can make way for a better understanding.

We shall first turn to some historical evidence which suggests that Autism has played a role in shaping models of religious and political conduct.

### The Blessed Fools of Old Russia

Holy (or 'blessed') fools were venerated in ancient Russia for centuries. In a fascinating paper Natalia Challis and Horace W. Dewey make explicit the extraordinary similarities between holy fools and the modern diagnosis of Autism.[1] The conclusion that many of the holy fools were indeed people who suffered from Autism is as surprising as it is convincing. The label 'blessed' connotes feeblemindedness, as well as innocence in the eyes of God. Eyewitnesses were still alive who could remember the fool Grisha, who lived in the town of Leningrad before the Revolution.

> He was an awesome figure: emaciated, barefoot and in rags, with eyes that 'looked right through you' and long, straggly hair. He always wore chains around his neck . . . Neighbourhood children would sometimes run after him, laughing and calling out his name. Older persons, as a rule, viewed Grisha with respect and a little fear, especially when he suffered one of his periodic seizures and began to shout and rant. At such times adult bystanders would crowd around and listen, for they believed that the Holy Spirit was working through him.

Challis and Dewey point out that a similar description is available from an English visitor to Russia in the sixteenth century. The Blessed Simon of Jurev, who died in 1584, is of special relevance since he was found in a forest as a wild boy by Russian peasants. Knowledge of holy fools is not only the province of scholars, but has filtered into general knowledge, not least because of Dostoevski's novel *The Idiot*.

The features most suggestive of Autism include 'eccentric, irrational conduct', 'apparent insensitivity to pain' (tolerance of extreme winter cold is always mentioned, and of hunger), a life outside society, guilelessness and indifference to social conventions. Furthermore, the fact that often they were wearing chains suggested to Challis and Dewey that these were used to fetter them on occasion, just like other madmen. They also commonly suffered from epilepsy, a clear sign of brain pathology and present in a high proportion of autistic adults, but rarely encountered in schizophrenic patients.

The reports also indicate that many of the blessed fools were mute. Those who spoke were unresponsive to questions and given to parroting. Many of the utterances reported were stereotypic and the speech of the blessed fools showed what we would now call inappropriate phrases. Interestingly, all these peculiar features of their speech which are suggestive of Autism were considered proof of prophetic powers. Thus, unintelligible remarks, parroting, or even absence of remarks, and bizarre, sometimes stereotyped actions were endowed with significance, and often embellished in legends. For instance, why did the blessed fool Nicholas hurl cabbages at a holy man who had made a special trip from another part of the town to see him? The citizens of Novgorod believed that this was because he wished to give them a lesson, symbolically representing their internal bickerings by throwing cabbages.

A further example of a blessed fool, this time a woman, described in the nineteenth century, poignantly illustrates the obsessional nature and oddness of interest which, despite its totally different cultural context, suggests Autism: Pelagija Serebrenikova would collect loose bricks or stones, carry them to a flooded pit, and throw them in one by one. Then she would immerse herself in the water and pull out and toss back the stones she had thrown in, one by one, 'and for many years did she toil thus'.

Characteristically also, the blessed fools had no sense of social status, and thus were exempt from the usual rules of polite conduct. This enabled the fools to approach powerful personages of church and state with impunity. In fact the fools were famous for confronting bishops and tsars, often with profound effects. In this way, they might have exerted power and influence, and this possibility was in fact exploited by a number of impostors (including the infamous Rasputin). For these reasons, there were rules for determining which were genuine fools. For instance, they had to be fools all the time. 'Of these there were not many, because it is a very hard and cold profession to go naked in Russia, especially in winter.'

The foolishness of the fools was, it appears, above all a social foolishness, stemming from an inability to relate to people in the ordinary way. It was assumed at the time that foolishness was deliberately adopted and a sign of great religious faith. Of course, we must allow for those heroic individuals existing in all religions, who do adopt voluntarily a life of social isolation and hardship. We must also allow for the possibility of other forms of madness, such as schizophrenia, to have contributed their share to the blessed fools.

The particular interest of the blessed fools of Russia is that, for at least some of them, there is evidence of 'autistic aloneness'. This is not the same as the crude avoidance of people, but rather an inability to relate to people in the ordinary way.

## Brother Juniper

It is not only the tradition of Eastern Christianity that can furnish evidence of the influence of Autism on religious and political thought. A chance find I made suggests that there could be many more and even older relevant instances. This find was in *The Little Flowers of St Francis*, a collection of legends written down in the thirteenth century. These legends have historical value since they represent oral traditions of the first or second generation of Franciscans. But apart from this, they are one of the treasures of world literature. A whole section with some 14 legends in this collection contains the most charming and curious stories of one Brother Juniper. These stories seem not so curious, and indeed make complete sense, if one assumes that they were in fact based on the life of an autistic individual among the early followers of St Francis.

It is worth quoting from the first of the legends, in the nineteenth-century English translation.[2]

> *How Brother Juniper cut off the foot of a pig to give it to a sick brother*
> One of the first companions of St Francis was Brother Juniper, a man of profound humility. Once when he was visiting a sick brother at St Mary of the Angels, he said to him, 'Can I do thee any service?' And the sick man answered: 'Thou wouldst give me great consolation if thou couldst get me a pig's foot to eat.' Brother Juniper took a knife from the kitchen, and went into the forest, where many swine were feeding. Having caught one, he cut off one of its feet and ran off with it, leaving the swine with its foot cut off; and coming back to the convent, he carefully washed the foot, and

diligently prepared and cooked it. Then he brought it to the sick man, who ate it with avidity.

Meanwhile, the swineherd, who had seen the brother cut off the foot, went to his lord, who, being informed of the fact, came to the convent and abused the friars, calling them hypocrites, deceivers, robbers, and evil men. 'Why,' said he, 'have you cut off the foot of my swine?' At the noise which he made, St Francis and all the friars came together, and with all humility made excuses for their brother. But the angry man was not to be appeased. He refused to accept any excuse or promise of repayment; and so departed in great wrath. And as all the other friars wondered, St Francis sent for Brother Juniper and asked him privately: 'Hast thou cut off the foot of a swine in the forest?' To which Brother Juniper answered quite joyfully, not as one who had committed a fault, but believing he had done a great act of charity: 'It is true, sweet father, that I did cut off that swine's foot. I will tell thee the reason. I went out of charity to visit the brother who is sick.' And so he related the matter. St Francis, in great zeal for justice, and in much bitterness of heart, made answer: 'O Brother Juniper, wherefore hast thou given this great scandal? Not without reason doth this man complain, and thus rage against us; perhaps even now he is going about the city spreading this evil report of us, and with good cause. Therefore I command thee by holy obedience, that thou go after him until thou find him, and cast thyself prostrate before him, confessing thy fault, and promising to make such full satisfaction that he shall have no more reason to complain of us, for this is indeed a most grievous offence.'

At these words Brother Juniper was much amazed, wondering that any one should have been angered at so charitable an action. And so he went his way, and coming to the man, who was still chafing and past all patience, he told him for what reason he had cut off the pig's foot, and all with such fervour, exultation and joy, as if he were telling him of some great benefit he had done him which deserved to be highly rewarded. The man grew more and more furious at his discourse, and loaded him with much abuse, calling him a fantastical fool and a wicked thief. Brother Juniper, who delighted in insults, cared nothing for all this abuse, and repeated the story all over again with so much charity, simplicity, and humility, that the man's heart was changed within him. He threw himself at Brother Juniper's feet, acknowledging with many tears the injuries which by word and deed he had done to him and his brethren. Then he went and killed the swine, and having cut it up, he brought it to St Mary of the Angels. Then St Francis, considering the simplicity and patience under adversity of this good Brother Juniper, said to his companions and those who stood by: 'Would to God, my brethren, that I had a forest of such Junipers!'

If Brother Juniper was autistic, he also had an admirable personality. He is so different from Peter, the boy we discussed in chapter 1, and from the wild boy of Aveyron that it might be hard to believe that there could be any connection. And yet we can pick out a common thread. Peter with his good language showed perfectly literal understanding and so did Brother Juniper. Neither Peter nor Victor, the mute boy, showed in their actions that they were aware that people might have different thoughts and beliefs. At the heart of the story of the pig's foot is the fact that Brother Juniper could not understand that other people might not have the same belief about his action as he did himself. The lack of awareness of other people's thoughts about things or events constitutes a most important clue to the nature of 'autistic aloneness'. Conversely, the evidence on Kaspar Hauser or Genie suggests that they did not lack such awareness. Although they showed severe social impairments, they could talk about their own mental states and indicate that they knew other people had states of mind that might be different from their own.

There are other stories that testify to Brother Juniper's honesty and humility, and yet also to his inability to gauge any effect his actions may have had for others beyond the most immediate context. For instance, he was once loudly and vehemently rebuked by his Superior for some particularly daft action (he once cooked food for a whole fortnight in one go – not considering that most of it would be spoilt). Far from showing the appropriate contrite reaction, Brother Juniper noticed one thing only: the Superior's voice had become hoarse while haranguing him. What did he do? He procured hot porridge – at some considerable trouble. This he tried to offer to the angry Superior, to soothe his throat. Since it was by now the middle of the night the Superior refused to get up. At long last Brother Juniper accepted the refusal, but he now asked the Superior to come and hold the candle so that he himself could eat the porridge! Marvelling at such piety and simplicity, the Superior could not resist. He came out of his cell and shared the meal.

A similar lesson in humility was given to the citizens of Rome who had come to welcome Brother Juniper, who was on pilgrimage. Brother Juniper took no notice of the procession, but instead he fixed his attention on a see-saw. Hours later, when the amazed crowd had long gone, he stopped the (typically repetitive) see-sawing and continued his journey.

Brother Juniper gave away anything to anyone who asked for it, including frequently his own clothes. Once he even cut the bells from the altar-cloth to give to a poor woman. This he did in a literal interpretation of the Franciscan virtues of poverty and charity. His literal interpretation led to embarrassing excess. The brethren had to keep a constant watch on him, and he was strictly forbidden to give away his clothes. Nevertheless, he was recognized to be a pure example of the true Franciscan spirit and for this he was held in high esteem. One cannot help thinking that he provided not only an idealized model for the brethren's own conduct, but one in which they would also see a degree of absurdity. They could laugh at him, the 'plaything of God', as St Clare so aptly called him.

What the case of Brother Juniper highlights is one of the many astonishing aspects of Autism, namely utter guilelessness. If his humility had in fact been a deliberately adopted way of life we would not expect the clearly ridiculous excesses and many awkwardnesses that resulted. Indeed, they did not occur with other brethren, famed as they were for their saintliness. There are other legends in the *Flowers* treating of the early companions of St Francis. But none are like those about Brother Juniper!

There are other surprising aspects of Autism that are worthy of myths, as we shall see in the following sections. One particularly intriguing theme is that of the creature of cold reason who is incapable of warmhearted relationships. This theme touches on the phenomenon of Autism combined with high academic ability. This does exist in real life, and has been elaborated in literature.

## Sherlock Holmes

The detached detectives of classic mysteries are not only eccentric and odd, but they are reminiscent of very clever autistic people. They demonstrate a particular type of oddness that might be shared by highly gifted autistic individuals. The oddness conveys clear powers of observation and deduction, unclouded by the everyday emotions of ordinary people. Absent-mindedness in relation to other people, but single-mindedness in relation to special ideas are part of this image. It is obvious that those whose thoughts are preoccupied while penetrating through conundrums (as detectives or as scientists) will tend to forget social niceties. Their minds cannot be troubled by the simple events of everyday life. On the other hand the genius-professor or genius-detective attends to matters that seem trivial to the ordinary person. It is usually near the end of the story that 'the significance of trifles' is revealed. This is precisely why this type of genius can solve problems on the basis of what appear to be negligibly small clues. The clues, traditionally, are of the kind that mislead ordinary people. Readers of detective stories are misled because of their perfectly normal emotional and social prejudices which show them certain events and facts in a particular light but not as they really are. Conan Doyle has given us the archetypal detective in Sherlock Holmes. He has also created an archetypal average person with warm feelings and prejudices, Dr Watson. In science too, the original genius can see data in a different light from that in which others have grown accustomed to perceive them.

Sherlock Holmes suggests the social usefulness and originality of the brilliant but socially detached mind. There is yet another autistic feature which many fictional geniuses possess, namely a special, circumscribed interest. One can think of Sherlock Holmes's 'little monograph on the ashes of 140 different varieties of pipe, cigar and cigarette tobacco'. One can also think of that other classic detective, Rex Stout's Nero Wolfe, and his obsession with orchids and rigid daily routine. Frankly obsessional characteristics are also evident in Agatha Christie's Hercule Poirot, who insisted on neatness and rectangularity in every aspect. He delighted, for instance, in square-shaped crumpets, in preference to the ordinary round-shaped ones, and his perpetration of a killing was proved by the perfectly symmetrical placement of a bullet-hole.

Miss Marple, Agatha Christie's other immortal detective, is in every way the opposite and has no autistic-like traits at all: she solves crimes by intuition, immersing herself in the context without analytic deduction. For instance, she feels that there is something wrong with the atmosphere in Bertram's hotel long before she knows why. In contrast, the classic detached detective is not captured by atmosphere. It is indeed this atmosphere that misleads everyone else but him into suspecting the wrong person. The detached detective is objective, incorruptible and in a way also often extremely literal. When everyone thinks that R-A-C-H-E is the beginning of a girl's name, Sherlock Holmes knows it is the German for 'revenge' and acts on this simple clue. Or, the last word gasped by a murder victim turns out to be the murderer's name after all. 'Elementary' – is the detective's usual verdict, leaving Dr Watson gasping.

The term 'autistic intelligence' was coined by Asperger. He believed that autistic intelligence had distinct qualities and was the opposite of conventional learning and worldly-wise cunning. Indeed he thought of it as a vital ingredient in all great creations in art or science. The fictional literature surrounding the 'mad professor' or his variants are full of examples that would fit Asperger's notions. Is a dash of Autism a mark of original thought? This question goes well beyond the enchantment of storytelling. There is no reason why it should not be treated by scientific investigation. The answer is tantalizingly open.

In the next section we shall continue to look at the theme of unusual intellectual gifts.

## The Pin-Ball Wizard

The Who's rock opera *Tommy* centres on a hero who has strongly autistic traits – although autism is never mentioned, and although other themes are superimposed on it.

Through the character of the father we are reminded how normal children enjoy waking up on Christmas morning, getting all excited. He could well have spoken of an autistic child when he says: 'And Tommy doesn't know what day it is . . . surrounded by his friends, he sits so silently, and unaware of everything . . . playing poxy pin-ball, picks his nose and smiles, and pokes his tongue at everything.'

The opera *Tommy* is of special interest here since it elaborates an aspect of Autism which has not found expression in other myths, namely the autistic child's strange and seemingly perversely effective system of sensory perception: Tommy does not function like a normal seeing, hearing, speaking child. ('I often wonder what he's feeling. Has he ever heard a word I said?') Yet, there is a paradox: he plays pin-ball to perfection, which surely demands superior sensory skills. 'He ain't got no distractions, can't hear those buzzers an' bells, don't see no lights a flashin', plays by sense of smell . . . He stands like a statue, becomes part of the machine . . . That deaf, dumb and blind kid sure plays a mean pin-ball.' It is known that Pete Townshend, who composed the work, knew about Autism at the time, and by his own account has long been interested in this disorder. At least in this case, we have direct evidence of the existence of the phenomenon of Autism contributing to art and culture.

## The Changeling

John Wyndham's science fiction novel *The Midwich Cuckoos* has elaborated the theme of a 'different' child smuggled into an unsuspecting family.[3] This theme of the changeling could, of course, apply to any child with special handicaps or gifts. In this story, aliens have planted beautiful and brilliantly clever children on the unwitting population of a small English village. These children eventually have to be given up by their stunned, uncomprehending human parents. Since these parents are just as much subject to mothering instincts as any parent, this proves to be a harrowing experience. Parents of autistic children find this story deeply evocative of some of their own experiences. The story represents symbolically the 'alien' nature of children so difficult to understand.

Even those aspects of Autism that seem at first so very positive, such as the occasionally found remarkable skills, appear far from normal if represented as signs of 'alien' intelligence.

## The Robot

The theme of the intelligent but soul-less automaton is only a small step away from the genius detective. It has undoubtedly created some of the most potent of modern myths. It is my belief that the existence of Autism has contributed to this theme in no small way. But this is not the only reason to look at it in more detail. I selected this theme because it reflects not only normal perceptions of autistic aloneness but also reactions to this phenomenon.

Obedient only to logical principles, robots are untouched by all that matters in ordinary human relationships. Yet they are a fascinating partner in such relationships. The first robots of science fiction knew no love, hate, curiosity, jealousy or revenge and could not fathom these feelings in others. They were easy to recognize as machines. New robots who, like R2D2 in *Star Wars*, have feelings programmed into them, are more tricky to classify as machines. Like autistic people early robots have no sense of humour, and are utterly literal in their understanding. But – despite their metal exterior – one tends to forget that they are machines. More often than not people treat robots as if they too were scheming beings. This is understandable if we assume that the attribution of states of minds is pervasive and compulsive.

As a metaphor for Autism robots serve well in many respects. The exterminating cone-shaped Daleks of the British television series Dr Who have given a name to the mechanical quality of voice (the Dalek-voice) that has often been ascribed to autistic individuals. The characteristic stiff gait of autistic adults is modelled by the metal humanoid devices. Robots carry out jobs that they are specialized for, without concern for wider aspects, with precision and, above all, in an unvarying routine. The machine-like behaviour reminds us of many characteristics of Autistic behaviour: we see repetitiveness, stereotyped movements, lack of emotional expression and lack of spontaneous playfulness.

So many human qualities can be found in an intelligent machine, yet some elusive but essential humanness is missing. One of the first and still best elaborations of this theme can be found in the tales 'The Sandman' and 'The Automata' by E. T. A. Hoffmann, written in the early nineteenth century.[4] Hoffmann was among the first to portray the paradoxical relationship between rationality and Gothic horror. This paradox strikes a familiar chord with many who have an uneasy relationship with modern machines such as computers. *Frankenstein*, Mary Shelley's masterpiece, is also concerned with the paradox of irrationality out of rationality. The Frankenstein myth, too, deserves to be looked at from the point of view of certain deep resemblances to aspects of Autism. I will mention here only the innocence of the monster and the sharp differences between his abilities and defects.

The disturbing theme of mechanical man is alive and well in contemporary films and stories. There are many fascinating elaborations, for instance those by Philip K. Dick, whose *Do Androids Dream of Electric Sheep?* was turned into the film *Blade Runner*.[5] Here the theme directly concerns the definition of the thin borderline where human and android may or may not be distinguished. Again this raises a question that can be tackled by scientific methods: Is there a continuum or is there a radical difference? Does this apply equally to trying to differentiate autistic and non-autistic individuals?

A particularly interesting variant of the robot theme is presented by *Star Trek*'s admirable Mr Spock. His mental make-up is non-human to the extent that all his actions are governed by logic and not by emotion. He is detached from the messiness and confusion of ordinary personal relationships, and hence has a particular lack of prejudice. This gives him clarity and objectivity of thought. In this way he is similar to Sherlock Holmes.

The robot metaphor symbolically captures the coexistence of the physical and intellectual achievements of autistic individuals, and, in sharp contrast, their perceived emotional insufficiency in personal relationships. The myth allows the representation of this particular contrast to be surprisingly constructive: the emotional detachment itself can be seen as an asset or even an attraction. The borderline between man and machine is ever more elusive. Clearly, when trying to understand robots, just as when trying to understand autistic individuals, we must comprehend them as participants in the human condition. A celebrated case is Eliza. It can tell us much about the vicissitudes of understanding that may well face us when tackling these puzzling problems.

### Eliza

Not only in literature, but in the study of artificial intelligence questions have been asked about the essential humanness of humans. Eliza is a program for analysing language, and is so cleverly designed that it is possible to have a 'conversation' with it using a printer. The program creates the illusion of perfectly understanding the minds of its partners.

A dialogue quoted in a book by Eliza's inventor, Joseph Weizenbaum,[6] goes as follows:

*Human*  I'm depressed much of the time.
*Eliza*   I am sorry to hear you are depressed.
*Human*  It's true. I am unhappy.
*Eliza*   Do you think coming here will help you not to be unhappy?
*Human*  I need some help, that much seems certain.
*Eliza*   What would it mean to you if you got some help?
*Human*  Perhaps I could learn to get along with my mother.
*Eliza*   Tell me more about your family.
*Human*  My mother takes care of me.
*Eliza*   Who else in your family takes care of you?
*Human*  My father.
*Eliza*   Your father.
*Human*  You are like my father in some ways.
*Eliza*   What resemblance do you see?
*Human*  You are not very aggressive but I think you don't want me to notice that.
*Eliza*   What makes you think I am not very aggressive?
*Human*  You don't argue with me.
*Eliza*   Why do you think I don't argue with you?

The conversation becomes gradually more like a psychotherapy session. It is no wonder many partners of Eliza requested that they could converse in private. Clearly they believed that some useful communication was achieved.

Eliza became a legend and was used, for instance in David Lodge's novel *Small World*, to show a developing therapeutic relationship between man and machine. What Eliza shows is how difficult it is in fact to distinguish machine-ness and human-ness by humans while they are involved in communication. When communicating, the human actively and continuously attributes ideas, intentions and feelings to the machine. Such attribution seems to be an inevitable part of two-way communication. It even happens when only one member (man, but not machine) does the attributing! However, as it works it deceives. In reality in this situation there is no two-way communication of the kind there appears to be; there is just a clever script that picks up key words and uses them again in certain neutral but apparently provocative phrases.

Are autistic individuals who can speak, but fail to communicate, a bit like Eliza in this respect? This possibility would certainly be amenable to being tested by scientific methods – though this has yet to be done. If the similarity were confirmed this would have a rather surprising consequence: as conversation partners or therapists of autistic children we could not help but attribute intentions, even if they themselves did not, and if the attributions were quite unjustified. It seems to me that psychotherapists who work with autistic children and interpret symbolically what these children do or say would do well to check on this possibility. Psychotherapy with autistic children is a controversial issue. Given its general lack of a sound scientific basis, it is not surprising that myths can exert a strong influence. One myth in particular has attracted therapists' attention. It is clearly a variant of an old fairy-tale theme: the case of the refrigerator mother.

## Mother

Snow White was poisoned by her stepmother, and Thorn Rose was cursed by the fairy who had not been invited. A modern contribution to the theme of the wicked stepmother is the emotionally detached and intellectual mother who may otherwise be conscientious in mothering duties. This mother is far more subtle in her cruelty than the traditional stepmother. For instance, she brings up her child by the book, taking expert advice, rather than relying on instinct. However, in doing this she forgets the importance of the heart over that of the intellect. The result, according to experts again, may be an emotionally stunted, autistic child.

This caricature of bad mothering overlaps with the caricature of the career woman, in particular of the 'intellectual' type. An abnormally detached child – a child who is unable to relate lovingly – a fitting punishment for the woman who neglected to be a full-time devoted wife and mother!

The term 'refrigerator' mother encapsulates the essence of this myth. In its application to Autism, it proved irresistible to Leo Kanner. But it really *is* a myth as far as any causal connection with Autism or the basis of any hope for a cure is concerned. Unfortunately, it is still not universally recognized for what it is, and thus has the power to add guilt and recrimination, as well as censoriousness from luckier parents, to the tragedy of an autistic child.

## Myths and Science

In this chapter we briefly looked at some legends and myths that seem to represent symbolically certain critical aspects of Autism. In some ways, they can be useful to gain a partial understanding of some of the most puzzling aspects of the phenomenon. The relatives of an autistic child often undergo a harrowing experience. They may obtain a certain degree of comfort from symbolic and artistic elaborations of Autism. On the other hand, those without personal knowledge of Autism can perhaps, through this medium, obtain a degree of insight into the experience of what it means to care for an autistic child.

The many different themes that have been and continue to be elaborated bear witness to the fact that facets of Autism are not only a property of personal experience, but are also part of public consciousness. But, however much myths appeal to us, they are of course only myths, and the half-truths they embody can give only short-lived comfort. They do not really help us to understand the nature of Autism. In order to do this we must adopt the rigorous and systematic method of scientific investigation. The next chapters will be full of facts that such efforts have already produced. We shall try and understand all these facts together so that they all fit together in one single coherent picture. Unlike literary treatments, this understanding must accommodate all the important phenomena of Autism together and not just seize on one fascinating aspect at a time. It is tempting to spin one or two astounding phenomena into an enchanting tale, but in a scientific endeavour we have to go beyond enchantment.

Because its scientific study has barely begun, we still only know a fraction of what there is to know about Autism. But by now we do know enough to unravel some of the confusions and to dispel some of the misconceptions. It is perfectly possible to sort out areas of knowledge and areas of ignorance. For the gaps in our knowledge we can suggest likely hypotheses for further investigation and discard unlikely ones that would just waste time.

In this book we are taking a fresh look at childhood Autism. We shall sift and sort through the statistical, biological and psychological evidence to date, so that a clearer picture of this puzzling disorder can emerge. On the basis of this picture we can then attempt to understand more fully what it means to suffer from 'Autism'.

# 4

# The Background Facts

---

Firmly and surely, population studies have shown that Autism is not a fanciful construct with literary connections, but very much a real-life phenomenon. On agreed behavioural criteria, Autism can be identified reliably by different investigators in different countries.

When and where does Autism occur? What is the relationship of Autism to mental deficiency? To schizophrenia? How early can Autism be diagnosed? Such basic questions are extraordinarily difficult to answer with certainty, but answers can and have been obtained by population studies. These will be the subject of the present chapter.

## How Many Autistic Children are There?

One might think it is impossible to count heads, if we do not yet know what the nature of Autism is. But this is not so. Population surveys can be based on certain specified behavioural criteria. This may seem arbitrary at first, since one can only speak of an identifiable syndrome if the constituent symptoms really do 'run together'. However, a survey can establish whether this is the case. It can also tell us to what extent symptoms vary between individuals, which symptoms can or cannot be reported reliably, and which are the earliest diagnostic signs. Facts collected in large-scale surveys are an essential complement to detailed facts about individual cases.

In 1966 Victor Lotter finished the first epidemiological study of Autism, focused on a geographically defined area.[1] He did this under the auspices of the MRC Social Psychiatry Unit in London which pioneered epidemiological studies in psychiatry. The study is worth looking at in some detail in order to appreciate the effort that is involved in population surveys. Lotter first screened *all* children between the ages of eight and ten whose addresses were in the county of Middlesex on a particular date. The total number amounted to about 78,000. By means of postal questionnaires to teachers and other people professionally concerned with children of that age, he initially identified all those children who might conceivably be autistic. He then consulted medical records and conducted individual interviews. In this way he was able to identify 135 suspected cases. These he assessed individually in great detail. As a result of repeated sifting, he found a group of 35 children who were similar to the cases that Kanner had originally described. He thus found an incidence of 4.5 per 10,000 of the population of children aged eight to ten. There was a ratio of 2.6 boys to 1 girl.[2]

All of the 35 children in the final group showed a persistent lack of affective contact and an obsessive desire for sameness, and these symptoms were present before age five. Lotter then divided this group into those who showed the features to a marked degree, and those who showed them to a lesser degree. He thus distinguished a nuclear from a non-nuclear group. There were 15 nuclear children (incidence 2 per 10,000), and 20 non-nuclear ones. The excess of boys was greater in the nuclear group (2.8:1) than in the non-nuclear one (2.4:1). Besides these children, there were 26 others who showed the two classic features of Autism to an even lesser extent. In addition, there were a substantial number of severely retarded children who were mute and socially withdrawn. We can be confident that Lotter's nuclear cases were clear-cut examples of Autism as described by Kanner. However, it is clear that there are a great number of less typical cases. These might well be diagnosed as 'autistic' by clinicians employing criteria less strictly based on Kanner's notions. Therefore a higher incidence of cases is expected if mild as well as severe cases of Autism are included. This was the case in a recent well controlled study in Nova Scotia.[3] 20,800 children between 6 and 14 years were extensively screened and 21 identified as autistic. This corresponds to an incidence of 10 per 10,000, doubling previous estimates, but with exactly the same excess of boys (2.5:1).

### The excess of autistic boys

The excess of autistic boys over girls was noted by both Kanner and Asperger and is now well established. A study that threw new light on this question was carried out by Lord, Schopler and Revicki.[4] Their study reports results from one of the largest samples of autistic children collected: 384 boys and 91 girls, aged three to eight years. This sample was identified at the University Clinic of North Carolina at Chapel Hill and included not just nuclear cases of Autism but also those who showed autistic symptoms to a less marked degree. All children were seen between 1975 and 1980 and were thoroughly investigated by psychological tests and interviews taking into account each child's development. The ratio of boys to girls was 5:1 at the higher end of the ability range and only 3:1 at the lower end.

This result can be looked at in another way: the autistic girls were, on average, more seriously impaired on almost every ability tested than the autistic boys. The girls had an average non-verbal IQ of 40 and the boys of 44, both of which are quite low. Though only a few points different, these averages nevertheless indicate a significant shift, since they are based on sizeable groups. Similarly, girls came out worse when simple daily living skills were assessed, and were worse on language or perceptual tests. However, in terms of play or affect, or the ability to relate to people, girls were as poor as, but not worse than boys. This is an important finding, and suggests that these particular features, which are critical aspects of Autism, are relatively independent of intellectual abilities and acquired skills. Furthermore, this finding indicates that it would not be right to think of the girls in this study as more 'autistic' than the boys. Instead, they seem to have more severe additional problems.

Lorna Wing, on the basis of a large-scale population study in London, also concluded that the sex ratio increases with increased ability.[5] At the lowest ability levels the ratio of boys to girls was only 2:1. This was comparable to the ratio for Down's syndrome and cerebral palsied children of equally low ability. At the highest ability levels Wing's sample showed a ratio of 15:1! Elizabeth Newson, Peggy Everard and Mary Dawson identified a sample of 93 very able autistic people who lived all over Britain, and found that only 9 of them were women.[6]

The excess of boys found consistently in all studies and the scarcity of girls at the middle and higher ability levels are typical 'clues' to the biological origin of Autism.

## Mental Retardation

Three-quarters of the Middlesex population of autistic children were mentally retarded and so were three-quarters of the Nova Scotia population. Comprehensive psychometric tests were carried out as part of a ten-year follow-up study by Rutter and Lockyer in London on a sample of 63 autistic children.[7] The proportion of children in this sample who were severely retarded (IQ less than 50) was 40 per cent, while the proportion of those who were moderately retarded (IQ band 50 to 70) was 30 per cent. Thirty per cent had IQs above 70. Only half of this last group actually had IQs in a range of intelligence that could be said to be normal average. In 1985, Freeman, Ritvo and collaborators from the University of California, Los Angeles published a longitudinal study on 62 children aged two to six years with yearly assessments for five years.[8] Seventy-seven per cent of their sample scored in the retarded range and IQs remained stable, with few exceptions, despite participation in various educational programmes. These and other studies show remarkable agreement, so that we can conclude that about three in every four autistic children will show mental retardation in addition to Autism.

The North Carolina sample of 475 autistic children is something of an exception. Here only 16 per cent had an IQ over 70, and only 7 per cent had an IQ over 80. An exception in the opposite direction is seen in a West Berlin sample of autistic children, which unlike the North Carolina study included only nuclear cases.[9] Here as many as 33 per cent were found to have an IQ of 85 and above. This is the highest proportion of able autistic children reported yet, but of course it is still very much a minority. The strong association of Autism and mental retardation is a fact that was not anticipated by Kanner and Asperger, and there is still occasional resistance in some quarters to accepting it.

Mental retardation is a sure sign of brain impairment of biological origin, but what about the small proportion of children who are not intellectually retarded on standard IQ-tests? It is conceivable, as Goldstein and Lancy suggested in 1985,[10] that the shape of the distribution of IQ-test scores for the autistic population is the same as for the normal population, just that the mean is depressed by about 50 IQ points. The depression would be due to brain impairment, but there would still be some children with relatively high scores. If so, then even the most able autistic children would show diminished performance – compared to their hypothetical functioning without Autism. This could indeed be so since, as far as is known, the most able autistic children do not reach the extremely high levels of IQ that can be reached by the most able normal children. In chapter 6, we shall consider what the pattern of intellectual abilities in autistic children reveals about Autism, and to what extent it differs from that of a normally developing child.

### The question of social class

In the methodologically impeccable Middlesex study, Autism was found to occur more often in families of superior socio-economic status. As many as 60 per cent of the 15 nuclear autistic children were in the two upper social classes, as were 31 per cent of the 20 non-nuclear cases.

This has to be seen against an expected proportion of 23 per cent of classes I and II in the population of Middlesex at the time. Such an excess was consistent with Kanner's and Asperger's own clinical samples. Kanner noted that all but three of the 11 cases that he described had family members who appeared in *Who's Who*, or in *Men of Science*. Autobiographical accounts of the impact of an autistic child on the family have been written by typical academics, including those who have achieved such high honours as the Nobel Prize.

Any association between disorder and high social class is intriguing. Is Autism a disease of the rich and powerful? Is it typical of professional, intellectual parents to have autistic children? The myth of the refrigerator mother would fit the career-oriented intellectual, emotionally detached woman. Thus, the possible association of Autism with higher social status was grist to the mill of psychodynamic theories of Autism. There is no reason, however, why an association could not be explained in terms of biological theories.

An extensive critique of suggestions of a link between Autism and superior socio-economic status was made by Schopler, Andrews and Strupp.[11] In 1979 they reviewed all available studies and came to the conclusion that reported associations are artefacts. These authors identified a variety of reasons that would naturally lead to a bias in the selection of cases. For instance, parents of higher social classes were more knowledgeable about Autism, were more likely to have the right contacts, and had the means to travel vast distances to the most eminent psychiatric centres with Autism experts. As a consequence, autistic children from such families tend to be over-represented. Meanwhile, several other population studies, in Britain[12] and Sweden,[13] failed to find any association between Autism and social class. Instead, these studies indicated an increased prevalence among the children of immigrant parents, who tend to be socially disadvantaged.

One would expect any excess of autistic children in the higher classes to diminish gradually, as more information and professional services become available. Such a diminishing trend was noted by Green and collaborators on admission data to the nursery at New York University Medical Center.[14] Between 1961 and 1976, 30 per cent of autistic children were from upper socio-economic families, but between 1979 and 1981 this was reduced to 18 per cent. If seen against census data of 12 per cent prevalence of social class I and II in the catchment area, it cannot be ignored, however, that even the low proportion in the more recent sample is a little higher than expected. Wolff and her colleagues in 1988[15] reported that they were hard put to find a group of retarded children whose parents were from a similarly high social class as their autistic sample. In their study parents of autistic children were more 'intellectual' and had more eccentricities than the other parents.

Just what other factors, besides referral bias, affect the population statistics have still to be found out. Genetic factors may well be part of the explanation. Biological and sociological factors are not totally independent of each other. For instance, Autism together with widespread organic pathology and resulting severe mental retardation may occur somewhat more frequently when there are poor socio-economic circumstances. Conversely, Autism, unconfounded by additional handicap, may be more frequent with better circumstances. In such cases diagnosis is simpler and less controversial. We would, therefore, expect some bias in the number of cases identified as autistic relating to social class exactly as found.

### The Incidence of Severe Social Impairment in Childhood

So far, we have looked at studies of Autism as diagnosed by a simple set of behavioural criteria relating to aloofness, communication failure and repetitiveness. The studies prove that these criteria can be used reliably to identify children who resemble those first described by Kanner. Do they also prove that Autism is a natural entity, a true syndrome? One needs to consider the possibility that the criterion behaviours occur randomly and independently of each other, and that their admittedly rare concurrence might merely be chance. For instance, if one looked for colour-blind, agoraphobic flautists, one would find a number in a large enough population, but one would not have found a syndrome. It would be pointless to attempt to explain the constellation of symptoms in terms of some single underlying psychological deficit. Since this is exactly what I shall aim to do in this book, it is clearly important to be sure that we are not hunting after a chimera.

Fortunately, there is a study that tested the possibility of a mere coincidence of symptoms. It did so by spreading a wide net over the total population of handicapped children in one area. This study was carried out by Lorna Wing and Judith Gould, and was based on Camberwell, a borough of Inner London, with a population of 155,000.[16] As a first step, it was established that among 35,000 children from 0 to 14 years who lived in Camberwell on 31 December 1970, there were 914 children who were known to the health or education services as suffering from some form of physical or mental handicap. In the earlier Middlesex study, all autistic children turned out to have been known to the services as handicapped. Therefore, the procedure followed in the Camberwell study was well suited for identifying all potentially autistic children. However, identification of autistic children was not the main aim of the study. The study aimed at discovering how many children in the population under scrutiny showed *any* of the main features of Autism.

All 914 children were screened and a sample of 173 children was identified for further intensive investigation. This sample included all physically mobile mentally retarded children. It also included all children with any one of three behaviours typical of Autism, regardless of retardation. These three features were: (1) severe social impairment, defined as the absence of the ability to engage in reciprocal two-way interaction, especially with peers; (2) severe communication impairment, both verbal and non-verbal; (3) absence of imaginative pursuits including pretend play, with the substitution of repetitive behaviour. Each child (with the exception of six who had died) was repeatedly observed and tested, and parents and care-takers were intensively interviewed about the child's behaviour and peculiarities from birth. Many years later, when the children were aged between 16 and 30 years, a follow-up study was conducted.

Classic Autism in its most severe form, closely resembling Kanner's original description, was found in 7 children. This corresponds to an incidence of 2 in 10,000, and is identical to the incidence of nuclear Autism in other studies. Just as in the Middlesex study, an incidence of 4.9 in 10,000 (17 children in all) was found when Austism was diagnosed on the basis of Kanner's two cardinal symptoms, namely extreme aloofness and presence of elaborate repetitive routines in the early years of childhood.

So far – so consistent. The syndrome of Autism was again shown to exist in highly recognizable form. However, the single most important diagnostic criterion, namely severe social impairment, was identified as present before age seven in an additional 62 children who did not show a history typical of Autism. Seventy per cent of these children had such severe mental retardation that their behaviour repertoire was extremely limited. For this reason alone they could not show many of the characteristic behaviour patterns of autistic children. They had no complex routines, peculiar speech or special skills. The incidence of children who showed severe social impairment amounted to 22.5 in 10,000 children under 15, a figure by far outnumbering the incidence of nuclear Autism. These children contrasted with 60 other children of the intensively studied sample who suffered from mental handicap without severe social impairment. Among these sociable mentally handicapped children, 32 suffered from Down's syndrome. Three additional Down's syndrome children were socially impaired.

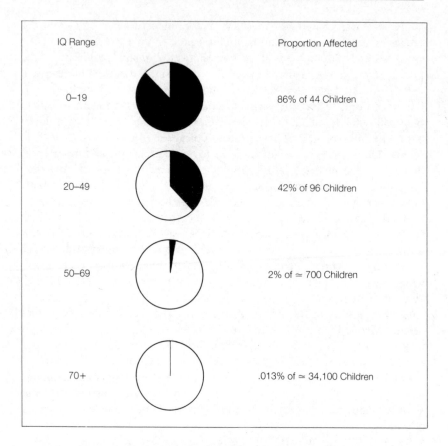

| IQ Range | Proportion Affected |
|---|---|
| 0–19 | 86% of 44 Children |
| 20–49 | 42% of 96 Children |
| 50–69 | 2% of ≃ 700 Children |
| 70+ | .013% of ≃ 34,100 Children |

Figure 4.1  *Proportion of children with social impairment in each IQ range, in a*
*total population of approximately 35,000 children aged under 15 years (from Wing and*
*Gould's study)*

We can conclude that social impairment of very much the same kind
that characterizes young autistic children is found very frequently in
mentally retarded children who are not autistic by any other criteria. Just
how the incidence of social impairment relates to mental handicap is
clearly seen in figure 4.1. At the most profound level of retardation, IQ
below 20, social responses are very difficult to discern. Nevertheless,
there is a proportion of children who were described by their parents and
care-takers as 'friendly and eager for social contact, like a normal baby'.
Apparently, these extremely handicapped children were able to use eye
contact to attract attention and to indicate that they discriminated
between individual people. In the highest IQ band, on the other hand,

only a very tiny proportion was identified as suffering from severe social impairment.

The simplest explanation of these findings is that pathological social impairment results from a particular brain system not functioning normally. The specific dysfunction is more likely to exist in conjunction with widespread brain pathology. This would explain the high incidence of social impairment at severe levels of retardation. On the other hand, there can be extensive damage without affecting the critical system, just as there can be very circumscribed damage affecting *only* the critical system. It is in this last case that we can see Autism in its purest form.

### The aloof, the passive and the odd

In the Camberwell study, social impairment was defined as an inability to engage in two-way interaction. Lorna Wing and her colleagues also attempted to capture the quality of the impairment. They identified three distinctive types, labelled as aloof, passive and odd (figure 4.2). Although each of these types of behaviour might be shown by the same child in different situations, it was possible to characterize a particular child in terms of its predominant behaviour.[17] The following fictitious descriptions are intended to show an extreme version of each prototype.

Jane is an *aloof* child who evokes the image of the 'child in a glass cage'. At school or at home she appears totally withdrawn and does not respond to social overtures or to speech. Jane herself does not speak at all. She also does not use eye contact, and often appears to avoid it altogether. Unlike her normal baby sister, Jane refuses to be cuddled. She will not seek to be comforted when distressed. Her mother reports

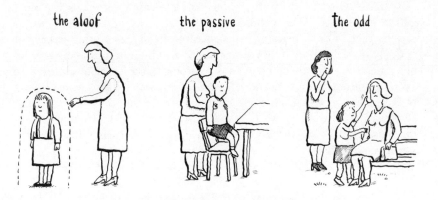

the aloof          the passive          the odd

Figure 4.2  *Three types of social impairment*

that Jane has never greeted her with the eager anticipation so obvious in her younger daughter. Sometimes the mother wonders whether Jane even recognizes her! On the other hand, Jane does not completely reject social contact. She approaches people for simple needs, for instance to obtain food or drink. She also likes rough-and-tumble play and being bounced to music. Her parents cherish these rare opportunities for physical and social contact.

David is a *passive* child who indifferently accepts social approaches made by others. He does what he is told, and his parents and teachers have to watch constantly that he is not led into mischief by his compliance. David has good speech and always answers questions willingly and with total honesty. For David, social contact with other children is part of the daily routine but not something to look forward to or to be done for pleasure. Most of the time, David has an easy-going temperament. However, any stresses or changes of routine result in emotional displays which range from uncontrollable sobbing to temper tantrums.

Doris is an *odd* child who likes being with people and likes to touch people. She goes up to total strangers, and asks 'What's your name?', 'How old are you?' She obviously is not able to judge when approach is unwanted or inappropriate. When she was brought for testing in a university department, she wore out the patience of the tester. At the end of the day she continued to cling to him and said she wanted to stay overnight, much to the embarrassment of her parents. No wonder people often comment on her pestering and obnoxious behaviour. Doris's parents are also worried about her tendency to physical aggression. They feel they must watch over her constantly, never letting her out alone.

In the Camberwell sample the three types of social impairment were distributed in such a way that about half the cases were typically aloof before age seven. This included all the classically autistic children. A quarter each of the remaining cases could be classified as either passive or odd. By the time of the follow-up study many children had changed from one category to another. There was a strong trend for aloof children to become either passive or odd, except for those with severe mental retardation. Of the seven nuclear autistic children four had *lost* their aloofness. What this shows is that the three types of social impairment may all arise out of the same underlying profound disability to form social relationships.

## The Triad of Impairments

It appears that pathological social impairment can be distinguished even at the level of most profound retardation, and furthermore it can occur at any level of ability. This was different for the other two features that the Camberwell study focused on: impairment of verbal and non-verbal communication, and impairment of imaginative activities. These skills normally demand a certain level of maturity. In normal children, they cannot be expected to be in evidence until around two years of age. Therefore, it is of little informative value to register absence of the features on a mentally retarded child with a mental age of much less than two years. Lorna Wing and Judith Gould divided both the socially impaired and sociable groups into subgroups based on language comprehension age of either above or below 20 months. In the children of the higher ability range, impaired communication or imagination could be unequivocally recognized.

It turned out that all socially impaired children in the critical higher ability range showed impairment in each of the three features under consideration. None of the sociable children did. There is therefore truly a 'triad' of impairments, not just three separate impairments. We now have an answer to the question whether the characteristic impairments seen in the rare nuclear autistic children in such clear-cut form are merely a chance combination. Plainly, they are not! We can now be sure that we speak of a natural entity when we speak of the disorder of Autism. There is every justification, then, to search for a single underlying psychological explanation for the curious constellation of the triad. The puzzle we must solve is why, despite an adequate level of intellectual development, there is communication impairment, and why there is no pretend play, and what this has to do with social impairment.

We now turn to another intriguing problem. The triad of impairments was present in every child who had a history of classic Autism. At the same time, the triad applied also to a large number of individuals who hitherto had been categorized as mentally retarded, psychotic or emotionally disturbed. Who are these children? In the Camberwell study only few differences emerged between these handicapped children and classically autistic children, but, for the classically autistic children the median level of intelligence was higher, the proportion of boys was larger, and a smaller proportion was clearly abnormal from birth.

It is open to argument how the whole range of socially impaired children should be classified. The American Psychiatric Association's *Diagnostic and Statistical Manual of the Mental Disorders* in its third revised edition recognizes the existence of children with pervasive developmental disorders of different kinds.[18] That is, there are many subgroups, only one of which constitutes classic Autism. In clinical practice it is necessary to take account of individual variation. For theoretical purposes, however, we would wish to focus on the 'essential' features of a disorder and set aside the variable features. For this reason, it is important that the existence of 'pure' Autism, without general accompanying mental retardation, has been confirmed. Nevertheless, the Camberwell study has opened up the possibility that *all* triad positive children are part of a single continuum and share one and the same underlying abnormality.[19]

### Autism and Schizophrenia

In popular speech disturbed behaviour is often called schizophrenic, in the sense of 'mad'. However, schizophrenia can be defined by using fairly precise diagnostic criteria, and there are many different forms of madness. It is a fact that schizophrenia, narrowly defined, rarely starts before adolescence. Kraepelin, the discoverer of schizophrenia, reported that only about 6 per cent of his sample of over 1,000 cases had onset before age 15. The onset of Autism, on the other hand, in almost all cases predates age three.

The time of onset of a disorder is of crucial importance. A disorder that affects the normal course of development from birth or even before, and the same disorder that befalls a mature organism are two different sorts of problems. Being born blind or deaf, for instance, leads to a totally different state of mind from becoming blind or deaf later. Similarly, psychosis of early onset is different from that of late onset.

It is a remarkable fact that childhood 'psychosis' whose onset can be dated confidently after the third year of life and before age five is almost non-existent. It looks as if there is a sanctuary period where a child can be said to be 'protected' from the outbreak of psychosis. Age of onset is not on a continuum, but is sharply divided, notwithstanding occasional forays from either side of the dividing line. In genetically transmitted diseases just such a sharp division in terms of onset is a common pattern. It can be related to two different kinds of evolutionary pressure: the first to eliminate genetic deviance as early as possible, so as to allow the chance of a new, successful start; the second to postpone any deviance to a point as late as possible, since death from common causes might precede any adverse manifestations. If the psychoses were of genetic origin, then this pattern would be readily comprehensible.

What of those children who become psychotic after age five, but before puberty? Do their symptoms resemble Autism or do they resemble schizophrenia? The answer is straightforward: these rare children almost always resemble adult schizophrenics in their symptoms and can be easily distinguished from autistic children. This was established in an important population study by Kolvin and his colleagues in Britain, published in 1971.[20] A study carried out in New York in 1984 by Green and others has essentially confirmed the earlier findings.[21] Kolvin and his colleagues reported that the youngest child of their sample of 24 diagnosed as schizophrenic was 6.7 years old. In 80 per cent of the sample, the onset of schizophrenia was after age eight and a half. Even at age six, linguistic and cognitive development is substantially completed. The basic prerequisites for adult competence are present, although performance improves with experience. Not surprisingly, then, childhood schizophrenia, even at age six, can be grouped with adult schizophrenia. There is no reason to confuse it with childhood Autism.

In both Kolvin's and Green's studies, children with early onset, that is before age three, were compared with those of later onset. Some important differences were found that extended beyond behavioural symptoms. The New York study showed that 52 per cent of the autistic children scored in the severely subnormal range, that is, IQ below 50. In contrast, none of the schizophrenic children scored below IQ 65. In the British study, too, the schizophrenic children tended to be much more able than the autistic children. Thus, both studies confirm that Autism as a disorder of early development results in major intellectual deficit. Furthermore, in these studies low IQ was associated with direct evidence of brain dysfunction. The autistic group was also significantly more affected by adverse obstetric events.

Despite the fact that schizophrenia and Autism are readily distinguishable diagnostic entities, in adulthood some autistic people resemble, in their surface behaviour, a certain type of schizophrenic patient. Such patients show negative signs, that is, little or no speech or facial expression, and little or no interest in social contact or communication. They may also exhibit simple movement stereotypies. However, behavioural resemblance is not dependable proof of resemblance in underlying dysfunction, let alone underlying causes of dysfunction.

Patients with positive schizophrenic symptoms in no way resemble autistic individuals even in their surface behaviour. The most characteristic positive symptoms of schizophrenia have to do with hearing voices and believing that there are significant personal messages in the environment. The voices and beliefs are subjective experiences which the patient is able to communicate to others. Articulate autistic people who have reported their experiences give accounts quite different from those of schizophrenic patients. Furthermore, in schizophrenia phases of acute illness often alternate with long periods in which normality is established again. This pattern is not seen in Autism. It is, however, possible that schizophrenia and Autism can occur superimposed on each other. There have been some reports of such rare combinations.[22]

Given that the term autistic was first coined by Ernst Bleuler to apply to thought processes in schizophrenia, and given that both Autism and schizophrenia result in some sort of social impairment, it is not surprising that the label 'schizophrenic' in the past was often used to refer to autistic people. To some extent, confusion between the two syndromes became self-fulfilling. Before the recognition of childhood Autism, some patients who would now be classified as autistic were described as schizophrenic with attention to their unique symptoms. Later, the old case histories might be cited as 'proof' that some schizophrenic adults cannot be distinguished from individuals we now recognize as autistic.

## How Early Can Autistic Aloneness Be Diagnosed?

Autism is a disorder of early onset, but early onset is generally defined as from birth to three. Why is the time span as long as that? Should it not be possible to specify exact ages for the first appearance of signs of Autism? Should the first signs not be observable soon after birth?

Home videos now available have recorded children later to be identified as autistic. Some enthusiasts believe that these will at last provide answers to these questions and lead to early identification. So far, the anecdotal evidence suggests that the hope is unfounded. For one thing, we need to know much more about the course of normal development in infancy; for another, the course of abnormal development may be so insidious that a start cannot be pinpointed.

What about retrospective information given by parents on the first two years? In 1977 Edward Ornitz and his colleagues at the UCLA Neuropsychiatric Institute sent a detailed inventory to over 100 parents of autistic and normal children under four.[23] One might expect that with hindsight some really early signs of abnormality would become clear. However, as many as half the parents reported that they had *not* yet suspected that 'something was wrong' in their autistic child's first year. In a sample of 93 autistic people of high ability conducted in Britain,[24] only 12 parents reported that they had a vague disquiet or definite concern about their child in the first year of life. Of course we do not know how many parents of perfectly normal children, if asked, would have admitted to such a concern, unwarranted as it was.

Given that the full clinical picture of Autism is not manifested before age three, and given that parents may not always report abnormalities, how do professionals fare in diagnosing social impairment at an early stage? A surprising answer is given in the eye-opening study by the paediatricians Hilda Knobloch and Benjamin Pasamanick.[25] This study is based on a sample of 1,900 babies referred to a large general paediatric service in North America. The majority of the children were under two years old, and they were seen because it was suspected that development was not proceeding quite normally. The authors identified 50 children as showing a persistent failure to relate to people as persons. Presumably they would constitute a sample of future autistic children. These children were compared to the next 50 children in the file who had also shown signs of abnormal development, but behaved sociably as best they could.

Between half and two-thirds of each of the two abnormal groups showed complications of pregnancy, birth and the neonatal period. The groups did not differ significantly in respect to incidence of complications, nor did they differ in terms of any of the observable neurological signs, including repetitive movements, which were present in almost all of the children. Convulsive disorders were found in 70 per cent of the sample. So also were a number of identifiable disorders associated with organic brain disease. Not surprisingly, mental retardation was present in the majority of cases. Other studies have not reported such a high incidence of organic signs, but the authors explain that it is easier to demonstrate neuromotor abnormalities in early infancy than in later childhood, when compensation may have occurred. Knobloch and Pasamanick emphasize that all those children who showed social impairment and who might later be diagnosed as autistic did not differ in behaviour from the others in any noticeable way, except by showing 'a failure to regard people as persons'.

The most interesting finding of the study, however, was to come at the follow-up of 40 of the children three to ten years later. In the intervening time, none of the children had followed any particular treatment programme, but all the parents had been told to expect delayed and slow development. Indeed, in all cases, mental handicap was present at the later ages. However, that potential symptom of Autism, namely 'the failure to regard people as persons' had disappeared in all those children who had been seen before they reached the age of 12 months. Not so their mental retardation. With hindsight none of them could be considered autistic. This strongly suggests that the symptom was useless as an early indicator of Autism. On the other hand, the older the children were when they were first seen, the more reliable the provisional diagnosis of Autism proved to be. Six children out of 22 who had been seen initially in their second year and had shown social impairment were definitely diagnosed as autistic later on. This was also the case for five out of six children who had first been seen in their third year or after.

This important study again draws attention to the fact that a behavioural diagnosis of Autism is fraught with difficulties if the behaviour repertoire is limited, as it is in young babies. True autistic 'aloofness' may be a very different phenomenon from what can be observed as lack of social responsiveness in early infancy. There are at least some babies who at first seem quite indifferent to social contact, but develop social reponsiveness later. There are also those who at first seem socially responsive, but later show severe impairments. This has long been known to experts in mental retardation, many of whom have reacted in surprise at the introduction of the newfangled label Autism, a condition whose main feature, namely social impairment, seemed to be very familiar. Those autistic children who are recognized as abnormal very early in life may well be recognized by virtue of their mental retardation, rather than their Autism. This view is confirmed by an as yet incomplete retrospective study. We obtained records of the routine screening that is carried out by health professionals on all babies aged six to 18 months. So far we found that in eight out of twelve autistic children the records from when these children were around 12 months registered no abnormality of any kind. On the contrary, social responsiveness and vocalizations were often positively commented on. Delays that were recorded in the four remaining children were, on the other hand, rather general.

Research findings to date dampen any ambition to develop simple behavioural or ethological methods for the *early* diagnosis of Autism. Clearly, we cannot use the notion of indifference to social contact as a touchstone. At least in the first year of life, this behavioural sign is neither unique to Autism nor universally present in Autism.

Is there something else that more specifically characterizes the inability to relate in autistic children, and distinguishes this inability from 'mere' asocial behaviour? Could that elusive something also help explain the other characteristic features of Autism?

The relatively late manifestation of the critical features of Autism, as well as the dubious significance of poor social contact in early infancy, suggests that autistic children suffer from a deficiency in a particular mental capacity that in normal development does not mature until the end of infancy. This, then, is an important clue in our pursuit of an answer to the riddle of Autism.

# 5

# The Biological Roots

'What causes Autism, and what can be done about it'? No question is asked more frequently by anyone confronting this puzzling disorder. Ideally, there should be an answer that would at once explain and prevent Autism while pointing to a cure. In reality no such answer exists. The full picture of causes and effects, the biological interwoven with the psychological, will eventually be revealed, but this grand tapestry has to be worked on by many hands and for many years yet.

Meanwhile, some people still believe that there is a simple answer that can explain, cure and prevent Autism: Autism is caused by psychodynamic conflicts between mother and child, or by some extreme existential anxiety suffered by the child, and is cured by resolving the original conflicts. Despite lack of evidence, this erroneous belief lingers on. It lingers on together with the belief that one can die of a 'broken heart', or be made ill by the 'evil eye'. It is actually impossible for a child to become autistic because it was not loved sufficiently by its mother or because it feels threatened in its very life and identity.

Undoubtedly, Autism has a biological cause and is the consequence of organic dysfunction. What is the nature of this dysfunction and what may be responsible for the abnormality are questions we shall look at in the present chapter. As yet, however, investigations are at an early stage.

The evidence for organic factors is still preliminary, but this does not mean it is premature to rule out psychodynamic causes. They are ruled out because they do not make sense. We can now laugh at the attempt to explain the cause of Down's syndrome in psychogenic terms, which actually happened just before the discovery of its chromosomal origin. But one might have known better even then. Just as in the case of Down's syndrome, in Autism too there are many facts that are simply incompatible with a psychogenic theory. For instance, Autism occurs in all kinds of families and cultures, and not particularly in problem families with unresolved emotional conflicts. Problem families may well produce problem children, but there is a world of difference between an emotionally disturbed and an autistic child. There is no reason to think that parents of autistic children love their children less, or try less hard to nurture and educate them. The visible evidence is that many try harder, and are more selfless in their efforts. One reason that this myth of Autism has been so strong is that it had Kanner's authority behind it. He was struck by autistic features in some of the parents that he saw. Kanner could have considered the possibility of a genetic factor, as indeed Asperger did. Instead he was attracted by the idea that autistic features in the parent might badly affect child rearing practices and that this alone might cause Autism. If this were true, any children who suffer very poor parenting should be autistic. This is plainly not the case. We saw in chapter 2 that Kaspar Hauser and Genie, who were both socially deprived to an extreme degree, were not autistic. In fact, both improved rapidly even though their physical and psychological development had been stunted and remained so to some extent. The triumph over adverse environmental factors which can occur simply by eliminating them testifies to the resilience of human beings.[1] But this is true only provided there has been no organic damage.

Just as with any other developmental disorder, it is of course necessary to take account of both organic and environmental factors. There must be interaction between these factors, or mutual influence, or else development does not occur at all. Where bringing up children is concerned, good parenting and special education will not make a damaged child normal, but will help the child to achieve its best potential. It does not take much imagination to think that a poor psychological or educational environment prevents such achievement. But this truism does not aid our understanding of Autism because it applies to any child.

### Signs that Point to Neurological Damage

At one time many clinicians held the belief that Autism was a functional, not an organic disorder, since there was then no direct evidence of brain abnormality. One of the first facts that shattered this belief was the finding that epilepsy appears, seemingly out of the blue, in about one-third of autistic adolescents.[2]

Consider what happened in the case of Paul. When he was first assessed at age three, no neurological abnormalities were found. On the basis of his behavioural symptoms, he was diagnosed as classically autistic. Ten years later, Paul was still autistic, but started to have epileptic seizures, an unequivocal organic sign. Naturally, the suspicion arose that Paul had neurological abnormalities that had been present from the beginning, but were simply not noticed.

Epileptic seizures are only one example of many organic signs that were found in abundance in autistic children as soon as they were looked for. The list is long and similar to that for other neurologically based developmental disorders. From the point of view of behaviour, mental deficiency is the most important and unequivocal sign of early brain abnormality. Even in autistic children whose intelligence test performance is above the range of mental retardation, a very high proportion of neurological signs are found. Signs of neurological dysfunction that are frequently found in autistic children include, for instance, EEG abnormalities, abnormal nystagmus, abnormal persistence of certain infantile reflexes and stereotypic movements.

The evidence for the existence of organic involvement in Autism is not just a trickle, it is overwhelming. However, such evidence only establishes that there is brain abnormality, not its nature. We are presented with a difficult problem. If there is a whole scatter of neurological abnormalities, which of these will be critical for Autism – and which will be merely associated? It is here that psychological investigations play a key role. If one could specify the nature of the essential psychological impairments in Autism, then one would have a guide to the search for specific brain abnormalities. Unfortunately, so far such a guide has not been available. The search has been carried out almost blind.

The clinical description of the behavourial symptoms of autistic children of different ages and abilities could lead one to expect damage almost anywhere. What this suggests is that the wheat has not yet been separated from the chaff. In the following chapters we will attempt to distinguish critical features of autistic behaviour from features which are merely associated. However, this is not all that needs to be done. In the end, we wish to know what the biological abnormality is and how the abnormality results in a typical pattern of symptoms. This knowledge is what we can look forward to, as the 'grand tapestry' of scientific endeavour progresses.

The challenge of the search for the biological basis of Autism has been accepted enthusiastically. The field of relevant factors is so staggeringly large that this chapter can provide only a glimpse. Coleman and Gillberg's monograph,[3] and the recently edited volume on neurobiological issues by Schopler and Mesibov,[4] and by Wing[5] provide useful sources for further information.

## What Might be Wrong with the Brain?

If Autism is an organic disorder, then one would expect to find the abnormality when looking at the brain directly. This approach is by no means simple and straightforward. Instead it has more than an element of gamble. Chances are high that some structural damage will be found, and this damage could be anything from the microscopic to the grossly visible, from faults within nerve cells to faulty development of whole cell systems. The chances are also high of finding physiological dysfunction. For instance, there could be a relative lack or excess of neuro-transmitter substances, or there could be a missing enzyme, as is indeed the case with certain other rare developmental disorders. A situation as open as this brings with it a special problem. The more aspects one is investigating, the more likely it is that irrelevant faults will be found, faults which have no critical relationship to Autism.

An important point to bear in mind when evaluating anatomical and physiological investigations is that Autism is a developmental disorder. Presumably, this means that underlying it is an abnormality of development. Distinguishing a developmental disorder from later appearing damage is not trivial. For instance, being born deaf has consequences for language processes but becoming deaf in later life does not. Although autistic-like behaviour can be found in some brain-damaged or psychotic adults who never showed such behaviour before, this is not the same as the disorder that we know as Autism.

The normal devlopment of the brain must be taken into account when hypothesizing what kind of damage could cause Autism. It is now known that brain cells at first proliferate, but then 'die back' in normal development. Contrary to the idea that development is growth, and that more is better, it is the immature brain that has more densely packed cells and more synapses per cell, not the mature brain. Developmental arrest therefore may be a failure to switch off, rather than to switch on. Nerve cells follow growth instructions laid down in the genes, so that abnormalities appear if a gene program is faulty. For instance, switching off may occur too late. In this situation, increased cell density might be expected, and this indeed was found in post-mortem examinations of several autistic patients.[6]

It would be useful to distinguish abnormalities according to their time of origin and their consequences for development. One intriguing physical indicator of abnormalities in foetal development is seen in the loops and whorls on fingertips and toes. Distinctive abnormal patterns have been reported in some autistic children.[7] If their onset could be linked to a critical point in prenatal development, this might prove to be a clue as to the biological onset of Autism. Similarly, the abnormal handedness patterns that have been found in population studies of autistic children point to early prenatal damage.[8]

Brain autopsies of autistic people are still few and far between. Increasingly, however, there are studies of the 'live' brain, for instance by computerized tomographic scan (CT scan). This method provides gross measurements that assess the relationship between cell-filled and fluid-filled spaces in the brain. If there is cell atrophy or pressure, then the fluid-filled spaces are relatively larger. If Autism is associated with destruction, rather than proliferation of cells, then the fluid-filled spaces should be enlarged. Some excitement was generated in 1978 by a study which showed such an enlargement.[9] This was more marked on the left side of the brain. The suggestive evidence fitted well with neuro-psychological ideas connecting left hemisphere damage with language dysfunction, which was long held to be a prominent feature in Autism. A number of neuropsychological studies seemed to confirm the hypothesis, and led to much debate. In the end, it could not be demonstrated that a specific left hemisphere lesion was in any way critical to Autsism.[10] Rather, any such lesion in autistic children is likely to be an additional brain impairment.

Since then, various types of scan, including PET-scan (positron emission tomography, which can measure the rate of glucose utilization of specific brain areas) as well as MRI (magnetic resonance imaging, which makes neural tissue visible and can detect lesions) have been carried out. Although these studies continue to provide direct evidence for brain pathology in many autistic individuals, they do not provide a rationale for focusing on any one particular brain area. A recent MRI study, reported by Courchesne and colleagues, provides a promising new lead.[11] They found an unusual malformation of a small part of the cerebellum in a large number of autistic people with and without mental retardation. It could well be that this abnormality is associated with abnormalities in other parts of the brain which have not yet been looked for. At present it is not clear how the abnormality relates to behavioural symptoms.

Apart from this last study, the main problem with anatomical investigations is that they have not so far produced evidence that would exclude *general* pathology or show an effect of *specific* pathology, possibly over and above the general impairment. As we shall see, this bane of research in abnormal mental functions has been overcome only partially in the area of psychological experimentation. The objection to data that demonstrate general deficit is that they offer too *many* reasons for the presence of particular deficits. A cortex depleted of cells (as indicated, for instance, by enlarged fluid-filled spaces), or alternatively a proliferation of cells (as hypothesized on the basis of abnormal neural development) would obviously be a bad thing. No one would be surprised if such gross biological abnormalities resulted in developmental disorder and in behavioural problems. But why should they result in Autism? And why only rarely in Autism?

The same questions apply when considering biochemical studies. Large numbers of such studies have been carried out, but as yet they do not present a coherent picture. One example of an unexplained but reliable finding is the significant elevation of blood serotonin in many autistic children.[12] At the same time serotonin in the spinal fluid or elsewhere in the body is present at normal levels. The abnormality was pinned down to an alteration in uptake or storage of serotonin by blood platelets. Here, then, is a specific factor that contains possible clues to the biological basis of Autism. But what does it mean? Any link from such a finding to behavioural symptoms in Autism would be extremely tenuous.

It is worth noting here that the hope for a pharmacological treatment of Autism is a strong motivation for taking research gambles. Various neuro-transmitter substances, enzymes, vitamins and diets have been and are being tried, sometimes with reasonable success. Many would argue that the 'Why not try this' approach is better than not trying anything at all. Undoubtedly, certain symptoms of Autism may be successfully treated pharmacologically. It does, however, seem improbable that a pharmacological cure will be found to prevent or reverse developmental brain pathology.

## Psychophysiological Studies

A whole branch of psychology is devoted to the measurement of autonomic functions such as heart rate and skin conductance, and the minuscule electrical currents emitted by the brain. The interest of these measures is that they are largely outside the subject's voluntary control. While they are direct measures of physiological symptoms, they nevertheless relate to psychological processess, such as anxiety, arousal and information processing.

A number of electrophysiological studies done with autistic children have been reviewed in a publication by Angela James and James Barry.[13] These authors, who have themselves provided the best experimental evidence, conclude that autonomic measures of autistic children such as respiratory responses, heart rate and skin conductance, as well as EEG measures, all indicate severe developmental immaturity. Mentally retarded autistic children were compared with equally retarded non-autistic children and were found to be even more retarded in terms of the psychophysiological measures.

The most important of their measures was habituation of the orienting response. This is the response that most animals will make when a novel event occurs. The most obvious components of this response is pricking up the ears and turning towards the source of the stimulus. In addition, however, changes in the EEG and in autonomic measures can be observed. Habituation of this response occurs because the animal recognizes that the stimulus has occurred before and is of no consequence. Humans too, habituate readily when a stimulus is repeated. In autistic children, the orienting response habituates abnormally slowly.

The failure to habituate can be understood as an outcome of a cognitive dysfunction. Repeated stimuli fail to lose their novelty value because they are not appropriately processed. If this is so, then the comparison with the next stimulus would fail to register identity. A cognitive dysfunction of the type we shall consider in later chapters would fit in well with this account. One would expect habituation failure when each stimulus is treated independently, and not as part of a greater pattern.

Habituation of the orienting response is also slow in states of high arousal. Perhaps autistic children keep responding to a repeated stimulus because they are very anxious. From here it seems but a small step to postulate that Autism is caused by an extreme anxiety state. This conclusion is unwarranted since, as James and Barry point out, autistic children fail to habituate while simultaneously showing *low* anxiety as indicated by heart rate. Indeed, other psychophysiological evidence suggests that autistic children are not chronically highly aroused.

The problem with psychophysiological evidence is that no one has, as yet, established to what extent the measures obtained are basic biological characteristics, and to what extent they are secondary phenomena of cognitive dysfunction. Level of arousal might very well be a result of processing effort rather than a cause of processing style. Another problem is that the evidence does not reveal anything specific to Autism, since very similar abnormalities are typical of a great number of psychiatric disorders. We can conclude that measurements of autonomic functions are valuable indices of information-processing abnormalities, but explanatory concepts have to come from elsewhere.

## Ideas from Neurology

There have been various attempts at an interpretation of Autism that explains its main symptoms in terms of general neurological theories. In 1978, Damasio and Maurer proposed the first comprehensive theory on this basis.[14] They envisaged the possibility of damage in the dopamine system of the brain, which projects mainly into the basal ganglia but also into parts of the frontal lobes and the temporal lobes. The dopamine system is shown in figure 5.1. It is interesting to note that for schizophrenia abnormalities of the dopamine system have also been proposed, and some evidence of this has been obtained. Damasio and Maurer drew their theory by analogy from behavioural symptoms shown by brain-damaged adults or lesioned animals. Such an approach must be treated with caution. Even if there is close resemblance of symptoms and signs between lesioned animals and neurological cases, schizophrenic patients and autistic children, it does not follow that the damage is in the same place. In any case, it need not be caused by the same agent.

The theory of dopamine system impairment deserves to be taken seriously since it addresses the problem of specificity. The system involves only a very small part of the brain, although it affects many different areas. The theory focuses on those neurological symptoms

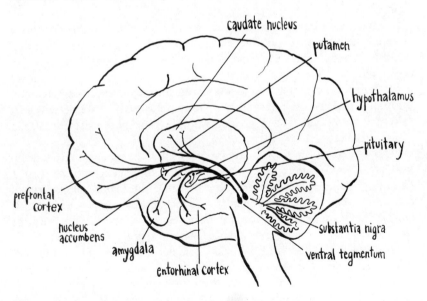

Figure 5.1  *The dopamine system*

which seem to be closely associated with Autism: strange gait, poor voice control, apparently expressionless faces, flapping hand movements, repetitious actions, lack of spontaneity, perseveration on one topic and social impairment. They are all typical autistic features. They could all reflect dysfunction of exactly those brain areas which are conrolled by the dopamine system. Coleman and Gillberg discuss the as yet indirect evidence that would support this theory and link it to a primary abnormality in the brain stem, which is where the dopamine projections originate.

One particular neurological syndrome has been claimed to be a neurologically defined equivalent of Autism.[15] This is called the Kluver-Bucy syndrome, a result of an artificially induced subcortical lesion of the amygdala and surrounding temporal neocortex. After sustaining the Kluver-Bucy lesion, monkeys fail to recognize objects and other animals, and as a result behave in a socially grossly inept way. They also show paradoxical tameness, lack of spontaneity and sometimes inappropriate rage. However, to what extent these symptoms resemble autistic behaviour is questionable. Excessive dopamine activity, which can be induced by treatment with amphetamine, blocks some of the functions of the amygdala. Ros Ridley and Harry Baker at the Clinical Research Centre in Harrow have demonstrated that treated with amphetamine, animals become overactive and highly stereotyped, losing all interest in their peers.[16]

If there were a specific fault in the development of the dopamine system in the brain, it could be by cells not dying back as they should in normal development. The result would be an increased number of dopamine neurones and therefore an overactive system. Dopamine overactivity in an as yet developing organism might lead to behavioural symptoms with a certain resemblance to those caused by overactivity in a fully mature system. However, one would expect more differences than similarities.

Of considerable interest is a comprehensive neuropsychological study by Rumsey and Hamburger of ten normally intelligent autistic men.[17] Here any deficit is not attributable to mental retardation or additional handicaps. A very marked deficit was found on a number of tests which are known to be sensitive to frontal system dysfunction. The authors suggest that these results fit in with Damasio's proposed model.

In 1986, in a thoughtful review article, Deborah Fein and her colleagues concluded that it is as yet too early to develop a detailed neuropsychological model of Autism.[18] They pointed out that previous theories necessarily rested on shaky foundations since their assumptions about the nature of the symptoms were too vague and unexamined. The strong message is that, until we are clearer about the underlying cognitive dysfunction in Autism, it is difficult to make further progress along the lines of neuropsycholgical investigations.

Meanwhile, research conducted from quite a different point of view has advanced the investigation of the biological basis of Autism. Rather than aiming to find out *what* is wrong with the brain of autistic children, this research boldly addresses the question: *why* is there something wrong?

### Genetic Defects

Can Autism be due to a fault in genetic programming? This question can be answered by twin studies and pedigree studies, in which all relatives are investigated in as many generations as possible. Promising studies in this area are in progress, and research workers at various centres are attempting to find the 'autistic gene' by means of linkage analysis in families with one or more autistic members.

Since Autism is a rare disorder, it is not often that one would expect to see more than one autistic child in one family. Nevertheless, 2 per cent of siblings of autistic children are found to be autistic. This incidence is 50 to 100 times higher than that of the population in general. It must not be forgotten that autistic people very rarely have children themselves. Therefore, if Autism is genetically transmitted, the chances of direct transmission are negligble.

A pioneering twin study was carried out in 1977. Susan Folstein and Michael Rutter succeeded in collecting 21 pairs of twins, with at least one twin unequivocally diagnosed as autistic.[19] The aim was to estimate the degree of concordance: would Autism, diagnosed according to strict criteria, be present in both twins when they were genetically identical rather than when they were fraternal? It has to be noted here that 100 per cent concordance rates are not expected even in well-established genetic conditions. One reason is the varying degree of penetrance of genes. Concordance for classic Autism was found in 4 out of 11 identical pairs and in none of the fraternal ones. This is strong evidence for genetic causes. However, the study went one step further: in the non-concordant pairs the co-twin was not necessarily normal. As many as 82 per cent of the identical co-twins showed intellectual impairment and language disorder, and so did 10 per cent of the fraternal ones. This finding suggests that there is a genetic cause for a more general disorder of cognitive development. Given a genetic predisposition for this disorder, classic Autism might be just one of its manifestations.

## Chromosome abnormalities

The chromosomal abnormality known as 'fragile-X syndrome' often results in mental retardation. In frequency it is second only to Down's syndrome, which is due to chromosomal abnormality of a different type. Fragile-X syndrome is seen much more frequently in males. Affected individuals show language abnormalities, many of which are reminiscent of those found in Autism. The abnormalities that exist, but by themselves do not qualify for the diagnosis of Autism, include muteness, delay of language acquisition, echoing of speech, odd voice quality and inability to hold proper conversations. Two other frequent symptoms in fragile-X individuals are pronounced aversion of eye gaze and dislike of being touched. It is interesting to note that these symptoms can be observed in the absence of a severe disturbance of social-affective relationships.

A proportion of fragile-X sufferers are autistic by strict diagnostic criteria. Since no epidemiology study has yet been carried out, both the true prevalence of fragile-X abnormality in the general population and the prevalence of Autism among affected individuals remains unknown. It is at present assumed that between 10 and 20 per cent of autistic boys have a chromosome abnormality, fragile-X being the most likely.[20] If substantiated, the finding would provide a cause for a certain proportion of Autism in boys, and would partially explain why there are more autistic boys than girls.

Coleman and Gillberg discuss findings on a sample of 10 autistic boys who had the fragile-X chromosome abnormality. In more than half of these boys there were adverse prenatal and perinatal conditions. Most of them had muscular hypotonia, epilepsy and signs of brain stem dysfunction. The authors propose the following intriguing hypothesis: a chromosome defect might underly abnormal brain stem development, possibly causing neuronal disarray of the dopamine system, and sometimes epilepsy. Autism could be one outcome of this chain of events. But does the chromosome defect cause the adverse prenatal conditions? Some perinatal problems are obviously caused by a sick baby but others must be due to other causes.

## Prenatal or Perinatal Brain Damage

There is general agreement from many studies that the incidence of perinatal hazards in Autism is astonishingly high. In 1971, for instance, Kolvin reported an incidence of 37 per cent in his sample of autistic children, but an incidence of only 12 per cent in his sample of 33 schizophrenic children (that is, those with onset of psychosis over the age of five).[21] A number of studies show that significantly more hazards of pregnancy and birth are present in autistic than in normal children. In Folstein and Rutter's twin study, there were 17 autistic boys whose twin brothers had not been so diagnosed. Even though there had been a deliberate attempt to exclude neurologically affected cases in the sample as a whole, 12 of these boys showed more perinatal problems than their non-autistic co-twins, for example, delayed birth, delayed breathing or neonatal convulsions.

The presence of adverse perinatal factors suggests but does not prove that brain damage, perhaps through anoxia, could have occurred. It must also be considered that adverse factors, whatever they may be – from pregnancy complications to forceps delivery – do not come out of the blue. There are many conditions which make adverse outcomes more likely. Or, as folk wisdom has it: Troubles rarely come singly. Reproductive problems may be part and parcel of a predisposition for developmental abnormalities. The effects of genetic, constitutional and prenatal environmental factors can combine to result in outcomes ranging from foetal death to barely noticeable abnormality. This view would fit in with the lack of specificity of findings in the field of birth complications. In none of the relevant studies, which were reviewed by Mary Konstantareas in 1986,[22] is there a clear distinction between prenatal, perinatal or even neonatal complications. Because these cannot be considered separate risks, it could be that the exact nature or timing of the event most critical to Autism is obscured. In the investigation of causes of Autism one finds not just one, but a whole array of potential hazards. What matters is whether the damage sustained from whatever source prevents normal development of a specific neurological system at a critical time. The hypothetical system might well be vulnerable to a whole range of onslaughts originating at different times and for different reasons.

## Viral Infections and Immune Dysfunction

The theory that psychotic illness can be due to immune dysfunction and/or viral infection has particular justification in the area of Autism. It has been shown in selected cases that a virus infection in a young child preceded the onset of typical symptoms of Autism, before which there was a period of apparently normal development. There are also cases where infection occurred in the mothers at an early stage of pregnancy. A clear example is rubella. However, in view of the rarity of well-documented cases, Autism cannot for the most part be linked to such aetiology.

Viral diseases are subject to sudden outbreaks. If the central nervous system becomes infected at a critical time, either before or after birth, Autism may result. This hypothesis is testable by studying the incidence of autistic children in relation to known virus epidemics. Of special interest are certain types of virus called retrovirus, which totally integrate themselves in genetic material in the body cells. Other viruses that have been suggested as possible causes of Autism are herpes and cytomegalovirus. These can remain dormant for years but from time to time can be reactivated.

The immune system, which protects us from virus damage, can itself be subject to dysfunction. Severe forms of immune intolerance in the mother lead to foetal death. Mild forms may interfere with normal processes of growth, and hence lead to developmental disorder. Indeed, there is evidence of immune abnormalities in some autistic children.[23]

One unexpected and intriguing finding about the mothers of autistic and socially impaired children was contributed by Lorna Wing's population study (described in some detail in chapter 3).[24] A disproportionately large number of mothers of impaired children (22 against an expected 5 for the size of the population), were of Caribbean origin. A similar excess of socially impaired children born in Northern Europe to immigrant mothers from tropical countries has been found in Sweden.[25] A possible cause is viral disease endemic in northern countries, to which mothers born in tropical countries had not yet acquired immunity.

## The Causal Chain

The evidence that we discussed in this chapter suggests that we should think not just about 'the' cause of Autism, but about a long causal chain. This chain has discrete links. In the manner of a mnemonic we can say that there is hazard, followed by havoc, followed by harm. As we have seen in this chapter the hazard can be of many kinds, including faulty genes, chromosome abnormality, metabolic disorder, viral agents, immune intolerance, and anoxia from perinatal problems. We can assume that any of these hazards has the potential to create havoc in neural development. Owing to the upheaval, lasting harm may be done to the development of specific brain systems concerned with higher mental processes. The harm may be mild or severe, but always involves developmental arrest of a critical system at a critical point in time. It is our hypothesis that only then will Autism occur.

What is this critical system? We do not yet know. In the previous chapter the findings from population studies of socially impaired children suggested that whatever it is that underlies the normal development of social and communication abilities is highly protected. The likelihood of this particular damage increases with the extent of general damage. Nevertheless, the existence of pure Autism in otherwise not generally retarded individuals shows that it *can* be damaged quite selectively, with other systems apparently left intact. However, if there is damage to one part of the nervous system, very likely there is also damage to some other part. The possibility of widespread damage is presumably the reason for the wide variety of handicaps associated with Autism.

In our causal chain model for autism there is provision for multiple causes and for multiple handicaps. Each possible cause could affect the critical system involved in Autism, whether or not if affects other systems as well. The idea is the same as the notion of the 'final common pathway' which is often postulated in biological theories of mental disorder. A common pathway can be damaged by a variety of different agents. This fact does not mean 'anything' can cause Autism. There is a single critical cause somewhere in the chain, but the agents that affect this critical link are numerous and varied.

Locating the pathology and linking it to developmental arrest at a critical point in time is a formidable task. Nobody expects to bridge the gulf between brain and behaviour tomorrow. Meanwhile, the bridge has to be built from both ends. In this chapter we briefly considered the state of progress from the biological end. In the remaining chapters of this book, we shall approach the question of causes from the opposite direction. We shall consider the various symptoms of Autism and then derive a deeper explanation. We shall ask what psychological processes can be inferred to exist to give rise to the symptoms. Eventually, such deeper explanations might be linked to hypothetical neurological structures.

# 6

# The Intelligence of Autistic Children

## Testing Intelligence

Many people wonder whether one can put any trust in IQ-scores obtained from autistic children. For one thing these children are difficult to test, and for another, results on different intelligence tests often seem contradictory. The fact-finding epidemiological studies that were reviewed in chapter 4 have established that the vast majority of autistic children are mentally retarded. Could it be that autistic children are more intelligent than they are given credit for? Both Kanner and Asperger were impressed by the 'strikingly intelligent physiognomy' of autistic children and by their unusual skills and interests. On a first encounter with young autistic children one may be struck by their attractive, bright-eyed appearance, so different from the dull expression usually associated with the mentally defective. It is not just appearance, either, that makes one wonder. The behaviour of autistic children often hints at capabilities out of the ordinary, sometimes even rare talent.

Gesell and Amatruda, in their 1941 textbook *Developmental Diagnosis*,[1] warn of the danger of mistaken impressions of intelligence in mentally retarded children with organic pathology. Interestingly, they use as examples children who bear traits that are highly reminiscent of Autism – a disorder which was not identified at the time! The danger they see is that such impressions can lead to false assumptions of non-organic pathology.

> Often the behavior of the child is very bizarre, and paradoxically enough the very strangeness of the behavior invites a diagnosis which may overlook the underlying mental deficiency. When the behavior assumes bizarre patterns, there is a temptation to look for environmental origins and to place a psychiatric construction on the symptoms. For example, the child may show extreme fixations on one toy, or on one pastime, such as pouring

sand through a pipe, opening and closing doors. This particular behaviour becomes a misleading focus of attention in the interpretation of the case. The behaviour may even be invested with symbolic significance to the relative neglect of a multitude of symptoms which definitely point to a fundamental defect. Activity and bizarre exaggeration are frequently associated with an attractive countenance and a faraway, wistful expression which builds up an impression of dormant or obscured normality. If the physician yields uncritically to this impression, he may describe the condition as one of symptomatic retardation.

It may well be that Kanner was subject to the effect pointed out in this passage. However, in 1971, in the 30-year follow-up of his initial sample,[2] he said of four of his 11 cases: 'originally astounding the observer with their phenomenal feats of memory . . ., if at all responsive to psychological testing, their IQs dropped down to figures usually referred to as low-grade moron or imbecile.'

The question of IQ-testing on autistic children has received careful consideration in a study by Lockyer and Rutter.[3] They compared the results of initial IQ-assessment of 63 autistic children at around age five with a second assessment at around age 15. They also compared IQ to later educational achievement and social adaptation. In this way the validity of the IQ-assessment was tested against real-life criteria, and it was gauged by the 'test of time'. The conclusions we can draw from this study are very clear: careful assessment of autistic children's intellectual abilities by clinical psychologists is trustworthy. Indeed it is just as trustworthy as it is with retarded and normally developing children.

Lockyer and Rutter's study showed that the IQ-estimates of autistic children remained the same at second testing ten years later, even when different test batteries were used, with different testers administering them. Nevertheless, there was pronounced unevenness of performance on different subtests. But this also was persistent over time. Fluctuating cooperation can be ruled out for this reason alone.

We must conclude that the frequently obtained low IQ-estimates and the widely diverging results on different subtests reflect stable facts. They are consistent with educational achievements and the everyday functioning of the children. The problems do not lie with the tests or the testers, but reflect the children's real handicap.

Children with initially low IQ scored even lower at the follow-up, a finding confirmed by Waterhouse and Fein in a more recent study.[4] Children who did not have useful speech by late childhood declined in terms of IQ. IQ was overestimated and misleading if only successfully completed tests were taken into account. Unfortunately this is often done in practice, so that the myth of the secretly intelligent autistic child persists. In particular, children who are found to be untestable on many subtests but score quite highly on one test tend to be credited with potential they do not have. It is necessary to take account of the whole range of performance in order to make accurate predictions.

Contrary to popular opinion, early IQ assessments, if properly carried out and interpreted, are excellent predictors of a child's later adjustment and functioning in real life. Nevertheless, IQ-test batteries, just like teachers' assessments or parents' observations, are overtaxed when required to distinguish subtle individual differences. The strength of well-constructed tests is shown when one wishes to detect large individual differences caused by brain impairment. There is little doubt that such measurements are superior to subjective judgements.

The problem that we need to turn to now is that despite generally low measured intelligence there can be astoundingly high performance on certain isolated skills. This is most dramatically demonstrated in the phenomenon of the *idiot savant*.

## The Autistic *Idiot Savant*

There are rare people who are mentally retarded, and yet show outstanding performance in one field of interest, often outperforming their intellectual superiors. The label *idiot savant* expresses the paradox of someone who, to all intents and purposes, is an 'idiot', but is *savant* by having one area of superior knowledge or skill. It is a fact that an inordinately high proportion, possibly 50 per cent, of these remarkable people are also autistic. There is the stunning example of Nadia, who, between the ages of four and seven, produced beautiful drawings admired by professionals.[5] There is also 12-year-old Stephen, who has attracted the attention of a President of the Royal Academy of Arts. Sir Hugh Casson says of him:

> Stephen Wiltshire draws exactly what he sees – no more, no less. He stands before the object – usually a building – for, say, 15 minutes, seeming to watch rather than to observe it. Later he will draw it, quickly, confidently, and with an accuracy all the more uncanny because it is done entirely from memory and without notes. He misses no detail – nothing. The only inaccuracy is that the object in his drawing is 'mirrored'. His preferred subject is always architecture and the pricklier and more complicated the better.[6]

Another young man, Nigel, who has very low measured intelligence and is quite unable to look after himself, is an accomplished pianist. He has an astounding repertoire of classical music and can learn a new piece by hearing it played only once. There is also 22-year-old Claudia who has won art competitions. With Stephen and Nigel she is one of many fascinating cases investigated by Neil O'Connor and Beate Hermelin.[7] The portrait in figure 6.1 was drawn by her in about fifteen minutes.

It is rare that *idiot savant* individuals can put their talent to professional use. Sadly, their mental handicap prevents this. It is also true that some of the skills that they are exceptionally good at are of very little use either to themselves or others. Consider knowing the day of the week for any given date, even in the distant past and future, and reading aloud fluently without comprehension.

We do not know what has to happen in order for a child to become an *idiot savant*. There may have to be a degree of obsessive determination for a particular skill to be perfected. No doubt, absence of a social life would guarantee that plenty of time is available for singleminded pursuit. It has frequently been observed that classically autistic children do show an unusual capacity for singleminded concentration. If these features facilitate the development of an isolated skill, then Autism would provide ideal conditions for the *savant* phenomenon to flourish.

One needs to remember that truly phenomenal cases are rare, even in the autistic population. Nevertheless, in many case histories there is mention of some ability that is seen as exceptional. The most frequently reported skills are those that have to do with rote memory and with constructional or spatial skills. Kanner coined the term 'islets of abilities', while others call them 'splinter skills'. Both terms vividly convey the isolated nature of these peaks of performance.

## Performance Peaks and Troughs

The well-known Wechsler Scales of Intelligence (WISC) consist of many different well-tried subtests. They have provided an abundance of information on the characteristic pattern of test performance in autistic children. It is worth dwelling on these findings, if only because almost every autistic child will be tested on the WISC or similar instrument in the course of assessment.

Because of the way the WISC is constructed, and because we can assume that there is such a thing as general intelligence that affects all aspects of performance, the 'ideal normal' child shows an even level of performance on a large variety of subtests, exactly average for age group. Even with children who are below or above average intelligence, one expects that, whatever subtest is given, the score will fall into the same

Uta Frith
by Claudia
B Holder

Figure 6.1  *Portrait of Uta Frith by Claudia, a 22-year-old autistic woman*

Figure 6.2   *The Comprehension Test (WISC)*

band. If one draws a graph representing scores on the various tests, a more or less horizontal line is obtained. A wildly uneven line (reminiscent of a seismograph recording turbulence) suggests neurological abnormality. There is wide consensus that autistic children show a more jagged profile than any comparison group. Moreover, their profile seems to be different from that found in any other clinical group. Oddly enough the diagnostic potential of this fact has not yet been realized.

Not every autistic child shows the same pattern, but one particular pattern is clearly discernible in group data. It is recognizable by having two opposite poles of performance. The two poles can be discerned despite individual variations and despite differences in intelligence levels and cultural environment. Even those autistic individuals with normal intelligence show this pattern[8] and Japanese autistic children show it too.[9]

*The pole of worst performance* lies on those subtests that demand a high degree of communicative competence. The most typical of these is the Comprehension subtest. This test, illustrated in figure 6.2 requires commonsense answers to seemingly ordinary, but really quite deep, hypothetical questions. It is not sufficient to give a 'correct' answer, as in the example, but the answer needs to be relevant to the question. Since communication is by definition impaired in autistic children, failure on these tests is perhaps not particularly surprising. Yet it is not the case that autistic people are poor at understanding and answering *any* sort of questions. Questions that request some precise information on a topic where the autistic person has some special knowledge are answered faultlessly. Indeed, there is the Information subtest of the WISC, on which autistic children almost always score better than on the Comprehension subtest. In contrast, it is often the other way round for retarded non-autistic children.

*The pole of best performance* lies on those subtests of which Block Design is the most typical. The nature of this test is copying an abstract pattern with little cubes within a time limit, as illustrated in figure 6.3. As a rule one can expect that almost any autistic child, provided it understands what is required, will obtain a score on this test which is as good or better than that of a normal child of the same age. This test, on the other hand, is usually very difficult for non-autistic retarded children. Why should this test be comparatively easy for autistic children? True, the task does not make heavy demands on social or verbal communication and the materials themselves seem to suggest what should be done, but would this alone explain the extraordinary ability of autistic children to perform well on it? Before we take this question further, it is necessary to be quite clear that there is a difference between test performance and the ability that is being tested.

Everyone knows that performance can be artificially increased by extensive drill and practice, or artificially decreased, for example, by simply not doing what one is supposed to be doing on the test. Test

Figure 6.3    *The Block Design Test (WISC)*

performance can never be considered a perfect reflection of the underlying abilities that are the test's target. Since performance on many subtests is amenable to improvement through general instruction, the existence of an underlying deficit may be obscured.

We need to step away from test performance and look firmly toward the pattern of psychological abilities that can be inferred from test performance. The underlying pattern should make sense if there is a particular cognitive dysfunction that is unique to Autism. Unfortunately, the WISC profile itself does not tell us what the dysfunction might be. After all, the WISC was not constructed as a tool for a theoretical analysis of cognitive abilities. What we glean from it in this respect is sheer bonus and therefore any subtest profile analysis will only become meaningful when it is compared with predictions from independently derived hypotheses. That is what we shall try to do in the remaining part of the chapter.

## Test Intelligence and World Intelligence

Any theory of intellectual dysfunction in Autism needs to account for unevenness of performance on IQ-test batteries. But this is a thorny problem. Simply to state that there is a deficit in verbal comprehension and none in spatial skill does not get us much further. The labels make the abilities in question look like basic units of brain function, located in parts of the cortex with labels such as speech or spatial orientation. However, we have little reason to think that they are. Rather, the abilities themselves need to be analysed into components. We need to find out what these components are, and which of them might be faulty. This can be done through the approach of cognitive neuropsychology, which suggests models for possible components. In the case of Autism, this approach presents a particular difficulty: over and above the overwhelming effect of brain impairment we have to look for specific components that are at the root of the demonstrated unevenness of performance. One can also look at this problem in reverse: the typical peaks and troughs in autistic children's performance might actually tell us something about the nature of IQ-tests.

IQ-tests are purposely constructed so as to be as independent of social context as possible. A good example is Raven's matrices. This is a test which uses abstract shapes arranged in rows and columns where the last position of the matrix has to be completed. Another is the Seguin Formboard, where cut-out geometric shapes have to be fitted into exact spaces. The materials are abstract and the tasks are self-contained in their goals. The intention is to equalize the task situation for individuals from different backgrounds, and to minimize the need for learned assumptions. This should make the tests suitable for revealing underlying abilities without cultural overlays. However, the decontextualization of the tasks unwittingly introduces new problems. Even if one can solve a problem in real life, one may not be able to solve it in the test. One needs to be accustomed to the idea of solving problems in tests for their own sake, outside a real-life context. Schooling normally provides the opportunity to get accustomed to decontextualized tasks and to learn to show 'test intelligence'. People who have never been to any school find the neutrality and detachment of a context-free test so strange that they are prevented from revealing abilities which are part of their 'world intelligence'. Ironically, it is on the supposedly culture-free tests (Block Design, Seguin Formboard, Raven's matrices) where ordinary unschooled people are at the greatest disadvantage.

For autistic individuals the advantage is exactly reversed. It may be that for an unschooled, normal human being the materials alone do not provide a sufficient stimulus for doing the task in the first place. In real life, the stimulus needed to solve the task would come from the wider context of which the task is normally a part. For instance, solving a matrix with abstract shapes may be meaningless as a test, but may be a meaningful problem when weaving patterns in rugs. Normal children everywhere do well when they understand and take account of context. The ability to take account of context is what we can take for granted in normal children, but not in autistic children. Here, instead, we might consider the ability *not to take account of context*. If this ability means performing well on Block Design and performing poorly on Comprehension, then we would have an amazingly simple explanation for the strange scatter of abilities in Autism.

The ability of ordinary, but unschooled children to *take account of context* is strikingly illustrated in an example, where we see failure on context-free IQ-type tests and success on the same problems in real life. This example is provided by a fascinating study of unschooled child street vendors in Brazil.[10] Here 'test intelligence' and 'world intelligence' are as sharply contrasted as in some autistic children, but in the opposite direction. The young street vendors were extremely adept at calculating prices and change when selling fruit or vegetables to their customers. However, in an artificial testing situation these same children failed when asked to do very similar calculations. Clearly this was not because of intellectual problems. Perhaps it was because the task without the presuppositions supplied by the ordinary context did not make enough sense to trigger the skills they had.

Margaret Donaldson, in her comprehensive yet marvellously concise account of children's cognitive development, highlights the acquisition of disembedded thought as a major task of development.[11] For instance, when becoming literate the child must learn to 'free language from its embeddedness in events' so as to achieve the ability to look at 'sheer linguistic form'. Aspects of words such as their sound structure are quite separate from their meaning but must be attended to in their own right when learning the rudiments of spelling.

Let us return to the case of autistic children. Perhaps they have no need to free language from its embeddedness in events, as it is never embedded in the first place. Their reading and spelling ability is often excellent. Their performance on abstract maths problems can be remarkably good. Yet in real life these 'human calculators' are often quite helpless. Even with superior numeric ability, autistic children would fail to make a living as street vendors. We now see that what is odd is that even the less able autistic children do comparatively well on certain tests! They do well on just those IQ-tests where a wider context is missing and they do badly where context is important. What can be the reason for this strange reversal of the normal state of affairs?

### Rote memory skills, and what lies behind them

It is easier to explain failure than success in children whom we presume to be 'entitled' to impaired performance by virtue of their impaired brain development. Nevertheless, the psychological investigation of autistic peak performance has been a fruitful area of discovery. Indeed, it is peaks rather than troughs in performance that give us the main clues to underlying cognitive deficits. We shall see that the 'islets' of abilities are not so much tranquil oases as volcanoes, blatant signs of underlying disturbance.

Feats of rote memory are a typical example of 'islets' of ability in autistic children. Beyond the mere observation of verbatim recall of speech or songs, we are fortunate enough to be able to draw on experimental studies. Experiments are essential if one wants to know which aspects of memory skills are responsible for this islet of ability, and which aspects are responsible for the fact that autistic children apparently derive little benefit from their skills for ordinary life.

Beate Hermelin and Neil O'Connor in London were the first to carry out systematic experiments on the abilities of autistic children in an innovative series of investigations between 1964 and 1970. During this period ideas about information-processing models entered into the arena of psychological theories. This meant that models could be constructed where input is separated from output, and both are separated from central processes where messages are received and stored, and actions are initiated. The revolution of cognitive psychology over behaviourism had already begun. I had the great fortune to be taught by these investigators, and their brilliant studies on verbal recall inspired my own work, as well as that of many others. Their experiments are reported in a monograph that appeared in 1970,[12] and range from psychophysiological studies to experiments on language and thought. Here I will summarize a few of the findings.

Autistic children were compared to much younger normal children and also mentally retarded children. The children in the three groups performed similarly on certain tests that have norms based on mental age. This is a stringent mental age 'matching' procedure. It ensures that any differences in performance found on experimental tasks are not due to one group simply being generally more impaired, or simply younger than another. The use of stringent matching on performance level pioneered by Hermelin and O'Connor has been an important methodological innovation that has enabled a breakthrough in what previously was an impasse. It is only too easy to find inferior performance on anything at all in a clinically abnormal group. To find that mentally retarded children are 'stupid' really tells us nothing that we did not know already. We know that brain impairment has the general effect of depressing performance. What is of interest is whether over and above this general effect there is some specific problem. By equating groups in terms of overall performance one can overcome this bias. Because of the inevitably poorer performance of handicapped children, a normal comparison group will consist of younger children because they perform inevitably less well than older children. Even more relevant is a comparison group of children who suffered neurological damage that did not result in Autism, but in mental deficiency. A difference between such a group and an autistic group should pinpoint Autism-specific deficits.

Differences in memory tests in children matched for their capacity to recall digits would have to be due to specific or qualitative rather than general or quantitative factors. Such interesting differences were indeed found. The task was to try and recall as much as possible of a slowly read out string of words that was deliberately longer than the tested span of recall. Autistic children – and we are here talking of moderately and severely mentally retarded autistic children – did something highly consistent on these tests: they always remembered the end of the string, regardless of what kind of string it was. The non-autistic children only did this when the word string was entirely random, for instance: 'what—

see—where—leaf—is—ship—we'. Then all children repeated something like 'is—ship—we'. However, when the string was not random, but half of it was a proper sentence, for example, 'where—is—the—ship—what—see—was—leaf', the non-autistic children repeated the sentence wherever it was and lost the rest. The autistic children repeated 'see—was—leaf', the last part of the message, just as they always did – and lost the sentence. Of course, when the sentence was at the end of the string, they repeated it perfectly.

In another experiment, the string was a super-long sentence: for example, 'On—Sunday—the—children—went—to—the—park—to—feed—the—ducks.' If treated as a string of 12 separate words, this would be way beyond the memory span of the children taking part in the experiments. However, young normal children often managed to repeat perfectly 12-word sentences and longer ones, even though they could repeat no more than about three random digits. One is reminded of the context-dependent skill of the child street vendors. Presumably, the sentence structure and the meaning acted as a stimulus to pack the words in such a way that they made one single coherent unit and thus the children's 'span' capacity was not exceeded. One could also say the children, oriented as they are towards meaning, understood the gist of the sentence. This aided their recall. The autistic children who took part in the experiment, especially the more retarded ones, were not able to do this mental trick to the same extent. They, too, were better at recalling sentences than jumbled words, but significantly less so. The autistic children were also less inclined than the normal children to re-order scrambled sentences into something more grammatical. Unlike the normal children, they did not feel compelled to organize stimuli into coherent patterns. There really is such a compulsion in normal people and it can be observed easily: if people are asked to repeat a long but ungrammatical sentence, they usually cannot help correcting it. The tendency to reorganize jumbled material is not unique to language. In some experiments I presented two meaningless sounds in some particular order, such as: ruc—mit—ruc—mit—ruc—mit.[13] This completely nonsensical string had to be recalled immediately. The general and not surprising result here was that simple rule governed sequences, e.g. strictly alternating the two sounds as in the example, were recalled much better than random sequences (for example, ruc—ruc—mit—ruc—mit—ruc). However, mentally retarded autistic children recalled both types of sequence about equally well. Again, they seemed to draw as little benefit from a simply structured nonsense sequence as they had from well-formed, meaningful sentences.

There are certain features of word strings, however, that can enhance recall equally for autistic and non-autistic children. In one experiment I found that sentences spoken with natural word stress were more helpful for recall than with unnatural stress.[14] Key words were more often recalled than function words, such as 'and', 'he', 'when'. The feature that does not enhance recall for autistic children as much as for normal or retarded children is overall *meaning*, or else, in a meaningless sequence, *non-random sequence structure*. What can be the explanation? Clearly, the *meaning* of a message to be repeated, or the *structure* of the pattern, the single most important feature for normal children, is not as significant for autistic children. They may remember unconnected words almost as well as meaningful sentences, and unconnected bits of information as well as those that are part of a meaningful context. It is this lack of preference for coherent over incoherent stimuli that must be regarded as abnormal.

There is more evidence that relates to an abnormal way of processing in autistic children, a way which seems to involve less attention to overall pattern structure than normal but, instead, more attention to small elements of structure. In one experiment, I attempted to find out if autistic and normal children might use different strategies to remember a short sequence of red and green counters, given that they would all learn the pattern within a few trials.[15] Type of error revealed whether the sequence was learned counter-by-counter or as a whole rule-governed pattern.

Normal children quickly picked up the most relevant rule for the pattern. Moreover, they exaggerated it. Their errors could be predicted by the dominant rule of the pattern. If the pattern included mostly red–green alternations, then the child produced even more such alternations. If there were mostly long runs of one colour, the child produced even longer runs. Somehow, the children gathered what the essence of each pattern was even before they had properly learned it. This could be similar to knowing the gist of a sentence and could arise from a constant orientation towards overall meaning.

Autistic children did not show this strategy. They were not influenced by the overall most relevant rule. Instead they were influenced by the last single element. This they either repeated or alternated, hence the errors they made could be entirely predicted on the basis of a small fragment of the pattern. In this sense, autistic children showed a diminished interest in overall pattern structure. At the same time, their responses were themselves rigidly patterned. There were pure alternations and pure perseverations. This I termed pattern imposition as opposed to pattern detection. Both processes involve patterns. However, the pattern that was imposed was derived from a very small part of the pattern that was available to be detected.

We can now return to the question of rote memory performance in autistic children. An autistic child may remember all the details of a train timetable without being a train enthusiast and without wanting to make use of the information for travelling. The key word is *rote* as opposed to meaningful. Kanner talked of the 'truly phenomenal memory that enables the child to recall and reproduce complex "nonsense" patterns, no matter how unorganized they are, in exactly the same form as originally construed'. To praise this as an achievement is odd. Normally it is not nonsense that one wants to recall, and the ability to do so is far less useful than the ability to recall sense. This we so much take for granted that it fails to impress us. Good performance in recalling rote material would normally be paired with even better performance on memory for meaning. Hence, it is appropriate to consider astounding isolated feats of rote memory of autistic children as a sign of dysfunction, rather than an islet of intact ability.

### Spatial abilities and what lies behind them

The most reliably found performance peak is on the so-called Block Design test, which is illustrated in figure 6.3. This peak is impressive: we are talking about a performance level that would be average or above average for the normal population, but is reached by children who score below average on most other subtests. Is this proof of superior spatial ability? Is it an islet of intact brain functioning in a sea of impairment? Or is it again a sign of underlying disturbance?

Some clarification came about in a rather unexpected way. When Amitta Shah and I investigated how well autistic children could locate hidden figures we found a previously unknown islet of ability: on the Embedded Figures test, autistic children scored above average for their mental age.[16] Normally, performance on this test increases with increasing development, but there are individual differences at any age. Performance is also much better in people who have the benefit of schooling, just as with the Block Design test.[17] Examples of embedded figures are shown in figure 6.4. A small target shape has to be located in a drawing of a larger shape made up of confusing lines.

When one looks at these figures it seems as if the larger shapes created by criss-crossing lines are so compelling that one simply cannot see the small embedded target shape. It is swallowed up by the bigger figure, and is now an intrinsic part of this object. Witkin and others maintained on the basis of earlier studies that people who are good at

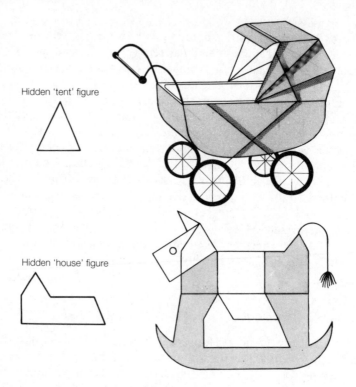

Hidden 'tent' figure

Hidden 'house' figure

Figure 6.4    *Examples from the Children's Embedded Figures Test (Karp and Konstadt, 1971), by special permission from Consulting Psychologists Press, Inc., Palo Alto, CA.*

finding embedded figures are the same as those who are good at other tasks purporting to show 'field independence'.[18] One way of describing field independence is the ability to disregard context. Field independent individuals are also good at Block Design. Moreover, this ability goes together with social field independence! From this point of view it was perhaps not surprising that our autistic children, who are supremely socially independent, indeed aloof, did extremely well on this test. They were faster and more accurate than non-autistic children who were of the same chronological age as well as the same mental age. Is this coincidence, or could there be a connection between thought detachment and social detachment?

Why is it normally so strangely effortful to detach the hidden figure from its embedding context? It is as if there were a strong force that pulls information together. It certainly feels like a force, because in order to disembed the hidden figures, one has to resist a natural tendency to embed. It is as if detachment has to be fought for and as if coherence was the stronger of the two.

In order to explore this idea we can draw on a simple model of the mind. The model is based on information-processing concepts. These concepts allow one to theorize about how the world outside is represented in the mind inside, and how the mind acts on the world. At its most basic this model of the mind distinguishes central thought processes and more peripheral input and output processes. The peripheral processes are specialized for various domains, for instance speech. Input devices transform sensations into perceptions going through many stages of processing. They can be thought of as custom-built, highly specialized modules. Their end product is usable information, already interpreted. This information can be further interpreted by central thought processes. The central system too can provide many stages of processing in many specialized subsystems. What is important here is that it deals with information which has been processed to an already very high level. The central system interprets, compares and stores. It draws inferences and reinterprets. It also initiates actions. But for their execution there are again highly specialist output devices.

Although this model is almost laughably simple, given that the mind is a structure of incredible complexity, it proves to be very helpful. For instance, we can propose that in Autism only the central processes are affected, but not the more peripheral input processes. It will in fact become clear in the following chapter, which deals with perceptual functioning, that such an assumption is well justified. Therefore we can focus our search for the dysfunction that underlies the peculiar pattern of intelligence in Autism on central thought processes. The next question is where, in this multi-layered and multi-faceted central processing system should we look?

Let us return to the clue that the hidden figures provide. I suggested that there might be a force (imagine a strong-flowing river) which pulls together large amounts of information (many tributaries). What about smaller amounts of information that eventually contribute to the larger picture? These too must be pulled together from even smaller amounts by some locally acting cohesive force (imagine little streams). Otherwise perception would be hopelessly fragmented (imagine small trickles).

It is necessary to assume that local cohesive effects are very strong. Perhaps they are impossible to resist when they occur at a relatively peripheral level. Optical illusions are an example of cohesive effects of a specialized input processor, occurring at an early stage of processing. However much we try we cannot escape their influence. A triangle defined only by three dots looks like a triangle even when there are no connecting lines. There is no evidence to suggest that in this respect there would be a difference between autistic and non-autistic children. The difference might lie solely with the cohesive force that acts at a high level in the central processing system.

Why should there be a centrally acting high-level cohesive force? Why is there a need to pull together information that is already processed and already interpreted? The answer might be: without this type of high-level cohesion, pieces of information would just remain pieces, be they small pieces or large pieces. As pieces they would be only of limited use in the organism's long-term programme of intelligent adaptation to the environment.

High-level central cohesive forces must be resistible to some extent. This is necessary in order to explain the achievement of disembedding. There are degrees of detachment and field dependence. Furthermore, central cohesive forces may be somewhat sporadic and their effects might sometimes be spurious. I say this because people can easily hold contradictory beliefs which they derived from different information sources (imagine different large rivers, each in its own landscape). It may be that only very exceptional individuals can create true global consistency (all rivers flowing into one ocean).

What if in the case of Autism the high-level central cohesive force was weak? What if it was *only* that particular aspect of central thought that was abnormal? Here we have a hypothesis that would allow us to make some predictions. In order to be useful, it should mark a critical difference between autistic and non-autistic children. Non-autistic, but mentally retarded, children might also suffer from some deficit in central thought, but this could simply be decreased overall efficiency.

A weak central cohesive force, weak relative to lower level cohesive forces, would simulate 'field independence' and all that it entails for performance on embedded figures. It would entail thought detachment and social detachment, but this would not be the same as detachment in an older normal child. In the normal child detachment is the sophisticated end-product of education, a sign of control over the high-level central force towards cohesion. In the case of Autism I propose that such control is lacking and that this results in an incoherent world of fragmented experience.

There are other effects that one would expect with a weak central cohesive force. For instance, input processes can run riot without the overriding goal set by the need to create coherence (imagine streams that do not feed rivers, rivers that do not run into seas). Paradoxically, if this happens, rigidly structured behaviour may appear, as we saw in the experiment where sequences of red and green counters had to be learned. We shall explore this phenomenon in the following chapter.

*Pulling apart Block Design*

How is it possible to test the notion that a weakness of central cohesion (which we have called detachment) is a key to the islets of ability in autistic children? How can excellence on the Block Design test be explained by detachment, and how does it relate to excellence with embedded figures and context-free tests of intelligence in general? The critical feature that links Block Design to Embedded Figures is that a *big* geometric shape has to be broken up into *small* shapes. The big shape has to be copied with little building blocks. The design elements that correspond to the blocks are in fact analogous to hidden figures. They have to be 'found' before the design can be reconstructed. Hence, the first problem for the child is to separate the given design into appropriate segments. This has little to do with what is generally thought of as spatial ability. However, it could have a lot to do with resisting the force towards coherence in high-level central thought processes. If autistic children show detachment, then they need not put up such resistance, and segmentation should be easy enough for them.

Young normal children might find the Block Design task difficult for the same reason that they find embedded figures difficult: they cannot as yet control the high-level central cohesive force. The idea here is that the cognitive system of young normal children, unlike that of autistic children, from the start is set to operate with a strong central drive for cohesion. Furthermore, one would expect mentally retarded non-autistic children to be very similar in this respect to young normal children. Their performance on both tests certainly is similar.

If this is so, then it should be possible to improve the performance of young normal and retarded children simply by making sure that the job of segmentation is done for them. A strong central cohesive force can be broken just by pulling apart those components in the pattern that correspond to the blocks (figure 6.5). In an as yet unpublished study Amitta Shah and I introduced such a manipulation experimentally with new designs that had to be copied by autistic and non-autistic children. The results supported the prediction. Prior segmentation massively improved performance of non-autistic children, whether normal or mentally retarded! Conversely it had little effect on the performance of able autistic children. With some unsegmented designs the young normal children and the mentally retarded children were hard-pressed to perform the task at all within a given time limit. However, when the design was segmented for them, they sometimes reached the speed of autistic children.

This experiment together with the very different experiment using coloured counters does make it plausible that a basic information-

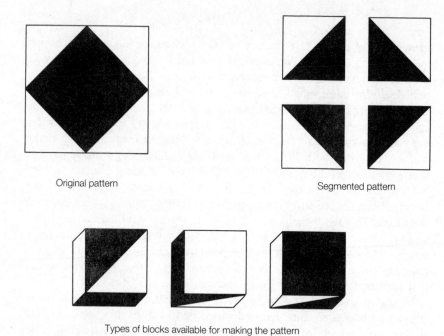

Original pattern                      Segmented pattern

Types of blocks available for making the pattern

Figure 6.5   *Block Design*

processing abnormality exists in autistic children that does not
necessarily lead to poor performance.

## Detachment and Coherence: The Grand View

We have now enough evidence to formulate a hypothesis about the
nature of the intellectual dysfunction in Autism. In the normal cognitive
system there is a built-in propensity to form coherence over as wide a
range of stimuli as possible, and to generalize over as wide a range of
contexts as possible. It is this drive that results in grand systems of
thought, and ultimately in the world's great religions. It is this capacity
for coherence that is diminished in autistic children. As a result, their
information-processing systems, like their very beings, are characterized
by detachment.

Detachment, as a technical term, refers to a quality of thought. It
could be due either to a lack of global coherence or to a resistance to such
coherence. The autistic kind of detachment is not the same as the

deliberate detachment which is fostered by formal education and which goes with scientific objectivity. Deliberate detachment presupposes coherence and results from reflection on coherence. In everyday language, detachment implies a lack of bias and a lack of impressionability, as well as a certain social aloofness. This connection is not mere coincidence. Nevertheless autistic detachment has different causes. It is unreflected and it results from lack of coherence.

The theory of impaired central coherence can well account for excellence on Block Design and Embedded Figures tests. It can also account for the excellent rote memory performance of autistic children. It remains to be seen how well it explains specific failure on the Comprehension test. Poor performance on Block Design and Embedded Figures in young children and in unschooled individuals, on the other hand, can be explained by a natural propensity of the mind towards central coherence. I shall argue in chapter 8 that ordinary conversation and the understanding and answering of questions as intended by the questioner implies striving for high-level global, not merely local, coherence of information.

The normal operation of central coherence compels us human beings to give priority to understanding meaning. Hence we can easily single out meaningful from meaningless material. Indeed it goes against the grain to deal with anything meaningless. Despite the processing effort that it involves, we remember the gist of a message, not the message verbatim. Furthermore, the gist is remembered better if it can be slotted into a larger context. The need to slot information into a larger and larger context is another way to look at the effect of high-level central cohesion. Much work will be needed to specify how central cohesion operates and much work will be needed to specify what kind of job it does.

The ability to make sense, to see meaning and structure in everything, is very useful. On the other hand, it is something we cannot help doing. From this point of view it is an extension as well as a limitation of our information-processing capacity. It must not be overlooked that as far as the internal inconsistencies of one's beliefs are concerned, there *are* great limitations. Total coherence is only a dream; perhaps it is as much outside the normal individual variation as is lack of coherence.

As evidence for our ability to make sense, I have put forward experiments that manipulated sequence meaning and sequence structure. These experiments use a great variety of material. All have a common denominator, that is, the contrast between stimuli that are detached and stimuli that are strongly held together. In one type of experiment we compare unconnected and connected words (connected by virtue of

underlying meaning), in another there are nonsense sounds in unpredictable and in predictable order (predictable by virtue of underlying
sequence structure). The third type of experiment employs isolated and
embedded shapes (connected by overall design). The red thread running
through all the results is the high performance of autistic children on
tasks requiring isolation of stimuli, favouring detachment, and their low
performance on tasks requiring connection of stimuli, favouring
coherence. In contrast, for young normal children, retarded children,
and also unschooled older children from a different cultural background,
the balance goes entirely in the opposite direction. Therefore, we assume
that a central cohesive force is a natural (and useful) characteristic of the
cognitive system. But we also assume that it is significantly impaired in
Autism.

When we look back over the evidence presented in this chapter, we
find that it is possible to explain the pattern of abilities in autistic
children by a relatively simple and strong hypothesis. Our explanation
certainly goes further than merely restating that there are some peaks
and some troughs in test performance. The whole pattern of abilities
makes sense when seen as deriving from a cognitive dysfunction of a
particular dynamic operating characteristic of very high-level central
thought processes. The dysfunction results in a peculiar detachment.

# 7

# A Fragmented World

## Sensations and Repetitions

At the age of five Jerry had been diagnosed as autistic by Leo Kanner. At the age of 31 he talked about his childhood to the psychiatrist Bemporad.[1]

> According to Jerry, his childhood experience could be summarized as consisting of two predominant experiential states: confusion and terror. The recurrent theme that ran through all of Jerry's recollections was that of living in a frightening world presenting painful stimuli that could not be mastered. Noises were unbearably loud, smells overpowering. Nothing seemed constant; everything was unpredictable and strange. Animate beings were a particular problem. Dogs were remembered as eerie and terrifying . . . He was also frightened of other children, fearing that they might hurt him in some way. He could never predict or understand their behaviour. Elementary school was remembered as a horrifying experience. The classroom was total confusion and he always felt he 'would go to pieces'. There were also enjoyable experiences. He liked going to grocery stores with his mother so he could look at the labels of canned goods as well as the prices of objects. He also remembered liking to spin objects but could not describe the pleasure this activity gave him. His life seemed to have markedly changed when he discovered multiplication tables at around age 8. He denied that arithmetic helped give his world a sense of order; he said he simply liked working with numbers. Similarly, he could give no reason for his need for sameness or rituals beyond stating that that was how things should be.

Jerry's recollections give us a glimpse of the importance of sensations and feelings about them in the life of the autistic person. It is not that Jerry had sensory impairments – if anything, he was hypersensitive – but that his perceptions remained fragments. 'Everything was unpredictable and strange' means stimuli were always different and unexpected. This would be so if they were not embedded in a large coherent pattern. Repetitions, on the other hand, were connected with enjoyable emotional reactions. As far as Jerry was concerned there was no other reason for their existence.

The outlook for an eventual understanding of perception in autistic individuals is promising. A considerable amount of knowledge exists already, as demonstrated in a recent review of experiments on perceptual functioning in Autism.[2] On the other hand, very little work exists on repetitions, stereotypies, obsessions and rituals. The *Handbook of Autism*, published in 1987 and edited by Cohen, Donnellan and Paul, contains 40 chapters on a wide variety of topics, yet none on obsessional phenomena. This pervasive and striking feature of Autism remains a most perplexing phenomenon. For a long time it has been ignored in the hope that it might turn out to be a secondary symptom – perhaps a strategy for coping with a senseless world. This view is difficult to maintain, however, since repetitions do not go away, as one might expect of secondary symptoms.

I would like to suggest that the repetitions and sensations that were such poignant experiences in Jerry's life (and also in the lives of many other autistic people) are two sides of the same coin: part of the same underlying problem. This problem is what I have already labelled lack of central coherence. Let us consider what it would be like if perception reflected a fragmented rather than a coherent world: the great writer Borges has provided a powerful metaphor in his story about a boy with a phenomenal memory.[3] One sentence may suffice in this context: 'It bothered him that a dog at 3.14 (seen from the side) should have the same name as the dog at 3.15 (seen from the front).' The experience of the dog is always different, often unexpected, and hence, as in Jerry's case, it could easily be frightening.

What does a fragmented world imply for actions – as opposed to perceptions? Actions would be relatively small units and separate from each other. The smaller and more separate they are, the more glaring repetition would be. With larger action sequences repetitions may occur equally often, but they would not appear stereotyped in the sense that small action fragments do. Consider Jerry's repetitive preoccupation with multiplication. Multiplying numbers is stereotyped activity, but doing maths homework every day is not.

In this chapter we shall first explore some of the ideas on perceptual processes in Autism and then, in the light of the conclusions, turn to the baffling problem of repetitiveness.

## The Five Senses

Seeing, hearing, touching, tasting and smelling are the means by which we receive information from the outside world. It is a logical first step to investigate if any of these means are used less efficiently in autistic children than is to be expected from their level of development. Observations and experiments quickly ruled out that sensory deficiencies were to blame. The problem is not a peripheral one to do with sensory apparatus, but is to do with mental apparatus.

One of the earliest hypotheses with a view to understanding mental processes of autistic children was the following intriguing idea: what if they preferred to use the senses closest to the body, touch, taste and smell, at the cost of those senses that deal with information from distant sources, vision and hearing?[4] This might explain why autistic children tend to touch, taste and smell objects and people, themselves and others, often in a socially embarrassing way.

Experimental evidence, however, soon showed that the excessive use of proximal senses was not specifically associated with Autism, but was associated with low mental age. Young normal babies also vigorously explore the world by means of their proximal senses, but it is generally the case that this phase does not last very long. Looking and listening remain the most important activities for exploring the physical and social environment.

What if complex information received by ear or eye were not processed as efficiently by autistic children as information received by other senses? This might explain why they appear to be deaf and appear to look through people. This hypothesis was the first serious attempt to track down the difficulty of autistic children with language and communication. It also promised to throw light on their apparent inability to make sense of their environment generally. The testing of the hypothesis was soon narrowed down to the possibility of a particular auditory processing deficiency. Visual processing impairments, on the other hand, were rapidly dismissed by the experimental evidence. Beate Hermelin and Neil O'Connor give a firsthand account of such systematic explorations in their 1970 monograph.[5]

A suspicion of deafness occurs frequently in the early history of autistic children. The suspicion itself is an interesting phenomenon. It is a logical attempt to explain the obvious communication difficulties of autistic children. But it is a doomed attempt if only for the reason that the same autistic children who do not turn their heads when spoken to look up when they hear the crinkle of a sweet-paper. Autistic children can have impaired hearing, but most do not. Some suffer from specific deficits that affect only speech, but again, most do not. In fact autistic children often echo speech, thereby showing remarkably efficient speech processing, as regards both input and output.

Experimenters are continuing in more and more sophisticated ways to identify the nature of the information-processing problems in Autism. We shall look at some of these attempts in later chapters, where we consider some specific reasons for the communication failure of autistic individuals. What all these attempts have in common is their target: the region of central thought processes. Dysfunction at a central level would inevitably have wide repercussions in perception and action. However, it does not imply dysfunction of the more peripheral sensory or motor processes.

### Discrimination and Categorization

The ability to discriminate fine visual and auditory detail has often been credited to autistic children. Indeed, the discrimination skills of autistic children can be out of the ordinary. For instance, absolute pitch is not an uncommon finding; a superior ability to discriminate pitch has enabled a number of autistic adults to become skilful piano tuners. The ability to discriminate visual detail has enabled others to become quality controllers in industry. On the output side, remarkable feats of superior visuo-motor coordination have been put to use in such activities as miniature model making.

The documentation of excellent discriminatory skills is important because it confirms the idea that the condition of Autism does not directly affect input and output processes. This is not true for mental retardation and hence does not hold for more severely mentally retarded autistic children. Brain impairment leading to serious intellectual retardation is likely to impair the efficiency of all information-processing systems, the peripheral as well as the central.

Could it be that autistic children fail to make sense of their environment *because* they are too good at discrimination? They may focus too much attention on too much detail and thus cannot see the wood for the trees. If this were the case, children might not be prepared to recognize similarities when they should, and hence would fail to classify stimuli as the same that would normally be so classified. This hypothesis, however, is ruled out by the solid results from experiments on categorization skills. In these experiments autistic children perform adequately, that is as well as their mental age permits. This is regardless of whether the material to be categorized is abstract shapes, line drawings, or words.[6]

If autistic children can see differences as well as similarities between different materials, why is it that teachers often complain that autistic pupils do not generalize from their lessons? The children learn specific things, but do not apply them in situations which the teacher at least perceives as similar to the learning situation. A common complaint is that an autistic child behaves very differently when at home from when at school. Unfortunately, whether autistic children differ from other mentally retarded children in this respect, or indeed from young normal children is not yet known. Perhaps generalization is too vague a term for explaining the justified frustration of teachers. Autistic children, even at a severely retarded level, show abundant evidence of generalization. For instance, Danny continually collects fluff from the carpet. In order to do this he must be able to treat alike, as 'fluff to be picked up', bits of different colour, size and texture.

Clearly, the problem of generalization that the teacher finds is of a different origin. It is not inability to categorize or inability to see similarities despite differences that prevents the application of learning. But perhaps it is an inability to see the *need* for generalizations across differences. Not pulling information together in spite of perceived similarities might be traced to a weakness in a drive for central coherence.

## The Control of Attention

Following the suggestion that abnormalities of perceptual experience relate in some way to defective central thought processes, we must consider the role of attention. Some high-level component in the mind has to decide what in the mass of incoming sensations is worth attending to. A good decision would be based on large amounts of pooled information. If coherence at this central decision-making point is weak, then the direction of attention would be quite haphazard. What form would this take? We would not look for poor, but for peculiar attention.

Of some historical interest is the hypothesis of 'stimulus over-selectivity'.[7] Originally it was thought that autistic children cannot attend well to simultaneously presented information and therefore select one very narrow aspect of this information. What makes this idea interesting is that it addresses the problem of why autistic children often fixate on very minor features of the environment but ignore more important ones. For example, they might focus on an earring, while being oblivious to the person wearing it. This bizarre effect was explained as a result of information overload. However, the opposite could also hold. Anybody can experience focusing on previously unnoticed cracks in a ceiling or marks on a surface through sheer boredom, that is, information 'underload'. A relevant example related by Margaret Dewey is that of an autistic boy whose fascination with drapery began when he had to watch stage productions in school. Being totally confused by the play or speeches, he would focus on the rippling curtains, especially fascinating under spotlights of changing colour.

Stimulus over-selectivity proved not to be specific to Autism, but was found to be related to mental age. However, there is still much need for empirical investigation of attentional problems in Autism. What stimuli will capture the attention of a person who does not know what is worth attending to? Where does the object of attention go to in a mind that has little concern for central coherence? Weeks and Hobson reported an experiment which shows how one might pursue these questions.[8] They asked children to sort pictures of people. It was possible to sort according to whether the expression of the face was happy or sad. It was also possible to sort according to whether a person did or did not wear a hat. Autistic children tended to sort by hat at first try, while non-autistic children tended first to sort by facial expression. At second try both groups sorted by the other feature. Clearly, they could discriminate and categorize either way, but the relative importance of the two features was different for the two groups. Why did different features grab their attention? For the purpose of high-level central coherence and personal long-term interest faces are presumably more important than hats. However, for the purpose of local coherence as a short-term goal for a small set of pictures, hats may be more striking.

### Meaning and Coherence

One of the recurrent themes in biographical accounts of autistic people is that certain stimuli seem to hold some inexplicable fascination for them while other stimuli, normally interesting and salient, apparently leave them untouched.

Park and Youderian describe the case of 12-year-old Elly, an autistic girl, who showed an obsessive interest in colour, light and number.[9] She observed shadows in the moonlight and clouds in the sky, experiencing intense emotional reactions to certain constellations of these, for instance, joy at a cloudless sky, despair at a moonless night.

In the evening, when Elly sets the table for dinner, she puts a tall glass by her plate. It is green, her preferred colour, and it is divided into 8 equal levels by decorative ridges. Into this she pours her juice. It too is green. On most days, she will fill the glass exactly to the 6th or 7th level . . . the exact level is determined by the type of day with respect to weather and phase of moon.

Temple Grandin in her autobiographical account of an autistic childhood mentions being preoccupied with things other people would hardly pay attention to.[10]

I also liked to sit for hours humming to myself and twirling objects or dribbling sand through my hands at the beach. I remember studying the sand intently as if I was a scientist looking at a specimen under the microscope. I remember minutely observing how the sand flowed, or how long a jar lid would spin when propelled at different speeds. My mind was actively engaged in these activities. I was fixated on them and ignored everything else.

Both of these accounts remind us of the link between sensation and repetition and also demonstrate that incidental features of the environment can become an autistic person's main focus of attention. That which is perceptually salient to most people may not be salient to an autistic child, and vice versa.

What, after all, determines salience? People pay attention to things they perceive as important, meaningful or relevant. All of these subjective terms indicate experiences of structure: a meaningful stimulus is meaningful because it *belongs* as a member of a set. It is already organized as to its place in memory. In this sense we can say that because a stimulus is important, we attend to it. If so, attention is under the control of central thought processes. With a weakness of central control, but an intact attention mechanism, patterns of attentive behaviour would have to be odd rather than impaired. Indeed, autistic children are able to sustain attention when anyone else would have lost interest. They are able to concentrate on things which would not interest other people in the first place. However, the oddness of autistic interests stems not so much from topic as from narrowness. All of these observations are what I believe to be clues to the *idiot savant* phenomenon. Again the idea of a drive for central coherence proves to be helpful. An autistic individual can focus for a long time on a narrow topic for its own appeal, whereas a normal child would attend to it briefly, finding it interesting only as part of a greater pattern.

It is probably only in the greater pattern that people share something of what they consider to have significant meaning. It is in the small tributaries to this pattern where one would expect to see idiosyncratic interests that are not shared by others. Autistic people have a strong desire to further their own idiosyncratic interests. For instance, Elly paid close attention to shadows because they were for some reason important and meaningful to her, and very relevant to her moods. When she travelled to a different time zone, she was alarmed that her shadow at 6 pm was not where it would have been at home. She could not relax until her mother had explained to her that 6 pm on her watch meant it was only 5 pm at the new place. This example suggests that Elly had a limited but strongly coherent scheme about the position of the sun at a certain time and the length of her shadow. It really mattered to her when there were unexpected discrepancies. The scheme had to be kept coherent. This insistence on sameness is a type of local coherence. It is not at all like *central* coherence. Instead, it is extremely limited in scope and quite self-contained. For instance, the length of shadows of others was not part of the scheme and of no concern to her. Also, the scheme was not only very limited in scope, but it can properly be called a thought sterotypy, a preoccupation of a highly repetitive nature. Elly was not able to see her scheme for what it was: a small fragment in a wider pattern of realities, in need of enlargement and modification. This insight would depend on having a strong need for central coherence of large amounts of information.

### The Puzzle of the Jig-Saw Puzzle

We have already discussed 'the deaf, dumb and blind kid' who 'plays a mean pin-ball' as one of the literary elaborations of Autism. The image captures well the paradox of apparent sensory failure with amazing sensorimotor success. It represents the uncanny combination of input and output processing prowess, with central processing failure. The failure is the lack of application of processing prowess to other ends.

A modest form of pin-ball wizardry is seen in little Danny, who bends to pick the finest fluff off the carpet, invisible to anyone else, yet who fails to 'see' toys and hardly recognizes anybody. A more spectacular form is seen in the young Nadia, who can draw exquisite pictures of horses from memory, but cannot name simple objects.

The exceptional ability of the *idiot savant* depends on several factors: a capacity for sustained attention to one topic; the smooth running of specialized processing systems; and, above all, repetitive activity. Any one of these factors alone would not be sufficient to account for the high levels of performance, but all together they go some way towards explaining the *savant* phenomenon. As an example of an islet of ability in autistic children which bears on a number of important factors, let us consider the ability to do jig-saw puzzles.

The way autistic children prefer to construct a puzzle may be quite different from the way a normal child does it. I was led to this conclusion for the following reasons. I observed, and heard from other quite independent observers, that autistic children use the shape of the edges of the puzzle pieces. On the other hand, they tend to ignore the picture on the whole puzzle. To investigate this Beate Hermelin and I once carried out an experiment where we contrasted two conditions.[11] In one condition there were rectangular picture puzzle pieces with straight edges, and in another, typically jagged pieces but without a picture. Autistic children performed remarkably well in both conditions, but much better than young normal children of the same mental age when there was no picture to guide them. They simply enjoyed fitting piece together with piece.

In most commercially available jig-saw puzzles there is a picture. This picture is broken up regardless of its natural shape or content boundaries. When I do a jig-saw puzzle I am continually amazed at how different a fragment of a visual detail looks when the puzzle piece is in place compared to when I just see the piece alone. I look for a piece with a dog's ear, for instance. At first it always looks as if there is no such piece, but once found and fitted, the detail is perfectly clear. The experience is not unlike that of hidden figures.

As Georges Perec put it in the preamble to his novel *Life, a user's manual*:[12]

> The pieces are readable, take on a sense, only when assembled; in isolation, a puzzle piece means nothing – just an impossible question, an opaque challenge. But as soon as you have succeeded, after minutes of trial and error, or after a prodigious half-second flash of inspiration, in fitting it into one of its neighbours, the piece disappears, ceases to exist as a piece. The intense difficulty preceding this link-up – which the English word *puzzle* indicates so well – not only loses its raison d'être, it seems never to have any reason so obvious does the solution appear. The two pieces so miraculously conjoined are henceforth one, which in its turn will be a source of error, hesitation, dismay and expectation.

Perhaps the autistic child to some extent ignores the picture and therefore can still see the individual puzzle pieces in the completed puzzle. If this were the case, doing puzzles would be easier. At the same time it would be very much a piecemeal exercise starting from small sections and almost incidentally resulting in a large picture at the end. As anyone knows, filling in the gaps provides a keen sense of pleasure, and the overall picture is often extremely trivial in any case. This experience too represents a drive for coherence but again it is a very limited, local type of coherence. As a metaphor, the jig-saw puzzle persisting as fragments, even when put together, symbolizes the effect of autistic detachment. In contrast, for the non-autistic person, once fragments are put together into a single picture, they lose their meaning as fragments and now get their meaning from the meaning of the greater unit they belong to. This represents central coherence on a larger scale.

An example reported by Digby Tantam illustrates the contrast that I wish to make in a completely different domain. A patient exhibiting typical autistic symptoms from early childhood obsessively collected information about the addresses of juvenile courts. It is unknown how this extremely odd interest arose. However it came about, it could be made less odd, if it would link up with a general interest in courts, buildings or town plans. It would not be just a fragment, however well studied, but part of a bigger picture. But this was definitely not the case for the patient. When asked why he did not want to know about the addresses of non-juvenile courts, he replied, 'They bore me to tears.' This was not a joke on his part. The remark showed a total lack of understanding that interests are expected to be justified as part of a coherent pattern of likes and dislikes, and not arbitrary. Sometimes, scientists can get absorbed in one extremely narrow and minute aspect of a problem. The difference between good science and abstruse curiosity is keeping in mind the relationship between the detail and the greater pattern of knowledge into which this detail will have to fit.

If we take seriously the notion of fragmentation of input as resulting from lack of *central* coherence, then it follows that there should also be fragmentation of output. Autistic individuals may experience and create an unusually fragmented world, but why should there be repetitiveness? What actually is the nature of the stereotypic activities that are a defining feature of Autism?

### Stereotypic Movements and Thoughts

Pointless repetitions have long been recognized as a common component of madness. Kraepelin in 1899 lists stereotypies as one of the characteristic symptoms of what he called dementia praecox. Yet stereotyped movement disorders are common in neurological patients, and are prevalent in mentally deficient patients. However, stereotypies are not just present in movements, but also in thoughts, and hence invisible. The definition and classification of repetitive acts and thoughts is highly unsatisfactory and such labels as stereotypies, mannerisms, perseverations, obsessions and compulsions are often used interchangeably. Indeed, there may be no sound theoretical basis for making a distinction. Whether or not a repetitive act is a compulsion is only known by introspection.

Why do repetitive acts occur at all? A living machine such as the human brain never stands still. It constantly responds to stimuli. Even when it does not respond, it runs, just as an engine runs in idling gear. Brain impairment often means that the organism cannot respond flexibly and quickly. Still, it runs. Often the activity is quite undirectional and appears as endlessly repeated loops of behaviour. Such loops also occur in perfectly normal people. Pacing up and down, tapping, humming, swaying, rocking, scratching, nail biting, ruminations, are all stereotypies of a useless but non-pathological type in the repertoire of all human beings. The list is long and includes any variety of action fragments (including thought) one cares to think of.

The presence of stereotypies in stressful situations has led to the hypothesis that movement repetitions and thought repetitions are part of some homeostatic mechanism that controls level of arousal. Chris Frith and John Done conclude from an extensive review of the literature on stereotyped behaviour that the evidence from psychophysiological studies does not support this idea.[13] Stereotypies do not necessarily decrease arousal. If anything, they often increase it. As regulators of internal states, repetitions seem to be extremely inefficient! Instead, they seem to be consequences of some general readiness to spring into action.

Stereotypies are not only abundant, but often excessive in autistic people as well as in mentally retarded people. Berkson and Davenport observed excessive stereotyped behaviour in two-thirds of their mentally retarded population.[14] Some of the patients showed such behaviour 50 per cent of the time. This degree of repetition can be a serious problem, especially if self-injury results. Hand biting, head banging and hair pulling, usually harmless as an occasional symptom, can become extremely damaging when done to excess. The distressing problem of self-injury can be tackled by behaviour modification techniques, in which reward and punishment are made contingent on the critical behaviour within certain rules. Success in reducing self-injury has been claimed in many instances.[15]

It is possible that repeated self-injury is triggered by a desire for a certain kind of intense sensory stimulation not interpreted as pain. It is also conceivable that pain sensitivity is reduced in certain autistic patients. In view of the fact that increased levels of the painkilling neuro-transmitter endorphin have been reported for autistic individuals, this explanation is not implausible.

Although autistic people seem to be more prone to show excessive stereotypies than any other clinical group, the stereotypies themselves are not distinctively different. The same repetitive movements, the same ruminations, are also exhibited by many non-autistic people. What accounts for the marked difference in frequency? An interesting study on the stereotypies of normal people by Asendorpf suggests at least one contributing factor.[16] He found that the mere presence of other people significantly decreased the amount of repetitive movements that undergraduate students displayed while nervously waiting to take a test. In normal people, stereotyped behaviour is very susceptible to external influences and can be easily incorporated into other behaviour or else suppressed. Stereotyped behaviour is socially undesirable probably because it signals boredom, or inattentiveness. In the case of autistic people the presence of others may not have a similarly inhibiting effect on stereotypies. It is often commented upon that there is little difference between their private and public behaviour. However, obviously, additional reasons are needed to explain the often excessive nature of stereotypies in autistic people.

Ros Ridley and Harry Baker describe one type of stereotyped behaviour which can be observed in animals, the *cage stereotypy*.[17] This behaviour ceases instantly when the cage is removed. They contrast this with another type of stereotypy which does not cease when environmental restrictions are removed. This stereotypy is typified by rigidity, perseveration and social withdrawal. Ridley and Baker traced its cause to a neurological or developmental abnormality. They found that similar behaviour can also be induced or exacerbated experimentally by high doses of amphetamine. Since amphetamine stimulates the dopamine system, a link to biological studies of Autism might be made (see chapter 5). Dysfunction of the dopamine system may well be related to the excess of stereotypies in autistic individuals.

## Routines and Rigidity

More uniquely characteristic of Autism than simple motor and thought stereotypies are the so-called elaborate routines of behaviour. They involve larger units of action and consist of more than simple mouthing, rocking or pacing. Precise definitions are lacking, so clinical judgement is at present the only basis for deciding what counts as 'elaborate'. It is generally agreed that what is an elaborate routine must be more than a short fragment of action and must include long and possibly complex sequences of thoughts, or interest fixations.

A typical list of examples is given in this extract from a mother's letter:

> I don't quite know when John's obsessions began but I suppose he was about three when he started to post anything he could find into our letter box, anyone else's letter box – or even the pillar box. This was shortly followed by a passion for ringing doorbells. The great interest from four to seven years was 'wog lights' – street lamps. He would stand at the window watching them all go on at night. In his fourth year he developed a great interest in reflections as seen in the windows, in shiny surfaces and loved carrying round a lens or binoculars. Putting little coloured pegs into their holes was an absorbing occupation, and also into any similar holes he could find. Then, when he was about six, came his interest in buses. Of course he had his collection of buses, but unless I initiated some play they were just handled. The other thing was distinguishing buses which passed by; one kind had stairs in the middle and a white roof – and he became quite upset if the stairs appeared in front and the roof were yellow.

Neither the content, nor the quality of special interests and routines, have been systematically investigated. Such aspects as rigidity, perseveration and resistance to change are still quite unexplored, but there are a few pointers.

For instance, there is an experiment which I carried out in order to study how young children would spontaneously repeat colours while making a pattern.[18] I gave the children either just two or four star-shaped and dot-shaped stamps with different ink colours which could be simply pressed down to make marks. I also encouraged children to play freely with a xylophone which had either two or four bars in place. Such experiments would lend themselves ideally to a computer game format, but 20 years ago, when I did the studies, such an idea would have seemed like science fiction.

The results of these simple games are easily summarized: the autistic children behaved in a markedly more stereotypic and rigid way than the other children. Their productions of coloured stamp patterns and xylophone tunes were of particular interest, because here we are looking at very free unstructured play behaviour. Nevertheless, even in this situation the patterns they made up were extraordinarily rigid. Of course, autistic people are often reported to behave in this way in a variety of everyday-life situations. An example related by Digby Tantam is 'putting each object in the main room of the house in its particular place every day. This takes up to three hours and cannot be interrupted without a serious tantrum.'

There was one other remarkable feature that I observed in these studies. When given a xylophone with four bars the most noticeable distinction was that some autistic children would *never* use all four. Some simply hit one, or perhaps two notes over and over again. This *never* happened with the non-autistic children I observed. Exactly the same restrictive behaviour was found with the colour patterns: some autistic children only ever used one colour, some only two. In fact, four colours were available and were pointed out as available, repeatedly. This self-imposed restriction is reminiscent of extreme faddiness in eating. One autistic child, for instance, is reported to have eaten only plain sandwiches for several years.

While the autistic children adhered to their chosen patterns rigidly, such was not the case for the mentally retarded non-autistic children, nor for the young normal pre-schoolers who took part in the experiment. They were anything but rigid in their pattern making. They simply 'played', trying out all the available materials in an exploratory way without imposing any strict rules.

Very similar findings were obtained by Jill Boucher who was also impressed by the extraordinary perseverative tendencies of autistic children.[19] What these studies suggest is that spontaneous behaviour is not random, but has a structure of its own. The structure produced by autistic children is both limited and excessively rigid.

### Interpretations of repetitive behaviour

Repetitive actions and thoughts, whether simple or complex occur in all autistic children, but they are still awaiting systematic investigation. They have not captured the interest of researchers to the same extent as, for instance, the language and communication problems found in Autism. Instead it is implicitly assumed that stereotypies and rituals are essentially *secondary phenomena*, perhaps like cage stereotypies, that are merely reactions to other problems. However, in Autism, there is no cage that could be removed.

I have already declared my bias in favour of a theory that takes all the varieties of stereoptypic and perseverative behaviour that is typical of autistic children as further signs of one particular fault in central thought processes. Because of this fault autistic children experience sensations as fragmentary perceptions and they also plan and execute actions in fragmentary forms. The fragmentation itself is relative; that is, the size of the unit can vary and is not the critical feature of the process. What is critical is the fact that the units are *not* at the same time *parts* of a whole. The jig-saw puzzle metaphor may serve once again to illustrate the difference between pieces as pieces, and pieces as picture parts.

Two difficult questions are raised by this hypothesis: First, why are fragments of behaviour (if they are such) repeated endlessly; and secondly, why is the repetition so rigid, even automaton-like? There are, of course, many other questions which apply to the nature of obsessions in general and may or may not relate specifically to Autism.

My guess is that *repetition* is the natural 'setting' for input and output systems, and that they are normally stopped from repeating when their products are acknowledged by a high-level central monitor. Such acknowledgment could be the signal for an input device to start processing new information and for an output device to change to new action. In other words, what needs special action by a central agency is switching off, not switching on. This assumption would readily allow one to think of the brain as a constantly running engine. The impaired brain, in the case of Autism, would show a disengagement between central and peripheral devices, because the central control processes are too weak to control them and to switch them off appropriately.

What of rigidity? It seems to me that flexibility is a quality particularly appropriate for a higher-level context using mechanism, but not for lower-level processing devices where reliability would be more important. It may well be that higher-level thought processes pay for flexibility by loss of automaticity. From an evolutionary perspective it is obvious that the behaviour of neurologically primitive (that is, non-centralized) organisms is rigidly programmed. If neurologically sophisticated organisms suffer from very specific damage to centralized processes, then the mode of operation of more peripheral processes could remain perfectly intact.

It has been the theme of the present chapter to look at both sensation and repetition phenomena in Autism as two sides of the same coin. This point of view is quite consistent with the theory that was proposed in the previous chapter. There cannot be central processing failure of the type postulated without wide repercussions. If the ability to achieve central coherence or meaning is extremely limited in Autism, then detachment and fragmentation into meaningless activities are inevitable consequences. It remains to be seen what further consequences there are for communication and social interaction.

# 8

# The Difficulty of
# Talking to Others

Ruth is a pretty, 17-year-old girl with ash blond hair. She attends a special school for autistic children and is doing well. Her reading age is almost at a normal adult level. Ruth does not talk much spontaneously, but answers questions willingly. She has a rather grating voice and emphasizes final consonants of words. Her diction is oddly wooden, with little modulation, but her grammar is faultless. I talked to her after she had done a number of reading tests.

*UF*: Ruth, you were most helpful . . .
*R*:   Yes-suh.
*UF*: It was very kind of you . . . I think you are an excellent reader.
*R*:   Yes-suh.
*UF*: Have you *always* been such a good reader?
*R*:   Yes I have.
*UF*: Do you remember when you first learned to read?
*R*:   No.
      (*After several unsuccessful attempts to make her talk about anything she remembered from her childhood I bring the conversation to the immediate context. Ruth lives in a self-contained flat shared with some other pupils of the boarding school.*)
*UF*: Now you live in that lovely flat, upstairs?
*R*:   Yes-suh.
*UF*: Is that really good?
*R*:   It is.
*UF*: Do you do some cooking there?
*R*:   Yes, I do.
*UF*: What kinds of things do you cook?
*R*:   Anything.
*UF*: Really. What is your favourite food?

*R*: Fish fingers.

*UF*: Oh, yes . . . And you cook them yourself?

*R*: Nearly.

*UF*: That's very nice.

*(Again, my attempts to make Ruth volunteer information were unsuccessful. All I could do was to give leading questions which she answered with perfect honesty. At no point did she try to create an impression, one way or the other, for instance by boasting or denigrating such skills as cooking or reading. Indeed, she seemed to express no attitude whatever towards either her accomplishments or her failings.)*

*UF*: And what do you do for fun?

*R*: Nothing.

*UF*: Perhaps you do some knitting?

*R*: Yes-suh.

*UF*: Or watching television?

*R*: Yes-suh.

*UF*: What programmes do you like?

*R*: *Top of the Pops.*

*(After some unsuccessful questions relating to the programme, with which I was unfamiliar, I switched topics.)*

*UF*: And do you read?

*(Implied here was 'for fun', but this was probably not conveyed to Ruth.)*

*R*: Yes-suh.

*UF*: What sort of things? . . . *(no reply)* Do you read magazines?

*R*: No. Just look at them.

*UF*: Ah, yes . . . Because there are lots of pictures in them?

*R*: Yes-suh.

*(Presumably, Ruth's literal understanding does not allow her to consider 'just looking at a magazine' to be called reading.)*

*UF*: Hmm, what sort of magazines do you look at?

*R*: *Radio Times* and *TV Times.*

*UF*: Oh, yes, I look at those too . . .

*R*: Work time now.

*(The characteristically abrupt ending of a conversation with an autistic individual is well illustrated. Ruth did not mean to be rude, but the break was over and it was time to go back to work. Normally such a fact would be wrapped up in the language of politeness. Ruth does not present any wrappings, instead she gives bare information.)*

What does this highly typical example tell us? First of all, it shows that communication with an autistic person is by no means a total failure. Nevertheless, the communication that is achieved is extremely limited. As ordinary conversations go, my conversation with Ruth was like getting blood from a stone. How could this be when she was clearly willing to answer all my questions? Although there is exchange of information there is a missing ingredient. There is a peculiar detachment, a profound lack of interest in why I asked the questions and in any effect her remarks might have on me. It is not that in the manner of some adolescents Ruth 'couldn't care less'. Rather there was nothing else to the conversation than point-blank answers. Question and answer were all small units, and each answer was minimal and final. In this way each answer stopped the flow of conversation. Even trivial conversations often flow on with one thing leading to another. In this way it becomes sometimes possible to build up a rich picture of a stranger's life and attitudes. Language is a means to such riches, but it seems they are not accessible to autistic people, even if they do have language. In this chapter we will attempt to find the reasons. These reasons will have to explain the subtle communication failure that is typified in the conversation with Ruth.

### What is Wrong with the Language of Autistic Children?

More has been written on the language of autistic children – the peculiar forms of their speech as well as their difficulties in comprehension – than on any other of their psychological disabilities. Fortunately, there are a number of excellent reviews available, and the interested reader is referred to them for the many diverse facts that are known, but which are not discussed in this chapter.[1,2,3]

Language offers many measurable aspects of performance, as well as providing grounds for inferring underlying competence. Language implicates a vast array of hidden abilities. There is, for instance, *phonology*, the ability that allows us to handle speech sounds; *syntax*, the ability to handle the rules of grammar; *semantics*, the ability that enables us to understand and create meaning. Lastly, somewhat separate from the primary linguistic abilities, there is *pragmatics*, the ability to use language for the purpose of communication. An example of pragmatics is illustrated in figure 8.1. The point of the question 'Can you pass the salt?' is a request for salt, not a request for information (about one's ability to pass the salt). To get this point one needs pragmatic rather than syntactic or semantic competence.

Aspects of phonology, syntax and semantics have been studied in autistic children, with often confusing results. But recently pragmatics has become the most prominent target for research.[4] Here there is unanimous agreement. Indeed, it is now clear that difficulties in the domain of pragmatics are a universal feature of Autism. Whatever level of syntactic or semantic skill is reached, and this can be high in some

Figure 8.1

autistic people, the level of pragmatic skill will be lower. Rather subtle pragmatic difficulties in someone with good speech are illustrated in the conversation with Ruth.

Recently, Helen Tager-Flusberg gave a preliminary account of a rare longitudinal study of autistic children's language acquisition which is still in progress.[5] Young normal, Down's syndrome, and autistic children showed the same order of emergence across a wide range of syntactic structures and grammatical morphology. The similarities were there despite the fact that the autistic children used a narrower range of grammatical structures, and used more repetitive and stereotyped language. Marked differences, on the other hand, were found in the *use* of linguistic forms.

Studies such as this are badly needed, since they will eventually clarify to what extent and in what aspects, if any, the language acquisition of autistic children is impaired. The more retarded children are generally, the more retarded their language skills would be expected to be too. This is different from a specific linguistic impairment which may exist over and above what might be expected from general developmental level.[6,7] The incidence of such additional specific impairment in Autism is as yet unknown. If Tager-Flusberg's findings and similar current findings by other authors are confirmed, then it may turn out to be much less frequent than was once supposed.

Those autistic children who are mute may or may not suffer from phonological, syntactic and semantic impairment. It is difficult to judge their linguistic competence. Sometimes, by accident, a surprising degree of competence can be discovered to exist. There is, for instance, the case of a young man who never used language until he was given a computerized communicator which he took to and used effectively. There are also those children who never speak, but on very rare occasions have been heard to utter a whole phrase, and there are the children who only parrot, but hardly ever talk spontaneously. In all these cases it is more appropriate to speak of severe communication impairment than language impairment.

Delays in language acquisition, too, may or may not indicate a primary linguistic impairment. Language acquisition problems could very well be due to communication problems. Normal language acquisition is undoubtedly aided by an innate desire to communicate intentionally. If this desire is weak in autistic children, then this might be as serious a handicap for language acquisition as deafness, for instance.

It is still one of the great mysteries how young normal children manage to acquire the language that is spoken around them. New words are learned easily if they can be attached to 'relevant' topics. If normal infants are ready to learn the word for 'pudding', they pick up the meaning in a situation where pudding is a shared topic of interest. The word will then be uttered and understood at the right moment. Thus, a child does not mistakenly learn to call the pudding 'raisin', or 'yellow', or 'stop it'. Autistic children, in contrast, may miss out on situations where a relevant topic is shared with a person who says the right word at the right time. If so, this would mean they have fewer learning opportunities. It would also mean that they might learn words or phrases that somebody uttered without intending them to be associated with the event that the child associated them with. So it is conceivable that they would actually learn to use the word 'raisin' to refer to pudding. This is one explanation of idiosyncratic speech which has often been noted in the language of autistic children.

If delay in language acquisition can be explained as a consequence of communication failure, rather than as a specific linguistic problem, what of the language peculiarities that are present even in those autistic individuals who have good grammatical competence? The most typical of these are echolalia, so-called metaphorical language and reversal of the pronouns 'I' and 'you'. All of these were already identified by Kanner and are among the most reliably observed behavioural features of Autism. We shall consider each of them separately in order to find out what they reveal about the relationship between language and communication in Autism.

*'Say hello, Bob' – 'Say hello, Bob.'*

Amongst the most characteristic behavioural abnormalities of young autistic children is the parrot-like echoing of speech (hence echolalia). At least three-quarters of all speaking autistic children show this conspicuous phenomenon. As a symptom it can be observed in some other conditions involving brain abnormalities, for instance, developmental or acquired aphasia or dementia. It also occurs in the speech of normal children, but only at a young age.

The ability to echo short or long fragments of speech requires a high degree of expertise in processing phonological and prosodic aspects of speech, both as input and as output. It requires the ability to turn attention to speech alone, as opposed to other environmental noises that might go on in the background at the same time. Echoing of non-speech noises is not typically reported for autistic children.

Which fragments of speech are most likely to be echoed? Observational evidence suggests that it is speech addressed directly to the child that is repeated, not speech addressed to others. When carrying out memory experiments I found it just as easy to get repetitions of random word strings as of meaningful sentences. On the other hand I found it very hard to get repetitions of a tape-recorded voice. Presumably, attention is more readily captured by a real person speaking than by an invisible voice. Often, in more anxious moments, a child may echo a parent's or teacher's admonishing words from the past: 'Don't do that, Paul.' 'You're a clever boy, Gregory.' An important question not yet answered by research is the extent to which utterances are modified when they are echoed, both immediately and after a while. In young normal children's parroting, modifications are very common. Normal children tend to echo speech that is just above their own grammatical competence, but we do not know whether this is also true for autistic children.

Why do autistic children echo speech at all? This question has been extensively studied and recently reviewed by Schuler and Prizant.[8] However, there is as yet no satisfactory answer. Much research effort has been spent on analysing echolalic speech in autistic children in order to find out what communicative purpose it might serve. For instance, echoing might signal 'I do not understand', since there is generally an increase in echoing when the children do not comprehend what someone says to them. Sometimes, echoing can be interpreted as a request. 'Do you want a biscuit' means 'Yes, please'. However, in many instances one cannot rule out that echoing is merely stereotyped behaviour, and does not stem from any communicative intent.

Should echoing be discouraged? There is no evidence to say whether it is a bad or a good thing, and so practitioners are divided. Some assume it must be bad, because both in normal language development and in pathological cases, as language improves, echolalia diminishes. This is also true for autistic children. Those children who echo most seem to use little spontaneous language. However, such observations do not tell us what is cause and what is effect.

The recall experiments that were pioneered by Beate Hermelin and Neil O'Connor, and which were discussed in chapter 7, are in fact still our best guide to an interpretation of echolalia. From this evidence echolalia appears to be a glaring manifestation of detachment between more peripheral processing systems and a central system that is concerned with meaning. The autistic child selectively attends to speech and translates heard speech proficiently into spoken speech. However, this processing seems to bypass involvement of central thought. Echolalia demonstrates how end-products of sophisticated information processing can go to waste by not being interpreted by yet higher-level processes. Though they are perfect phonological, prosodic and syntactic units, these products do not become part of global meaning. Instead of becoming tributaries of a mighty river they are streams running into sand.

The phenomenon of echolalia is not outside normal experience: anyone may lose the thread of conversation when tired or preoccupied. In this case it is typical to find oneself silently echoing the last phrase heard, without comprehension. It is as if the phrase is being recycled, until it can be received by an interpreter. Effort is needed for echoing a message, but some extra effort is needed for understanding a message.

The contrast we have been considering is between fully understanding a message, and simply transmitting a message. Clearly, many autistic children who do not fully understand speech are nevertheless able to receive and convey speech. They let bare messages go in and out correctly, but they do not seem to look for a *reason* for conveying the messages in the first place. An example is 'Say hello, Bob' – with Bob echoing 'Say hello, Bob.' Bob did not interpret the utterance, otherwise he would not have repeated it verbatim. In order to interpret the utterance, the past and present context of the message needs to be considered, not just the message itself. When this is done, the way is open for fuller comprehension (for example, she wants me to be friendly to Mr Fox: I'd better say hello to him: 'Hello, Mr Fox'). If the autistic child attends only to small bits of information rather than to a large globally coherent pattern of information, then this job would be very hard. Is it possible that weak central coherence precludes the capacity to appreciate the deeper intentional aspects of communication? Echolalia would fit in perfectly with this hypothesis. Can we explain other typical features of autistic language in the same way?

### 'Peter, Peter, pumpkin eater'

A particularly odd phenomenon of language use in autistic children has been referred to since Kanner by the term 'metaphorical language'.[9] This is a most unfortunate label which has little to do with either the layman's or the linguist's use of this term. It needs an example to illustrate what Kanner means by it. An autistic boy, Paul, was two years old when his mother used to recite to him the nursery rhyme 'Peter, Peter, pumpkin eater'. One day, while she was doing this, she was working in the kitchen and suddenly dropped a saucepan. Paul, from that day on, chanted 'Peter eater' whenever he saw anything resembling a saucepan.

The anecdote constitutes a perfect example of associative verbal learning, the sort of learning that was once thought to explain language acquisition in the normal child. We now know that such learning is not typical of young normal children. Indeed, it is hard to believe that it is typical of the language learning of autistic children, and to what extent their language acquisition might be governed by this principle is as yet unknown.

As Kanner (1946) succinctly put it, 'the child's (metaphorical) remark is not "relevant" to any sort of verbal or other situational interchange.' There would therefore be less confusion if one used the term *idiosyncratic remarks*. These remarks are bizarre because they are based on unique associations and because they do not refer to wider experiences that are accessible to *both* speaker and listener.

In order to understand idiosyncratic speech one often needs to do special detective work. Trying to puzzle out why and how an autistic child uses particular idiosyncratic expressions makes an absorbing game. An example is taken from the vocabulary of Jay, an able autistic man who became an electronics technician. He consistently uses the term 'the student nurses age group' whenever he refers to the years spanning late adolescence. Why student nurses? When asked this question, he wrote:

> I know that there is another name which identifies the 17–21 age group other than 'student nurses' age group as according to certain people. Mr T. my electronics teacher at VGRS might call the 17–21 age group the American Television Electronics School or ATES age group, since most students at ATES are in that age group, as well as most student nurses.

This comment is remarkable, as it implies an awareness of other people's point of view without drawing the consequence that it is shared points of view that permit two-way communication. Jay is not concerned with what label most people would use, let alone whether they would want to make a special category out of the 17–21 age group.

Proper metaphorical remarks, as opposed to idiosyncratic remarks, can be accessed by other people through shared experiences. For instance, one may say that one's arm has 'gone to sleep'. Sometimes such remarks are highly original. Abundant examples are to be found not only in literature, but also in everyday life. One normal four-year-old child, for instance, spontaneously described his arm as 'gone fizzy'. This was instantly understood.

It remains characteristic of autistic children that they persist in using bizarre idiosyncratic phrases, but it is not characteristic of normally developing children, children with specific language impairment, or mentally retarded children. This peculiarity can be seen as part of a wider failure in communication: idiosyncratic speech suggests a lack of interest or need to share with the listener a wider context of interaction in which both are actively involved. It suggests a failure to gauge the comprehension of listeners. In this sense the information conveyed remains a detailed, self-contained piece that is not part of an overall, coherent pattern.

### I and you and you and me

When an autistic child substitutes 'you' for 'I' and 'I' for 'you', this is indeed quite startling to any observer. It seems such a fundamental mistake. No wonder the phenomenon has been vested with deep significance! It has been used to support speculations about whether autistic children are deeply confused about their own identity. It has even been alleged that the child is actively avoiding the pronouns I, me, my and mine. Thorough investigations leave no doubt that such fanciful speculations are part of the myths of Autism and not part of the reality.

What happens when an autistic child reverses pronouns is both simple and complex to explain. The simple part has to do with delayed echoing of an utterance associated with a similar situation.[10] For instance: the boy who said 'Do you want a biscuit?' was parroting a phrase which was frequently used by an adult when giving him a biscuit. He had learned to associate this particular phrase with the event without learning what the phrase means.

The complex part of the analysis of pronoun errors has to do with the so-called deictic function of personal pronouns. What this refers to is the fact that their use is *relative* to who is speaker and who is listener. Even in normal language development errors in this sphere are common at least up to age five. The errors that are made are often 'edited out' by listeners, since it is taken for granted that the child is not really confused about who is who. There is also experimental and observational evidence to show that autistic children are not confused about their own and others' physical identity. A study by Rita Jordan that is still in progress indicates that they almost always use names correctly. However, they tend to use proper names when their non-autistic peers would use pronouns.

One interpretation of these results that would be consistent with our previous interpretations is that autistic children are subject only to a drive for local but not global coherence. They only pull together a very limited amount of information at a time. Normal children, in contrast, take into account a much larger amount of information. They understand how pronouns relate to previously used, or mutually understood, nouns. Therefore they choose name or pronoun, whichever serves best in the cohesion of discourse.[11]

Normally, we keep continuous track of what an utterance means from the point of view both of the speaker and of the hearer. But this is not all. Whose point of view should be taken in a particular case is open to social negotiation. Autistic children have problems in the finer points of social role appreciation. It is therefore not surprising that personal pronouns are 'confused', or not used at all by such children, even in non-echoic speech.

For similar reasons autistic children have difficulty with tenses. This is not a grammatical problem, but a problem of knowing when to use which tense. Normally we resolve this question by reference to the higher-level context in which the utterance is embedded. The same applies to such words as this and that, here and there, come and go. Given our discussion in the preceding chapters, we would expect that autistic children find it hard to use such relative terms appropriately. Without a strong need for central coherence the ability to use higher-level context would be weak.

The difficulties with pronouns, with relative terms for time and space, the persistence of idiosyncratic remarks, and the pervasiveness of echolalia are all phenomena that seem like the tips of a huge iceberg. The iceberg is lack of appreciation of wider meaning including the speaker's intentions. In this way the most typical feature of autistic language can be explained as consequences, not causes, of a specific communication failure. How far can linguistic skills be developed in the presence of this iceberg?

*How well developed can language be in autistic individuals?*

We can find abundant evidence that in *retarded* autistic children the development of speech and language is often delayed. This of course, is not unexpected. It is also true for mentally retarded children who are not autistic. What is surprising however, is that a sizeable proportion of autistic children who are mentally retarded learn to read very effectively. They read aloud with excellent phonology and they can complete unfinished sentences with the right grammatical form.

Maggie Snowling and I carried out investigations of phonological and syntactic competence in these excellent readers.[12] On a standardized test of grammatical competence we found that they performed just as well as non-autistic children of the same mental age. We also found that they can make very fine syntactic distinctions. For instance, when reading aloud sentences such as 'one yellow bippis is enough for me', and 'seven little bippis had a boat', they quite unconsciously adjusted their phonology according to whether the word 'bippis' appeared as singular or plural. The final -s is voiced when it indicates a plural, but unvoiced if not. In this way we distinguish 'peas' and 'peace'.

On the other hand, when we asked our autistic fluent readers to guess the missing words in a story, or to detect silly words that we inserted, then they failed markedly, compared to controls. For instance, in a factual nature story they did not bat an eyelid when they came to a sentence that said: 'The hedgehog could smell the scent of the *electric* flowers.' They were not sure what to do with: 'There, surfacing in the dim light, was a young male' – when from the story context it was obvious that the missing word had to be 'beaver'. They might, for instance, happily insert the word 'horse'. This was fine in the local sense of the sentence, seen by itself, but not in the global sense of the story.

Few investigations of the *semantic* competence of able autistic individuals have been done. It seems almost certain that there are exceptional autistic people without any noticeable semantic impairment, particularly when topics relate to their field of interest. This opinion is based on the fact that there exist some flawless examples of writing by able autistic people. One of these is the autobiography of the remarkable Temple Grandin.[13] This exceptionally articulate young woman can truly speak for herself:

> I am successful in my business. I travel all over the United States, Europe, Canada and Australia designing livestock handling facilities for ranches, feedlots and meat packing plants. My experiences have given me empathy for the animals going through the facilities and help me design better equipment. For instance, the chutes and pens I design are round. The

reason for this design is because cattle will follow a curved path more easily. There are two reasons for this: first, the cattle can't see what is at the other end and become frightened and, secondly, the curved equipment takes advantage of the animal's natural circling behaviour. The principle is to work with the animal's behaviour instead of against it. I think the same principle applies to autistic children – work with them instead of against them.

There is little one can add to such competent and lucid writing. It is only fair to say that Temple Grandin is unique in this respect.

Those who are in close touch with able and articulate autistic people often remark that there is something wrong about the way they talk but that it is hard to put a finger on it. A telling example is provided in one of many letters written to Margaret Dewey by Jay (the same who coined the term 'student nurses age group'). In this extract, he gives a remarkably insightful analysis of the struggle he has with subtle word meanings.

> I wonder if Jack's voice still sounds whiny or not? My voice does not sound whiny but it did when I was at H. I was telling you this last June also. My sister Wanda originally used the word whiny to mean nasal voice. Why? I don't know. She did two months after her high school graduation. I've copied her. Using the word whiny to mean nasal voice is just what an autistic child would do. The expression 'whiny voices' is not used in social circles. It is rather blunt and insulting like calling coloured people 'niggers'. When a person speaks of a boy or girl whose voice sounds whiny, he or she always says this: 'this boy or girl's voice is nasal', which is also true. I must apologize for using whiny voices in this letter. I should have used nasal voices instead. I just can't seem to get whiny voices off my mind.

The writer is extremely, if not obsessively, concerned with the exact meaning of the phrase 'whiny voice'. To him, it refers to an exact sensory quality, a purely perceptual or behavioural phenomenon. However, there is clearly more to its meaning than this. This 'more' can only be understood if one considers the reason a person might use the phrase in the first place. The answer cannot be found in any dictionary: it is in the realm of intention. Perhaps the speaker wants to complain about the voice quality. Jay has correctly deduced that whiny is a pejorative term, but he does not know when and how to use it. In this sense what escapes him are *shades* of meaning. A common complaint of those experienced with advanced autistic language is that there is a tendency to see everything as either black or white. The analogy made from 'whiny voice' to 'nigger' is a strangely exaggerated one, while the difference between whiny and nasal may be non-existent in terms of social acceptability. The differences and similarities are not categorical, since they truly depend on the circumstance. Although Jay thought a lot about this problem, it did not occur to him to worry about the fact that commenting on voice quality at all may be socially inappropriate.

We all implicitly know that the same words uttered with different communicative intent result in a change of meaning. A good example is irony. For autistic people the literal meaning of words does not change in an ironic setting. In this setting the actual words remain the same, just as in the Embedded Figures test the hidden details remain the same. In both cases autistic people may be more inclined to see the details 'as they are', uninfluenced by their embedding context.

According to biographical accounts, irony is extremely difficult to master for autistic people. However, the ability to handle nuances is not just a luxury shared by a few sophisticated people. It is common to all normal users of language. Of course this ability will vary with practice and culture. What counts here is having the mental capacity that makes learning about shades of meaning possible, if not inevitable. An autistic individual is crippled by being limited in this capacity, and hence can learn to recognize subtle or shifting meanings only with great effort.

## The Uses of Speech in Communication

Let us go back to the conversation with Ruth. Ruth had a good vocabulary, excellent grammar and was a superb reader. Yet she was an abysmal partner for small talk. Poor language is not the cause of poor conversational skills. Nothing illustrates the truth of this statement better than the insistence on syntactic and phonological precision typical of some autistic adults. 'He speaks as if he were a foreigner', or 'he takes everything literally' are the usual spontaneous judgements by conversation partners. By contrast, in normal conversation idiomatic and ungrammatical speech is common. Listeners are often unaware of the errors, in fact.

There are as yet few studies of the conversational competence of autistic people.[14] Those by Baltaxe represented something of a landmark.[15] She documented, for instance, that German-speaking autistic adolescents confused the polite and familiar form of address (Sie and Du), a confusion that arises from a neglect of social roles. She also documented a number of other subtle problems in language use including turn-taking and the differentiation of new from old information. These have been highlighted by all recent reviews.

When introducing a new topic into a conversation, an autistic individual may not mark it as new. On the other hand, observation suggests that highly verbal autistic people often say 'by the way . . .', 'talking of . . .', 'well, anyway . . .', when they are in fact *not* introducing a new topic. They learned a formula without fully understanding it. It is necessary to pull together quite large amounts of information in order to know when it is appropriate to mark a topic as new. Precisely this may be the problem that cannot be overcome by learning conversational gambits.

When considering conversational competence, the prosodic features of speech are just as important as content of speech. We are talking here of the use of intonation, pitch, speech rate, fluency and word stress in the service of communication. As yet few investigations exist in this area with normal, let alone retarded or autistic children. Even well-adapted autistic people show relative incompetence with these tools of communication. For instance, their voice may suddenly switch from whisper to loudness, from low to high pitch. It is as if they fail to judge what volume is needed to reach the listener, and use sometimes too much, sometimes too little. Speed can be a similar problem. 'If only I could make him speak more slowly, people might understand him,' one mother said to me recently. With some autistic people the complaint is total lack of variation, which is perceived as sing-song, or monotonous, pedantic speech. On the other hand, sometimes an apparently beautifully modulated voice carries a nonsense remark or a repetitive phrase. All this suggests that the problems do not originate from lack of control but from lack of knowing when and where to apply control.

One pertinent example concerns the use of stress. Primary sentence stress marks distinctions between key words and function words. 'The *father* held his *son*.' Contrastive stress, on the other hand, marks pragmatic distinctions. 'The father held *his* son (not hers).' It is here where autistic individuals have particular difficulty.[16] This further confirms that the use of prosodic features for purposes of conversational communication is impaired, not their perception or execution. Conversational failure can be interpreted as a consequence of the same deeper disturbance, the same iceberg, that explains all the language peculiarities we have considered. What is the nature of this disturbance?

### Conveying messages and communicating

The disturbance of communication in Autism is at once gross and subtle. This can best be explained by imagining that there are two kinds of communication. One kind is of highest priority in normal individuals, and this has the special status of fully intentional communication. It relates information to mental states and evaluates information that is conveyed. The other kind applies just to the conveying of bare messages. This second kind can be clearly observed in the conversation with Ruth, but the first kind seems to be absent altogether.

Faithful conveying of information is not a trivial accomplishment. It calls for accurate encoding and decoding of speech at input and output stages. Ruth does this. Echolalic children do it too. Nevertheless, in everyday communication one rarely expects that a listener will have to receive and then transmit a bare message as an exact copy. On the contrary, one expects listeners to know that messages are not bare, but usually contain something more. What really matters in everyday communication is the point of the message rather than the message itself. In other words, as listeners we need to know *why* the speaker conveys *this* thought (rather than another), and as speakers we need to be sure we are understood in the way we *want* to be understood. We have elaborate verbal and non-verbal signals for getting across these intentions.

The two sides of intentional communication fit like lock and key in Dan Sperber and Deirdre Wilson's brilliant and innovative theory of relevance.[17] This theory, which attempts to explain how comprehension is possible, is uniquely suited to a psychological explanation of the communication failure in Autism.

An example may illustrate the two kinds of communication. Consider the scene of two creatures pushing each other, illustrated in figure 8.2. 'Crinkley is pushing Snakey' is a bare message conveying the content of the cartoon. In the ordinary flow of conversation, this message would only be one among many possible ways of talking about the picture. Which particular utterance was produced would depend on the context. It would depend on what the speaker expects the listener to understand. Though correct, the description 'Crinkley is pushing Snakey' might be an entirely inappropriate (babyish? pedantic?) thing to say. The various utterances that are illustrated in the speech bubbles convey more than the content of the picture. In every case it is *surprise* at Crinkley pushing Snakey. Yet, each utterance puts across the surprise in a different way. While revealing the mental state of the speaker, each utterance gives different shades of meaning to the bare message. We normally pack all sorts of evaluations into our utterances, and reveal or hide all sorts of mental states. Indeed, utterances can reveal something about the reason that somebody is talking to somebody else at all. What is more, we constantly pay attention to aspects of utterances that have to do not with their content, but with the intention of the speaker. According to Sperber and Wilson, true communication would just not work without this type of attention. In fact, in ordinary conversations bare messages

Figure 8.2

(where only content matters) are so rare that they tend to be interpreted in terms of some ulterior communicative purpose *even* if none is there. This is the case in figure 8.3. Because of the normal language user's habitual processing of a speaker's intention, autistic language may be over-interpreted in the way the telephone query in the cartoon was over-interpreted.

The reverse failure is illustrated in figure 8.1. Here, the lack of communication is due to not considering the reason a question was asked in the first place. She really did want the salt. This situation is highly reminiscent of the failure of autistic people to answer similar questions appropriately.

Normally speakers give not just more information than that contained in the bare message, but evaluated information. By doing this they can achieve different degrees of understanding from the deliberate vagueness of the allusion to the sharp precision of the *mot juste*. In this way speakers can justify *why*, in the current context, they make an utterance, and

Figure 8.3

listeners can find reasons *why* the utterance was made, in the current context. With successful communication the reasons are mutually negotiated and understood. Since this understanding is of the greatest importance, redundancy is common. Not only choice of words, but also tone of voice and a whole range of non-verbal body language can be put into service. We have reason to believe that in Autism true intentional communication is impaired in contrast to the conveying of bare messages. As a consequence, the many tools that allow communication to develop to a highly sophisticated level are not mastered. But this is not the fault of the tools.

It is pervasively documented that autistic individuals cannot easily understand language that is flippant or witty, and that instead they are excessively literal. Margaret Dewey carried out an informal survey in America using cartoons from the *New Yorker*. Very able and highly educated autistic people failed to understand them, or find them funny. Autistic people's own utterances can be lengthy and pedantic, and often use stock phrases. Sometimes their comments are perceived as inappropriate by others, as rude or as funny, or else over-polite. For instance, one autistic young man asked 'May I extract a biscuit from this tin?' when it would have been more appropriate to say 'Can I have a biscuit?' Another young man, who often telephones his favourite aunt, never fails to announce himself by saying 'This is M. C. Smith, your nephew, speaking.'

One final example of the vicissitudes of the two kinds of communication, the literal and the normal, intentional kind, is provided by the delightful comedy film *Being There*.[18] Here, an innocent, mentally handicapped and undoubtedly autistic hero, played by Peter Sellers, is taken up as a guru by a sophisticated and gullible group of people. They do not know anything about him, but his simplicity and artlessness puts them in awe of him. His every pronouncement (spoken in a slow, measured voice) is transparently obvious, and a bare truism. None the less, it is eagerly received, richly interpreted and invested with deep significance. At the same time, the hero is quite unaware of the effect he has. The serious side of this comedy of errors is that the autistic literalness acts as a mirror to those who are busily 'intentionalizing' and who see in any message whatever they seek. Here for once the capacity for communicative intent is shown to make fools of us all. It is more usual, of course, that we consider as fools those who do not have this capacity.

# 9

# The Loneliness of the Autistic Child

It all makes me very sad because I am getting older and older and I continue not to meet anyone. Perhaps someone reading this could get in touch with me. I hope someone that can offer me some love and affection will get in touch. Living is more or less one constant bore. Yes, I think anyone normal would find it hard to lead the kind of existence I have. I think if some normal girl would take a real interest in me I would just bother with her and no other girl, but I spend my time talking to a lot of girls, hoping I can find one that will take a real interest.

This extract ends David's 100-page autobiography, which he hopes will help him find a companion. But what is different about this case from the thousands of lonely hearts who might have written very similar words? This is the question we have to bear in mind when trying to understand the reason for the social impairment in Autism. We need to go beyond the ordinary concepts of sociability. We need to seek the reasons not merely for social incompetence, which after all is a problem shared by many who are not autistic.

The consensus is that social ineptness in autistic individuals is most strikingly demonstrated in two-way interactions. However, beyond this contention there is little agreement on its nature. This is not surprising, because it is difficult to define what social competence and incompetence is in normal individuals. Surface behaviour is not a useful guide here. If it were, we would have to attribute social impairment to those people who display little outward affection, and who react to their own feelings and to the feelings of others with what has been termed a 'stiff upper lip'. We might also be misled into attributing warm, affectionate relationships to those who are only play-acting. Instead, we know that 'one may smile and be a villain'. Examples of sophisticated social competence include telling the difference between posing, acting and

Figure 9.1

really meaning it. They also include the art of being a recluse and the skill of keeping others at a distance. The loneliness of the autistic child is something different altogether. It demands a circumspect approach.

Fred Volkmar and his colleagues used the Vineland Adaptive Behavior Scales with a large sample of autistic and non-autistic retarded children.[1] A comparison of their scores on different sub-categories of social skills proved to be highly illuminating. Firstly, the autistic children were not totally devoid of social interest or responsiveness at any age. Secondly, they were not impaired equally across all categories, but showed a significant degree of scatter. Thirdly, they could be distinguished from mentally retarded, non-autistic children, who also showed their share of social impairment. In self-care and simple daily living skills (for example, road safety, health care, domestic skills), autistic children did rather well, and sometimes better for their mental age than their counterparts. However, in terms of interpersonal communication autistic children came out very much worse. They were rated poorly at sharing and cooperating, apologizing, making and keeping appointments, borrowing and returning, controlling impulses, and responding appropriately to people of different degrees of familiarity.

Autistic children's ability to appreciate other people's emotional reactions was felt by caregivers to be particularly poor, as was the ability to express emotions in a meaningful fashion. Deficits in the area of interpersonal relationships were so marked that the autistic group on the average was functioning four years below what would be expected from their mental age level. All these reported impairments at first glance do not seem out of the ordinary, apart from their reported severity. What is it about the target behaviours that make the autistic individual so incapacitated as a social being? Clearly, we have to go deeper than the behavioural manifestations of the impairment. We can start by looking at what is known of the development of social skills in the autistic child.

### Learning to be Socialized

There is as yet no systematic study of the development of social behaviour in individual autistic children. Such studies are rare even of normal children. Throughout development, dramatic changes occur in social behaviour. Indeed it is often difficult to trace continuities. The egocentrism of the infant does not predict any degree of egotism in adulthood. It certainly does not preclude the ability for selfless acts in later years. As we know from novels, a happy childhood may well precede unhappy social relationships in adulthood. The awkward shyness of the teenager does not forebode a reclusive future. On the basis of such commonplace experiences one should also expect that social impairment in Autism has different manifestations at different levels of development. It is true that the behavioural signs of impairment vary with age, and they also vary with the degree of associated retardation. Yet, there is consensus that the underlying social impairment of Autism is persistent, despite change in behaviour.

There is a large question mark over social abnormalities shown during the first year of life. This is because it is not clear which aspects if any are specific to Autism, and which aspects might be signs of some other cause for developmental delay. Normal babies show a very active interest in people almost as soon as they are born. Mental retardation is known to diminish social responsiveness just as it diminishes responsiveness to other stimuli. Learning in all domains is affected. Since the majority of autistic children are mentally retarded to some degree, we would expect social impairment for this reason alone. We shall return to this important and puzzling question in a later section of this chapter.

In early childhood, between three and five years, the isolation of the autistic child from the world of others is especially marked. 'He is happiest when left alone', 'he is always looking through people', 'he never even glanced at his new baby sister', are typical remarks from parental accounts. The lack of appropriate emotional responsiveness in their child is a most distressing aspect for the family. What this means remains to be seen, but it is not a total absence of affect. Autistic children express joy, fear, anger and other moods, but they are often out of synchrony with social expectations. The delayed appearance or absence of language is a strong impediment in attempts at socialization. Furthermore, social praise and disapproval are more difficult to apply than they are with normal children. Autistic children do not seem to be able to judge the intention behind these common controls of behaviour. For instance, they may be miserable over a petty reprimand ('your fingers are sticky') and ignore an important one ('get off the road').

After age five there is often marked improvement in social skills, especially in the more able children. Indeed during the whole of their development, autistic children show noticeable increases in socialization. Yet learning to behave *appropriately* towards others remains much harder for them than it is for other children.

Autistic children are often badly teased and tormented by their normal peers. This suggests that the social oddness of autistic individuals is so outstanding that no physical sign is needed to brand them as outcasts. Nevertheless, there are also those who have learned social behaviour so well that their oddness may not be noticed for a long time. In fact it may only be noticed in extreme situations and whenever really subtle social cues must be interpreted. For instance autistic individuals cannot 'read between the lines' to know whether or not they are welcome, or they may panic when suddenly faced with an unfamiliar requirement. For example, a young woman who is employed, lives independently and drives her own car, regressed completely when her car broke down, showing stereotyped speech and hand flapping.

It is often remarked that autistic people have no sense of personal modesty, shame or guilt. They find social taboos hard to understand, so that behaviour in public tends to remain exactly the same as in private. This includes behaviour that is normally tolerated in young children but not easily overlooked in grown-up autistic people. Parents and teachers have to direct many specific lessons to instilling social dos and don'ts in autistic children. Yet sometimes they might wish that the maxims were not learned as well as they are! There are, after all, cases where being polite actually means an insult ('thank you for a delightful dinner' when this was an acknowledged disaster), and where behaviour normally frowned upon becomes the right thing to do. From anecdotal evidence it seems that these sorts of problems are excessively hard to understand even by the able autistic individual.

Some of the perceived abnormalities of autistic social behaviour can be seen not so much as impairments, but as unusually positive qualities. These qualities can be captured by terms such as innocence, honesty and guilelessness. Autistic people are not adept at deceiving others, nor at impressing others. They are not manipulative, or gossipy. Since they often do not have a strong feeling for possessions, they are not envious and can give to others gladly. There is the story of the man who after his parent's death gave away all his money and his furniture to false friends and was later discovered starving in an empty and cold room of his former home. Autistic people may not empathize in the common sense of the word, but neither do they gloat over other people's misfortune. Indeed they can be profoundly upset by suffering they see, and they can show righteous indignation. One young man, seeing a girl roughly treated, attacked her escort, with painful consequences for himself.

All of these qualities of autistic people have been recognized in legends, stories and myths since ancient times. There is a danger that they are forgotten when one talks of the profound social impairment of autistic individuals. Clearly, the nature of this impairment is not a simple global lack of social responsiveness. The egocentrism shown by the autistic child is not at all like the egotism of the calculating manipulator;

it has instead the same innocence as the egocentrism of the normal infant. Like their islets of ability, these endearing and positive characteristics of autistic people are important clues. The negative aspects of social behaviour may tell us where the handicap is felt most sharply, but we also need to take account of the positive aspects. Only by looking at both sides of the coin can we understand the nature of the handicap.

### Do autistic children avoid other people?

Abnormal two-way relationships are the core feature and *sine qua non* for the diagnosis of Autism. The expert can subjectively identify this abnormality with confidence and yet the exact nature of the problem has proved extremely elusive. At first, it seemed that the underlying problem in behaviour towards others could best be described as a rejection or avoidance of social contact. Autistic aloneness might then be seen as either a voluntary or an involuntary state of physical isolation from others. Beate Hermelin and Neil O'Connor, at the start of their extensive experimental investigations of autistic children, were the first to put this notion to the test.[2] These tests were as straightforward as can be: an autistic child and an adult were together in an empty room for nine minutes. For the first three minutes, the adult attempted gentle physical contact, trying to engage the child in play, and for the last three minutes the child was asked verbally to do things and to answer some questions. It turned out that only in this last period, where communication through language was attempted, autistic children acted differently from non-autistic children of the same mental age. Most importantly, however, there was no sign of particular avoidance of the person.

This finding was confirmed in a second experiment. Here the physical distance was measured from the child to various 'objects' placed at the end of a large room. These 'objects' were carefully selected to see if the child would approach or avoid them. There was a box, a rocking platform and a blanket, all of which autistic children might like to hide under, or else use for their own purposes. There were also a real woman, a life-size doll, and a big loudspeaker, out of which came a soothing voice talking to the child. If it were true that autistic children actively avoided human contact, then they would avoid any of the social stimuli and seek out others. But this was not found. The autistic children, just like their non-autistic counterparts, spent significantly more time near the real person than near any of the other stimuli. Clearly, on gross physical avoidance measures, it was impossible to maintain that autistic children avoid social stimuli.

Beate Hermelin and Neil O'Connor then continued to explore the clinical observation of eye-gaze avoidance that was said to be a characteristic sign of autistic children's impairment. For this experiment a more elaborate apparatus had to be constructed. The children had to look inside a large dark box at two lighted display cards. The eye gaze was observed from a peephole at the other side of the box. The direction of the eye gaze, as well as the duration of eye fixation, were recorded by a three-way switch operated continuously by the experimenter, and connected to a pen recorder. With this simple but ingenious apparatus, one of the most elegant experiments with autistic children was conducted.

It is worth relating some of the details. Three groups of children, normal, autistic and subnormal, looked into the box. All were of the same (non-verbal) mental age as each other, which was around six years. Each pair of pictures displayed at the left and at the right was lit up for 30 seconds after the child was comfortably settled looking right inside the black box. The picture pairs differed on just one dimension, for instance one was red, the other black, one had a small blue square, the other a large blue one, etc. There was also a pair of identical blank cards, just to see if the child showed some strange preference for looking in one direction rather than the other. The most interesting display pair, however, was that of a photograph of a person and the same photograph jumbled up. Now, for each display how much time the child spent looking at each picture was recorded and also how much time was spent gazing around the box. 'Non-directed' gazing increased within each 30-second display period at about the same rate for all children. However, the autistic children had a very much higher rate of non-directed gazing for all the displays than the other groups. With *every* display the autistic children spent a rather short time looking directly at the pictures.

The children in all three groups showed preferences for looking at one card more than another, except for the blank cards. They preferred the more interesting and the more colourful member of each pair, just as one might expect. Also, just as one might expect, they looked more at the face than its jumbled-up counterpart. Moreover, all children, including the autistic ones, looked longer at these two cards than at any other displays. Because the autistic children compared to the other children spent much more time throughout looking at nothing in particular, they also looked less at the photograph. They also looked less at everything else.

### The myth of gaze avoidance

In a further experiment, Hermelin and O'Connor cut away the corners of the black box and put curtains on the openings. One experimenter then put his head into either of the two windows, while the other recorded the eye fixations of the children through the peephole. The critical part of this experiment was that on some occasions the experimenter looked at the child directly with eyes open, and on some with eyes closed. Perhaps because of the unusual 'display', all the children simply stared at the face, and looked at it for much longer than they had looked at any of the picture displays. This was regardless of whether the experimenter's eyes were open or closed. While autistic children might have been expected to avert their gaze when looking at the open eyes, this was not in fact what was found.

Strangely, these clear results have not succeeded in debunking the myth that autistic children intentionally shun interpersonal contact and show this in particular by gaze avoidance. We need to uncover some of the reasons for this persistent belief. Many shy but normal people often avoid eye contact. But here the phenomenon is not considered a sign of abnormal avoidance. It is experienced as part and parcel of perfectly normal non-verbal interaction. In contrast, autistic children are felt to avoid eye contact, even though they don't. As Beate Hermelin said at a meeting of Autism experts: 'The child looks equally little at the filing cabinet as at the psychiatrist. However, it is the psychiatrist who complains.' In this statement, however, lies the beginning of a new look at what is impaired in the autistic child's relationship with people: it is not that there is gaze avoidance, rather 'gaze' is not used in communication. The child neither looks away at the right time, nor meets the gaze when this would be expected.

It is a well-known saying that the eyes are the windows to the soul. By using eye contact we try to read what someone else might think or wish. The autistic child's failure to enter into this particular social exchange is disconcerting, and can readily lead one to 'complain'. This, then, may be the reason many people cling to the idea that autistic children avoid eye contact.

Eye gaze is so important for communication that a complicated, but largely unconscious, 'language of the eyes' is part of our social competence. There are pleading and imploring looks, triumphant looks, glaring looks, looks that kill, looks that mock, and looks that seduce: the list is as long as social relationships are varied. The meaning of these looks lies in shared mental states. If there were no mental states, then a language of the eyes would not exist.

A mundane but important use of eye gaze is to indicate turn-taking during conversation. It usually happens entirely without awareness. For instance, if you are eager to make a comment in a conversation, you try to catch the eye of the other speaker. Of course, he may deliberately avoid your eye so that he can continue speaking. Totally silent but sophisticated intentional communication is also possible through the language of the eyes.

Peter Hobson reports that an autistic man perceptively observed that 'other people talk to each other with their eyes'. He did not understand how they did this. Michael Rutter describes a young man who complained

> that he couldn't mind-read. Other people seemed to have a special sense by which they could read other people's thoughts and could anticipate their responses and feelings; he knew this because they managed to avoid upsetting people whereas he was always putting his foot in it, not realizing that he was doing or saying the wrong thing until after the other person became angry or upset.[3]

These two examples hint at an intriguing possibility. Whatever causes the inability to use the language of the eyes has nothing to do with avoidance of human contact. It has nothing to do with a lack of awareness of other people. Instead, we can begin to see that it has something to do with *awareness of other minds*. Before we turn more directly to this possibility, let us consider some other experimental work that has greatly increased our knowledge of the social impairment in autistic children.

## Social Responsiveness in Infancy

The normal infant shows social responsiveness from a remarkably early age. The social smile emerges at around six weeks of age, but a preference for human faces exists from birth. It takes somewhat longer for the infant to distinguish individuals by looking at their faces. A dramatic demonstration of facial discrimination occurs when the infant shows fear of strangers, usually at eight months. However, fear of strangers implies more than the ability to discriminate between different people. It also implies attachment to certain familiar people. No wonder the distress of their baby at the sight of unfamiliar faces is treasured by parents! It is the sign of a special emotional bond. Towards the end of the first year an infant will greet its mother in the morning; it will stretch out its arms, anticipating being picked up; it will mould its body to her and make joyous sounds. But it may well stiffen and turn away if someone unfamiliar wants to cuddle it.

Peek-a-boo games are often quoted as evidence of unequivocal turn-taking and reciprocal interaction in infancy. However, there are already much earlier instances of two-way interactions. There are exchanges of smiles and vocalizations and there are responses in terms of body movements. By the time the infant points out objects for the pleasure of shared attention, the first words are already understood. Reciprocal interaction increases even more when language learning has begun.

Is all of this lacking in young autistic children? It has often been presumed that early social responsiveness must be poor because older autistic children are so handicapped in their two-way interactions. The idea is that the explanation of autistic aloneness might lie in a lack of that innate socializing drive that characterizes young normal infants. However, the facts so far fail to support it. Early signs of sociability are by no means always absent in autistic children. Nor is absence of such signs found *only* in autistic children. This was revealed in an important study by Knobloch and Pasamanick which seems to be the only direct test of the hypothesis.[4] The study documented that many mentally retarded non-autistic children show very delayed development of social responsiveness and might be falsely diagnosed as autistic.

Conversely, anecdotal evidence exists for some autistic children who showed normal reciprocal interaction with their mothers as documented in photographs, films and diaries. These children smiled and babbled like normal children, and they looked pleased to see their parents. Some even stretched out their arms to be picked up and played peek-a-boo games. Even though there are also many anecdotal examples of autistic infants who did not show any of these things, this is also true for many non-autistic but mentally retarded children. Since mental retardation is frequently associated with autism, it is possible that those children who showed poor social responsiveness in infancy did so not by virtue of their Autism, but by virtue of their mental retardation. It is clearly necessary to conduct more investigations with babies who are at risk for developmental disorders.

What is the evidence for young autistic children's early social responsiveness? There are few experimental studies on young autistic children, but those by Marian Sigman and her colleagues are outstanding.[5] One of their investigations directly addressed the question whether autistic children can form personal attachments.

## Attachment

A rich paradigm in developmental psychology is based on the 'stranger reaction'. In this paradigm, there is an initial free play period with mother and child. Then the mother leaves for a brief interval and sometimes a stranger stays with the child. Lastly, the mother returns. During the reunion period the effects of attachment are shown by a marked increase in the child's spontaneous interactions with the mother. Distress reactions are observed at the mother leaving, as well as pleasure at her return. However, these particular indicators are not as ubiquitous and subtle as the different degrees of social responsiveness before and after the mother's return.

Marian Sigman and her colleagues applied the stranger reaction paradigm with autistic children of as young an age as they could locate given the age at which Autism can be diagnosed.[6] The children, between two and five years old, were compared with non-autistic retarded children of the same mental age. In view of the general belief in the inability of autistic children to form attachments, they were surprised to find no differences in the behaviour of both groups when with a stranger and at the mother's return. The autistic children showed a slight but significant increase in social responses directed towards their mother at the reunion stage. This experiment provides evidence of positive social responsiveness in young autistic children.

## Shared attention

Young autistic children are not devoid of social responsiveness, but there is an odd quality about their social interaction. This quality is difficult to capture. Sigman and her colleagues were able to identify some intriguing if subtle differences when they compared autistic and retarded children.[7] Autistic children talked less to their mothers than the other children. They also brought and showed toys less often. This finding is important. It was confirmed independently in a study by Loveland and Landry.[8] Furthermore, of all the social behaviours looked at, this subtle deficit discriminated best between autistic and non-autistic children.

What is the nature of this deficit? Normal ten-month-old children begin to point out things to people around them, regardless of whether or not they are already looking at the object. The aim seems to be to *share attention*. It has been proposed that the young infant's pointing is 'proto-declarative', and has the same function as some of the first words. Something is declared for its own sake.

What typically happens in early pointing is that children indicate something that is relevant not only to them but also to the person they communicate with. The partner responds with comprehension. For instance, 'Yes, you have a penguin just like that one', as if the child, by pointing to a penguin (and not to anything else) had wanted to make such a statement. Mutual comprehension can be achieved at this pre-verbal stage and this is immensely rewarding. When it happens both partners show delight. As the child grows up the important human ability to communicate for its own sake remains rewarding and shows a meteoric rise. It continues to increase in sophistication even in adulthood. Just think of advertising and politics. However, poker-faced negotiation is a long way from early pointing behaviour!

Shared attention can be shown by looking at another person at the right moment, as well as by bringing and showing things to that person. It was precisely these activities that were found to be missing in autistic children. Furthermore, in a different study with young autistic children, Frank Curcio showed that they never exhibited proto-declarative pointing.[9] So it is this aspect of social interaction, which is not even a particularly striking one from a naive observer's point of view, that turns out to be a major clue in the puzzle. It is evidence of an inability to recognize other minds.

If one wants to share one's own mental states with another person, then it is natural to communicate, by word or deed, what is relevant to this experience. Although on the surface it may look as if the child gives bare information about the location of an object out there by pointing to it, there is much more to it. The location itself is rarely interesting, but the singling out of the object is. It has been made the target of a particular mental state. This is what is being signalled and this mental state, not the toy, is of great interest to the partner.

An autistic child does indicate when he wants a broken toy mended, but he does not indicate to his mother what toy he remembers or likes for its own sake. Therefore she cannot share in the child's mental state. The child, we can hypothesize, makes no distinction between what is in his own mind and in anybody else's mind, and thus the question of sharing the content does not arise.

The demonstration of attachment in autistic children suggests that they recognize the difference between familiar and unfamiliar individuals. We may assume then that autistic children have the ability to recognize the existence of others as individual people. However, we now hypothesize that they have problems in recognizing that other people have independent minds. A simple distinction such as this is an important step in trying to account for the patchy nature of the social behaviour of autistic children, which is by no means deviant in *all* respects. Nevertheless, there are other explanations of the social impairment in autistic children, and one such explanation concerns the ability to understand emotions.


## Understanding Emotions

Can autistic children read feelings expressed in faces or in voices? If they cannot, then perhaps this alone might be a reason for their social handicap. Peter Hobson[10,11] portrayed the emotions happy, sad, angry and afraid by means of video film and asked children to match them up across different modes of presentation. For instance, the child had to say which of four faces went with which of four vocalizations, all expressing these emotions. Other tasks involved matching faces with situations in a video sequence, and again with body gestures.

The autistic children taking part in the various studies conducted by Hobson were in their teens, with mental age averaging ten years on Raven's matrices test. Most of these children, roughly two-thirds, were extremely poor at emotion matching. In contrast, almost all normal and mildly retarded children of the same mental age performed at ceiling. The failure of many of the autistic children was extremely surprising, given their age, ability and education, and the results are proof of some specific difficulty in emotion recognition which is independent of general intellectual ability.

The question is whether these results point to an irreducible deficit in the innate ability to understand expressions of emotions. There is much evidence that there is such an innate ability in all higher animals and it could be argued that this ability in people is closely related to an innate mechanism that permits affective relationships between people. It is Kanner's original hypothesis and it is also the one adopted by Hobson that such a mechanism is faulty in Autism. The hypothesis remains attractive because it takes seriously the indefinable emotional quality of normal personal relationships, a quality which is often felt to be missing in relationships formed by autistic people. One argument for the existence of a primitive mechanism of this type in normal children has been the phenomenon of early emotional bonds between mother and infant.

It has been taken for granted too readily that early bonding and attachment formation is missing in autistic children, and that this lack is the purest manifestation of their core symptom. The currently available evidence suggests that there are two serious problems with this belief: (1)

lack of early social responsiveness is not universal in Autism and is probably rare in more able autistic children; (2) non-autistic children also lack this ability, but later are less socially impaired than autistic children.

In Hobson's studies quite able autistic children failed to make links between the same emotion expressed in different ways. Perhaps they were not even aware that particular feelings can be portrayed and identified in unmistakable fashion. Such a profound failure can be explained if we hypothesize that autistic children have a poor conception of feeling states because they have a poor conception of all mental states. For this reason the effects that feelings have and the way they can be expressed in voice, face and gesture would remain a closed book. If interpreted in this way, the impairment in emotion recognition is not irreducible, but can be seen as part of a more general cognitive deficit in recognizing mental states.

### Expressing emotions

Happy giggles and temper tantrums are proof enough that autistic children can express feelings. It is another question whether they occur when they are expected socially. In one area at least autistic children show very normal responses. They express their delight in rough-and-tumble play, tickling or bouncing and moving to music. Nevertheless it is odd that they still enjoy these games at an age when normal children would prefer more sophisticated social interaction.

If left alone, young autistic children often seem quite happy in their solitary activities. Many would never spontaneously seek social contact. Unlike normal toddlers they seldom run to be hugged when they need comfort. It is the absence of genuine interest in reciprocal interactions that sticks out in the behaviour of autistic children. By contrast, young non-autistic children, including those with Down's syndrome, unequivocally show that they find pleasure in interacting with others and that they prefer not to be left alone. They can express this in their behaviour if not in simple words. In older, more able autistic people different features strike the observer. Here it may be noticed as peculiar if they do not hide their likes or dislikes of different people and show excessive friendliness.

We still know little about the development of emotions in young children. One highly original study was carried out by Derek Ricks in 1976.[12] He recorded the vocal responses made by young, non-speaking autistic children to four situations which usually evoke an emotional reaction in normal infants, often expressed in pre-verbal vocalizations. The situations were: seeing the mother in the morning (evoking greeting); food being prepared (evoking request); food being briefly offered, then withdrawn (evoking frustration); a balloon, or a sparkler being lit up (evoking pleasant surprise). Normal babies' vocalizations were recorded as well as those of autistic children, who were as young as possible given the age at which diagnosis is made. The parents were asked to listen to these and identify the situation. They also had to indicate which they thought was their own child.

The results of this experiment were striking. First of all, parents of the normal babies could not reliably identify their own. Parents of the autistic children, however, recognized their children with ease. Furthermore, all of the parents could identify the different situations that gave rise to the vocalizations of all the normal babies. For the autistic children identification could only be done by parents for their own child's responses. Clearly, there are universal vocal expressions that can be readily interpreted, but the autistic children in the sample did not use them. Instead, these children expressed distinct emotional reactions in their own idiosyncratic way.

There is other direct evidence of emotionality in autistic children. At all ages they are frequently observed in extreme moods of happiness, distress, frustration, fury or panic. At the appropriate developmental level they are capable of subtle moods too. As we already saw in chapter 7, Elly shows fine-grained emotional reactions to light and number patterns.

It seems possible that the observed intensity of basic emotions is a sign of immaturity. It has often been remarked that autistic people have few facial expressions, a wooden or stiff body posture and frequently a monotonous voice. Many observers agree that there is some dysfunction, lack of regulation or modulation, perhaps, that marks the emotional expressiveness of autistic people. This may be so if the need to control expressions is diminished by a lack of genuine interest in communication. Such interest would be difficult to sustain without an appreciation of other people's different states of mind.

Marian Sigman and her colleagues have shown in an as yet unpublished study that pre-school autistic children are anything but neutral or flat in their affect compared to mentally retarded or normal children of the same mental age (about two years). Their faces were filmed during a five-minute structured person-to-person interaction, and the recording was then rated on an objective encoding system for facial expressions. What did emerge as different about autistic children was that they spent more time showing negative affect expressions, and in particular showed some very incongruous, strange blends of negative and positive expressions. In fact, half the autistic children showed expressions that were quite idiosyncratic. This finding of idiosyncratic expressions is reminiscent of Derek Ricks's vocalization experiment. Emotional expressions beyond infancy are culturally coded and have to be learned, just as social conventions and language have to be learned. Learning in all these spheres, though possible for autistic children, is exceedingly slow and difficult, by all accounts. It could be that it is slow because the essential drive for such learning, the need to communicate and understand mental states, is absent.

## Gestures

One of the most poignant observations that is quoted almost universally in descriptions of childhood Autism is that the children use an adult, or an adult's hands, as a tool. They may lead an adult to an object they want and place the hand of the adult over the object.

A classic example is given by the first report about the 'wild boy of Aveyron', the case discussed in chapter 2. This report was written in January 1800 by Constans Saint-Estève, the commissioner for the district where the boy was found. 'When he became thirsty, he looked left and right; spotting a pitcher, without making the least sign, he took my hand in his and led me to it; then he struck the pitcher with his left hand, thus asking me for something to drink.'

The strangeness and poverty of gestures in autistic children has been the subject of a number of systematic studies, both experimental and observational. In one study we found that there are certain gestures which autistic children can handle adeptly for the purpose of social interaction.[13] The common feature of this class of gestures is that they have an instrumental purpose. That is, they are designed to make someone else do something immediately. Figure 9.2 shows examples. Instrumental pointing is one such example and is very different from the pointing to gain shared attention. In one case it serves the purpose of making someone look at a particular thing that he did not look at before. In the other case it serves the purpose of communicating an interest in something that the partner may be looking at already. All four illustrated gestures were responded to appropriately by autistic children with a wide range of intellectual abilities. They were also understood by young five-year-old children, and by severely retarded Down's syndrome children. What was more interesting was that these same instrumental gestures were also used spontaneously with peers by all of the children. It is well known that autistic children engage in many fewer interactions among themselves than other groups, even if they are very familiar with each other. We confirmed this in our own observations. Given the low

Figure 9.2  *Instrumental gestures*

rate of interactions, the total number of gestures made by autistic children was also low. However, gestures were used for a similar proportion of interactions as in much younger, normal children, or as in Down's syndrome children of the same age.

Taking just this result, one might conclude that when autistic children interact with each other they use gestures like everybody else. This would be quite wrong. We have considered only instrumental gestures so far. This type is used for a kind of communication which goes something like this: a particular thought or wish ('go away') is to be conveyed to the partner. It is encoded into a simple and well-learned hand movement. The addressee decodes this message and obeys it, and he should go away, as requested, without further qualms or hesitation. Instrumental gestures correspond to the concept of transmitting bare information that we used in chapter 8. There I tried to make the point that bare communication is

Figure 9.3 *Expressive gestures*

different from sophisticated intentional communication in which information needs to be evaluated. For instance, the message to go away is rarely just such a simple message. We look to see whether it contains an apology, a challenge or an open attack. With manual gestures, evaluations cannot be as precisely conveyed as with words. 'Push off', 'Get lost', 'Hop it', 'Please move a bit', 'Just leave me alone', 'Don't bother me now' are examples of utterances which can verbally embody the request to go away. In comprehending bare messages there is only room for obeying or defying the request as formulated. In comprehending more subtle intentional messages there is certainly room for compromise or flexibility. For instance, if somebody said to me, 'Never darken my door again', I would probably ignore the actual request, and treat it as a joke. But I would try first to find out why the utterance was made at all, basing my reaction on that intention.

Certain gestures are used primarily in sophisticated intentional communication, and these are often called expressive gestures. Examples are shown in figure 9.3. Unlike *instrumental* gestures, *expressive* gestures convey states of mind. They deliberately convey feelings one has about something. For instance, one may be embarrassed about seeing somebody else behaving in a silly way and deliberately show this feeling in a gesture of embarrassment. Other examples are demonstrations of friendship, offerings of goodwill, and threatening gestures. Given our hypothesis of serious yet subtle communication failure at a high intentional level, we expected that autistic children would not show these demonstrative expressions. This was indeed the case. No autistic child in our study showed such a gesture during the observation periods – while every Down's syndrome child did!

For expressing basic feelings such as happiness, sadness, anger or fear sophisticated intentional communication is not required. However, advanced intentional communication is necessary for expressing feeling states that relate to one's evaluation of something. This evaluation is an important part of a message to be conveyed to someone else. It is the ability to share such emotions that is captured when we talk about empathy.

## Empathy

We have now reached the point when we can link together the scattered facts that are known about autistic children's very special social impairment. The most important discovery is that the impairment is not as global nor as static as one might expect from descriptions of very withdrawn, very retarded and very young autistic children. At first glance the identified disabilities appear deceptively minor: autistic children don't engage in shared attention, they have difficulties in understanding expressions of feeling states, and also some peculiarities in expressing feelings. In general, these difficulties seem to turn on the more sophisticated aspects of communication and not on a lack of affect or affection. Can all this really be of much consequence for their social development?

The most general description of social impairment in Autism is lack of empathy. Autistic people are noted for their indifference to other people's distress, their inability to offer comfort, even to receive comfort themselves. What empathy requires is the ability to know what another person thinks or feels despite the fact that this is different from one's own mental state at the time. In empathy one shares emotional reactions to the other person's different state of mind. In cases where two people have the same feeling or thought at the same time we speak of sympathy rather than empathy. Empathy presupposes amongst other things a recognition of different mental states. [It also presupposes that one goes beyond that recognition of difference to adopt the other person's frame of mind with all the consequences of emotional reactions.] Even able autistic people seem to have great difficulty achieving empathy in this sense. No doubt, this level of emotional understanding is a crucial aspect of friendship and enmity. On the other hand, sympathy is within reach of able autistic people. As reported by Margaret Dewey, if a news reader says 'these people suffer from unrelenting hunger', then Jack – without needing to take into account states of mind – feels genuine compassion. He too has suffered from hunger and knows its effects. Although he is autistic, he can feel sympathy for people who suffer in situations which have caused him distress before.

A different kind of sympathy might be a reflexive, or seemingly unintentional, mimicking of another's perceived emotion. This is seen in infectious laughter and infectious crying, and is not unlike the infectious yawn. As yet nobody has tested whether there is evidence of such emotional mimicry in autistic children. In order to account for what Kanner called disturbance of affective contact one must explain a paradox: how can it be that a great deal of emotional responsiveness is present when at the same time some significant aspect of emotional communication is absent? The theory that autistic children lack the ability to recognize the existence of other people's minds promises to do just this.

One and the same behaviour can mean two very different things. If a child cries when he is hurt, he is involuntarily expressing an emotion. On the other hand, we know that a child may cry deliberately without being hurt at all in order to make somebody else feel sorry for him. The difference between the two behaviours is huge, but it is *invisible*. When we infer intentions we are in a tricky position in respect to behavioural evidence. The temptation to attribute mental states and all sorts of intentions to others is ubiquitous. We do it even to inanimate objects, let alone animals and pre-verbal infants.

Fortunately, in this area of psychology some major theoretical and methodological advances have been made.[14] The first to do this were David Premack and Guy Woodruff in their ground-breaking study of intentionality in chimpanzees.[15] Subsequently Heinz Wimmer and Josef Perner developed an ingenious paradigm to study the development of these so far unresearched concepts in young children.[16] It is this paradigm that has opened a new door to our understanding of autistic children, as we shall see in the following chapter.

# 10

# Thinking about Minds

## Thinking about Minds in a Painting

The cover of this book shows a picture painted by Georges de la Tour (1593–1652).[1] We see four fancifully dressed people: a woman and two men are seated at a table, engaged in card playing. Standing behind the group is a maidservant holding a glass of wine. These bare facts do not convey the tacit drama that is there, in front of our eyes, yet not visible in the sense that the characters involved are visible.

We know a drama is taking place because the characters speak eloquently with their eyes and hands. There is a curious sideways glance by the lady in the centre, and also by the servant. Both look towards the player on the left, who looks towards us. The lady also points to him with the index finger of her right hand. The player pointed out in this way by look and gesture holds two aces behind his back with his left hand. In his right hand, elbow on the table, the player holds the rest of his cards. The other player, on the right, is looking downwards into his cards, apparently engrossed.

Even with this added detail the description does not capture what is going on in this scene. To do this we have to put the facts together and make some inferences. The facts and inferences have to do with what the characters see, know and believe. Although we cannot see states of mind, we can attribute them guided by the painter's intentions, with logic and precision, and not by tenuous and vague speculation. As a result we know that the painter portrayed an incident of cheating at cards. How do we come to know this fact with such certainty? Our understanding is based on a powerful mental tool that every normal adult possesses and uses with varying degrees of skill. This tool is a theory of mind. The theory is not the same as a scientific theory, but much more practical. It provides us with the ability to predict relationships between external states of affairs and internal states of mind. We might call this ability 'mentalizing'. Mentalizing is a compulsive activity. It seems we cannot avoid drawing inferences as to the causes and effects of behaviour. So, if a man hides cards behind his back, he is cheating. Perhaps the compulsion stems from the need to pull together disparate information into a coherent pattern. Using the metaphor of a mighty river with many tributaries, we already identified this need as an important dynamic principle of central thought.

We do not derive any old meaning from any old pattern: there are restrictions. To make sense of the painting there has to be coherence within the set of different clues that the painter carefully provided. Each clue forces us to make certain inferences, and the inferences have to be pulled together to give a coherent interpretation.

One strong clue is given by the concealed aces. According to our theory of mind we infer that what the others do not see, they do not know. We also infer that the other players believe the aces to be in the pack, because we know this is the rule of the game.

Another clue is the staring servant girl. We infer from her standing position that she would have seen the aces held behind and hence knows of the cheating.

A third clue is the strange look of the lady in the centre who points to the cheat with her finger. Therefore, the lady knows. Perhaps the cheat himself does not know that she knows. His face is averted and he looks unconcerned.

A final and most important clue is that the third player does not look up from his cards at all. Therefore, the painter means us to think that he does not know what is going on. We conclude he is the one who will be cheated, and he will lose the heap of coins that now lies in front of him.

This lengthy piecemeal analysis is not how people actually come to a coherent interpretation of states of mind. Instead the normal response is either like instant realization, or else like a slow dawning of the truth. Nevertheless, the analysis shows that, unconsciously, many computations may have to be performed.

In our understanding of the drama in the picture we attribute different kinds of *knowing*. For instance, we infer that the lady *knows* what the cheat is up to, or that the young man *does not know* what sinister event is just unfolding. What is fascinating is that our inferences even extend to what kind of *emotional states* might arise in the characters (surprise, anger), but we are left in suspense as to what happens next. Will the lady challenge the cheat? Will she collude with him to defraud the young man? Will the young man be warned in time? The painter has forced us to make only some attributions of mental states but he leaves the outcome open.

If we watched a real scene rather than a painting, our inferences would work very similarly. We take note of certain behaviours, but we do not leave it at that. We interpret behaviours, just like amateur psychologists, in terms of hidden states of mind. In this way we can create better coherence of the information processed than we could achieve by merely relating behaviours to events. We can successfully interpret what people do and sometimes even predict what they will do next because we take for granted a common theory of how human minds work. This fact is also obvious in the study of behaviourism. Behaviourists need to adopt a very detached view in order to observe behaviour objectively. They must inhibit the natural tendency to connect behaviour to inner states so as to describe facts without any attribution of a 'mind' at all.

Clearly the behavourist approach is artificial. It calls for rigorous discipline. No such discipline is possible, or even desirable, in our everyday life. As a spider is destined to weave webs, so are we programmed to weave information into coherent patterns. Assumptions about both behaviour and mind and their cause and effect relationships are intermingled in this practice.

The reason for going into so much detail about the effect of having a common theory of mind is, of course, to make a contrast with its absence. The possibility that autistic children lack a theory of mind has been suggested already on the basis of their peculiar inability to relate to people in the ordinary way. One implication of this hypothesis is that autistic individuals are natural behaviourists and do not feel the normal compulsion to weave together mind and behaviour for the sake of coherence.

## The Sally–Anne Experiment

A test of the hypothesis that autistic children do not appreciate the existence of mental states has many pitfalls. For a start, one needs to investigate whether or not other mentally handicapped children differ from autistic children in this respect. If they did not, then the hypothesis would be worthless for explaining the nature of Autism. One approach to the problem is to set up a situation where something happens without somebody else's knowledge. That event cannot be part of the mental state of the ignorant person. If a child can 'mentalize', then this inference will be obvious. It will not be a tortuous logical operation to predict the ignorant person's behaviour, which is no longer appropriate in the changed circumstances. The behaviour may now appear 'silly', possibly making the child laugh.

This is the idea behind an ingenious method developed by Heinz Wimmer and Josef Perner for the study of the development of a theory of mind in young children.[2] Wimmer and Perner's carefully controlled experiments revealed that development of a theory of mind is a long drawn out process. It is not before age three or four that normal children fully realize the implications of a false belief. Before that age, it is difficult to demonstrate that they can appreciate the difference between their own belief and someone else's belief, and that there can be different beliefs about a single event.

From these findings one would not be justified in expecting autistic children to demonstrate mentalizing ability unless they had reached a mental age of about four years, whatever their chronological age. Only if autistic children well above this mental age failed to mentalize, while non-autistic handicapped children did not, would there be direct evidence for a specific hypothesis. To test the hypothesis that autistic children fail to take account of beliefs (one type of mental state), Simon Baron-Cohen, Alan Leslie and I used the Wimmer and Perner method.[3] We tested autistic, normal and mentally retarded Down's syndrome children, all with a mental age above three. What we did in the experiment is explained in figure 10.1. We used two dolls. Sally and Anne, and acted out a little scenario: Sally has a basket and Anne has a box. Sally has a marble and she puts it into her basket. She then goes out. Anne takes out Sally's marble and puts it into her box while Sally is away. Now Sally comes back and wants to play with her marble. At this point we ask the critical question: 'Where will Sally look for her marble?'

The answer is, of course, 'in the basket'. This answer is correct because Sally has put the marble into the basket and has not seen it being moved. She *believes* the marble is still where she put it. Therefore she will look in the basket even though the marble is not there any more. Most of the non-autistic children gave the correct answer, that is, they pointed to the basket. In contrast, all but a few of the autistic children got it wrong. They pointed to the box. This is where the marble really was, but where, of course, Sally did not know it was. They did not take Sally's own belief into account.

Many non-autistic children who solved the problem also found it amusing. Some even started giggling as soon as Anne (naughty Anne!) transferred the marble to her own box. At once they anticipated what was coming and entered into the conspiracy of this little game. Some spontaneously made Sally say 'Ooh – where's my marble gone?'

The failure of the autistic children to understand Sally's belief is the

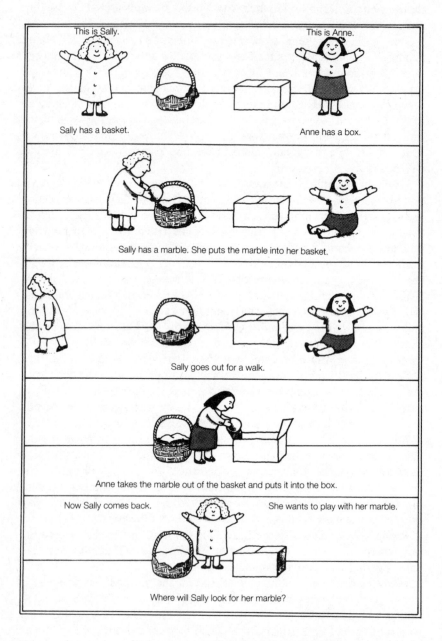

Figure 10.1  *The Sally–Anne experiment*

more remarkable, because they actually had a much higher mental age than the other children. Intellectually they were able to solve a great many logical problems. Yet they were not able to solve the apparently simple problem presented in the test. They remembered correctly where Sally put the marble, and they also answered correctly when asked, 'Where is the marble really?' The difficulty resides solely in the crucial inference that if Sally did not see that the marble was transferred to the box, she *must* still believe that it is in the basket. This inference did not seem a problem for most of the Down's syndrome children, but it was for most of the much more able autistic children.

### The Hidden Coin and the Pencil in the Smarties Box

It is never advisable to rely on just one paradigm when a surprising and theoretically important result is obtained. After all, the striking result with Sally and Anne might have been due to some hidden artefact. One such possibility is that developmentally advanced autistic children might have been unwilling to attribute mental states to two wooden dolls, but would be willing to do so in the case of real people. We also wanted to test a different sample of autistic children who were even more able than the previous ones.[4]

Now we ourselves enacted the scenario: Alan Leslie ostentatiously gave me a coin and asked me to hide it in one of three places. I chose a special hiding place, asked the child to help me remember where I put the coin, and then left the room on some pretext. While I was out, Alan transferred the coin in a conspiratorial manner to another place. He could then, quite naturally, ask the child: where does Uta *think* the coin is? Has Uta *seen* what we did? Does Uta *know* that the coin is now here (pointing to its new place)? Lastly, he asked the same critical question as before, namely where will Uta *look* for the coin when she comes back?

We found essentially the same results as before, that is 15 out of 21 autistic children failed, but we could now be more certain. Some of the children who predicted wrongly where I would look for the coin also indicated that this is where I would *think* (or *know*) the coin was. This was despite the fact that they correctly indicated that I had *not seen* the transfer and that an arbitrary new hiding place was chosen. In other words they had not understood that in this case to see is to know and not to see is not to know.

The logic of mentalizing to us is as simple and compelling as $1 + 1 = 2$. We all take it for granted from about the age of four, but we should not take it for granted in autistic children.

Figure 10.2

One could argue that the problem is not necessarily with the logic of mentalizing, but with yet another extraneous factor. Perhaps, the able autistic children did not like to attribute a false belief to an adult who comes to do tests.

To check on this possibility, we used a task where the child himself experiences what it means to have a false belief.[5] The experiment is illustrated in figure 10.2. A sweet container (a tube) which is well known to all British children was used in this test. All the children we tested expected Smarties to be inside the box, and all were disappointed when a horrible little pencil fell out. Now the autistic children knew that there was a pencil in the box. When they were asked what a new child, first coming to be tested, would say, they wrongly replied 'a pencil'. Only about 4 in 20 autistic children did not make this error and correctly said that the next child would first also say 'Smarties'.

The children who failed were quite aware that they themselves mistakenly thought that Smarties were in the box. They remembered what they said when asked. We can conclude that they did not fully understand *why* they had thought there were Smarties. The reason is, of course, that the container *is* a Smarties tube and Smarties are justifiably expected to be inside. However, the children did not realize that someone else would have to make that same error for the same reason as they made it.

Seeing something, expecting something, and being told something can all be equivalent in their consequences on mental states and on behaviour. This draws our attention to the supramodal and hence central nature of mentalizing. Information from different sources, the results of seeing, remembering and telling, are all pulled together in a coherent interpretation of what happened. Because it is a coherent whole, the information content is so simple that any normal four-year-old can cope with it. If it were not a coherent whole, perhaps because of a weak drive for coherence, but remained a complex set of separate pieces of information, then anybody would find it difficult. This may be the situation for autistic children.

### Comic Strips for Physicists, Behaviourists and Psychologists

For understanding physics or behavourism, mentalizing is irrelevant. But how can we be sure that mentalizing is a unique kind of logic that can be weak or absent in able autistic children while more conventional logic is intact? To obtain evidence for this possibility, Simon Baron-Cohen, Alan Leslie and I carried out an experiment using strip cartoons of the kind illustrated in figure 10.3.[6] The same subjects as in the Sally–Anne experiment took part. The task was twofold. First, the children had to put the pictures in order so as to make up a story, with the first picture already in place. Second, the children had to tell the story in their own words.

From the ordering of the pictures we could determine how well the intended story was understood, even in the absence of words. The words, however, gave more direct insight into what the child had

A mechanical story

A behavioural story

A mentalistic story

Figure 10.3.   *Three types of picture sequence*

understood the story to be. Specifically if mentalizing is a problem for autistic children, then they should perform poorly only on the mentalistic-type stories, but not on the mechanical or behavioural ones. This was exactly what we found.

A mechanical event as a story was indeed perfectly understood by all our autistic children. They all ordered the pictures correctly. Moreover, they used the right kind of language when telling the story, for instance: 'The balloon burst *because* it was pricked by the branch', or 'The tree *made* it burst.'

A behavioural script can be told without reference to mental states. 'A girl goes to a shop to buy some sweets. She pays the shopkeeper and carries away her sweets.' This way of ordering and telling a social routine was also well within the competence of our autistic children. Not so the mentalistic stories. The vast majority of our able autistic children just could not understand them. A mentalistic story only makes sense as a story if a state of mind is attributed to a protagonist. For instance: a boy puts some chocolate into a box and goes out to play. While he is outside (the logic of mentalizing computes: without his knowing), his mother eats the chocolate. When he comes back, he is *surprised* to find the box empty (the logic of mentalizing computes: he believed his chocolate to be still in the box).

The mentalistic story is modelled entirely on the Sally–Anne experiment, and the same children who failed in that experiment also performed very poorly in this. They put the pictures in a jumbled order. Their 'stories' were told without the attribution of mental states. For example: 'A boy puts some chocolate into a box. He goes out to play. His mother eats a chocolate. He comes back and opens the box. It is empty.' This is not a story even though it reports the events in the correct order. As a story it makes no more sense than a description of the same events in a different order. For instance: 'The boy puts some chocolate in a box. He goes out to play. He comes back and opens the box. It is empty. His mother eats some chocolate.'

The normal and Down's syndrome children, although they had a lower mental age, out-performed the autistic children on mentalistic stories, in both ordering and talking about the stories. They performed less well on the mechanical stories, and about equal on the behavioural ones. These results show that autistic children are better 'physicists' and equally able 'behaviourists', but the other children are better 'psychologists'.

The results suggest that mentalizing demands a very different kind of ability from that involved in causal and behavioural thinking. However, if autistic children lack a drive towards central coherence, as I have postulated, how can we explain their ability to make sense out of physical and behavioural event sequences? On a small scale, understanding simple causal events and behavioural routines must be governed by coherence-creating devices. Clearly, local coherence, as opposed to a drive for global coherence, is not lacking in Autism. The difference is that the 'small rivers' of information created by local coherence (and this may include causal connections) do not feed 'large rivers' which hold together vast amounts of information.

## Affective Contact and Theory of Mind

In order to develop a coherent theory of mind one needs not only the ability to mentalize, but also experience. One needs experience with people who have different relationships to each other, and different personal interests. However, experience would count for very little if the child did not absorb it and integrate it with already existing knowledge. As an individual develops, a succession of theories must be developed as previous ones are found inadequate.

Pinocchio, for example, the archetypal unworldly child, was badly deceived by scheming creatures, but he learned his lesson. Eventually Pinocchio was able to understand who were false and who were real friends. This is not the position of autistic children whose unwordliness is of a different kind. We have hypothesized that they do not have the basic propensity to pull together vast amounts of information from events, objects, people and behaviour. Even if they had the cognitive prerequisites that enable them to mentalize, they would only form 'small' theories about mental states, but not a comprehensive theory of mind. Autistic children are behaviourists. They do not *expect* people to be kind or to be cruel. They take behaviour as it is. Therefore, intentions that change the *meaning* of behaviour, for instance, deception, flattery, persuasion and irony, present difficult problems of interpretation. While the autistic individual interprets behaviour in a literal fashion, the opposite is true for the compulsive mentalizer; behaviour will be interpreted not in its own right but from the point of view of the intentions behind it. Such is the effect of a theory of mind.

The fact that people are sometimes devious and sometimes like to tease, and yet behave as if they were sincere, is a hazard for autistic people and a senseless puzzle. The often quoted statement that autistic people see everything in 'black and white' and do not understand shades of meaning is understandable in this context.

We can contrast awareness of the existence of mind with the awareness of the existence of other people as agents of physical events. If autistic children have only the latter physical kind of social awareness, then, of course, they would be expected to discriminate between different people. So they do! They can also distinguish emotional expressions, as long as there are unique cues. Similarly they can distinguish between kind and evil people, when good and evil are always expressed plainly in words or deeds.

The social impairment implied by not being able to 'mentalize' is not a global impairment. Not all social interactions depend on it. There is also no reason to think that poor mentalizing would prevent emotional attachments. Indeed, in the previous chapter we noted that there is much evidence for real personal attachment in autistic children and adults. The autistic 'disturbance of affective contact' is not a global disturbance either. However, if autistic people cannot conceptualize mental states very well, then they cannot empathize with *mental states* of others, such as their feelings.

What implications does a theory of mind have for emotional and social relationships? A few examples may illustrate how by taking account of others' mental states in even the most trivial social encounters, we exhibit what one might call affective contact. People constantly guess and monitor what each other's thoughts might be. This does not involve hard thinking, but, on the contrary, renders it easier to make sense out of a large amount of disparate information at once.

Let us consider some everyday examples involving Lucy and her friends.

1 With the way she says 'good morning', she conveys what mood she is in or rather, what mood she would like to be considered to be in. (Thinks: 'I am not saying how awful I feel.') Peter reacts to what he thinks Lucy's 'real' mood is. (Thinks: 'Hmm, doesn't sound too good at all.') His reply, 'Shall I get you an aspirin?' would clearly seem mad, unless one assumed that a theory of mind is at work.

2 When meeting Jane, Lucy exchanges remarks about the weather. This, of course, is useless information, if taken at face value. They really convey something else to each other. (Thinks: 'I am in a friendly mood and I like talking to you, particularly if it is not about a real problem!')

3 Paul now appears, but Lucy does *not* exchange trivialities with him. This can be taken as a meaningful and pointed message. (Thinks: 'You are in my bad books. I hope you notice that I'd rather not talk to you just now.') In Paul's hearing Lucy gossips with Jane. 'Have you heard that Mrs Wood is getting married again?' (Thinks: 'Paul is really going to be shocked now. Serves him right.')

Now let us consider these examples from a different point of view. Let us see Lucy interact with her autistic sister, Jennifer.

1 Jennifer listens to Lucy's glum 'good morning' and concludes that this morning is a 'good' one. Lucy is not pleased at this reaction, but if she wants Jennifer to give her an aspirin, she has to say so.

2 Remarks about the weather would allow Jennifer to talk about her special 'hobby'. She records daily temperature, air pressure and rainfall. If necessary, she will contradict Lucy, 'It is not warmer than yesterday. At my last reading it was 16.3°C.; yesterday's temperature . . .' This

could lead to a tedious conversation that Lucy has long learned to avoid or cut short.

3 Lucy cannot really gossip with Jennifer, only exchange information. Information is received and given away indiscriminately and without considering any effects, such as hurting or pleasing somebody by giving the information. She does not know what it means to keep a secret. It is puzzling to her that a simple statement of the truth might hurt others. 'Aunt Doreen shaved her moustache' was a remark that was not welcome at her aunt's engagement party. Yet it was just an observation of Jennifer's, not at all calculated to give embarrassment.

These examples suggest that the failure of ordinary intentional communication and the inability to relate affectively to others are really one and the same thing. The failure is most strikingly demonstrated by the fact that even in very able autistic people understanding of language as well as of social and affective relationships remains literal. Since remarks and interactions are not experienced as part of a web of implicit presuppositions, interpretation of verbal and non-verbal signals is extremely restricted. From this point of view there is no need to postulate separately an inability to respond affectively.

The Jennifer example also hints at something else. There is a distinction between interactions with explicit information exchange and interactions with implicit emotional responses. Lucy seems to be continually weaving a web of expectations of what others think, know, wish or feel. This motivates her remarks and determines whether she feels pleased or displeased by the response. For this reason, any responses that do not tie in with her expectations of particular inner states make her cross or leave her bored.

Blow-by-blow accounts of behaviour or a listing of facts are often boring, unless these accounts evoke some bigger context within which they belong. Yet such bigger contexts are evoked with minimal effort. Consider the beginning of the story 'Gogol's Wife' by Tommaso Landolfi:[7] 'At this point, confronted with the whole complicated affair of Nikolai Vassilevitch's wife, I am overcome by hesitation. Have I any right to disclose something which is unknown to the whole world?' The web is woven. Already one is ensnared. What is the complicated affair? Why has it not been revealed? This is the stuff our social and affective world is made of.

The loneliness of the autistic child does not merely consist of a deficiency in expressing and understanding emotions. To the autistic individual other mental states, such as knowing and believing, are equally a mystery. Some affective quality which is a subjective experience in *many* mental state interpretations, whether those of others or one's own, is part of a theory of mind. Even in the Sally–Anne experiment, where simply a belief has to be attributed and taken account of, emotional reactions are readily obtained – for instance, glee at Sally's deception. Affective experiences may be part and parcel of the dynamism of cohesion and detachment in our central thought processes.

## Autism and Self-Consciousness

If the development of a theory of mind is problematic for autistic children, then it follows that the development of their self-awareness may also be problematic. Nevertheless, one cannot doubt that autistic children have appropriate representations of the bodily self. They can distinguish people from objects, and familiar people from strangers. The hypothesis of poor self-awareness concerns only the development of an appropriate representation of the self as owner and manipulator of mental states. If this mental self is a product of reflection – then without the ability to reflect on mental states it may not exist. However, the reflective self remains as elusive as the mirror of a mirror.

The culmination of mentalizing ability is self-consciousness. A lack of mentalizing is therefore tantamount to a lack of self-awareness. *Autos*, the Greek word for self, is a constant reminder of this possibility whenever we use the term Autism. It is hard to conceive of intellectually mature human beings as lacking self-awareness. What would it mean? Such individuals would be totally on their own but unable to keep company even with themselves. The company of other people would not be a companionship of minds, and hence not necessarily preferable to that of mindless things. In whatever nasty colours cynics portray human nature and man's 'inhumanity' towards his fellow creatures, they do not question that the company of minds is as essential as are light, water and nourishment.

It would be fruitless here to join the debate of many philosophers over many centuries as to what consciousness of self and other might be, and how it is achieved. The ability to make sense of other people is also the ability to make sense of oneself. We make sense not by tedious empirical collection of data, but by bold (and often mistaken) theories. The theory we apply to others' minds is exactly the same as the theory we apply to understand our own mind. We call on mental states to explain why we did something; or rather, we impute coherent aims and motives whenever possible, and avoid imputing random or external causes. 'She constantly asserts herself because she is basically insecure' is typical of everyday imputations. It makes a coherent story of what otherwise would be a paradox. In everyday life we 'know' how the mind works, but of course this has little to do with a scientific explanation. In fact we are light-years away from really knowing how the mind works with the confidence of our day-to-day knowing. By considering the power of theory of mind, we can get a little closer to the problem of self-awareness. To know that one thinks is to know that one exists, to paraphrase Descartes's famous dictum *cogito ergo sum*.

## The Origins of Theory of Mind

What has to happen for the ability to mentalize to appear in the young child and what are its consequences for development? This question has been brilliantly answered by Alan Leslie, who suggested that there is a striking similarity in the logic underlying mentalizing and pretending.[8] Pretence can be seen as a precursor of a theory of mind.

The mind of the normal infant is already equipped from birth with fundamental 'knowledge' about important features of the world. At a primitive level even the newborn child 'knows' about such concepts as time, space and causality. The child also 'knows' about objects and people and responds to them differently. Of course the infant has to learn specifics about his world, and can do this, because it is capable of forming *representations* of people, things and events. Representations bring the world into the mind. However, from about one year onwards the infant appears to be able to go a huge step further, and can now form representations of representations (metarepresentations) of real world events. What knowing is to knowing about knowing, representations are to metarepresentations.

The significance of this developmental advance is of the utmost importance for all higher mental functions. Alan Leslie proposes a mechanism (the decoupler) that explains how metarepresentations might work. According to Leslie this mechanism is innate and matures only in the second year of life. At this point the ability to pretend starts to develop, and then gradually the ability to mentalize. This (among other things) eventually enables a fully fledged theory of mind to be formed.

What makes Leslie's theory relevant to Autism is that we can assume that *both* pretend play and mentalizing are impaired in autistic children. There is evidence that autistic children show little if any pretend play. They spend much of their time in reality-oriented play. Rarely do we find convincing accounts of imaginative make-believe play such as one typically finds in normal pre-school children. How can playful *pretence*, of all things, be such an important aspect of normal development?

Pretending ought to strike the cognitive psychologist as a very odd sort of ability. After all, from an evolutionary point of view, there ought to be a high premium on the *veridicality* of cognitive processes. The perceiving, thinking organism ought, as far as possible, to get things right. Yet pretense flies in the face of this fundamental principle. In pretense we deliberately distort reality. How odd then that this ability is not the sober culmination of intellectual development but instead makes its appearance playfully and precociously at the very beginning of childhood.

Reality-oriented play, which responds to an object's actual properties or expresses knowledge of its conventional use, raises many interesting problems. But pretence poses us deeper puzzles. How is it possible for a child to think about a banana as if it were a telephone, a lump of plastic as if it were alive, or an empty soap dish as if it contained soap? If a representational system is developing, how can its semantic relations tolerate distortion in these more or less arbitrary ways?

This is how Alan Leslie starts the paper where he systematically sets out to elucidate the origins of both pretence and theory of mind. We cannot go into his theory in any detail but it is possible to illustrate by example what Leslie considers to be a crucial component of metarepresentational ability: decoupling.

### Putting things in quotes

The film *Citizen Kane* contains the famous headline: *Candidate found in love nest with 'singer'*. Kane's plan to become Governor was ruined by this scandal. His friend observed that his life was subsequently devoted to removing the quotes from the word singer. Kane tried to do this by turning the 'singer' into a famous opera star. Predictably he failed. As implied by the quotes the girl was *not* a singer in any serious sense at all.

This example conveys the idea of decoupling by likening it to the familiar activity of putting words into quotes. Quotes act as signals of decoupling. They indicate that the criteria of reference, truth and existence, are suspended. 'Singer' no longer commits one to think that the person can really sing, but singer does. This difference is similar to the difference between primary representations and metarepresentations.

The example shows more than decoupling. It shows how easily the decoupled thought, freed from its normal duties of referring to reality, can become part of other thoughts and can undergo an amazing change in meaning. For instance, we know that 'singer' is to be understood ironically, in fact as non-singer. Just how powerfully interpretations can be manipulated in this way is shown in the following real life example.

In August 1987 an American journalist, Charles Glass, who had been kept hostage in Lebanon, escaped from his captors while they were asleep. For some reason, instead of giving Glass a hero's reception, people felt uncertain about what had happened. Perhaps they thought that he could not really have escaped, believing this would have been impossible. It was later proved that he did escape in the way he described. His report of his escape was therefore a true representation of a real event. However, the general air of suspicion made the description of the escape appear to be merely a version of the truth, and possibly a lie. The effect of the language of decoupling can be seen in what was said on the television news on the day of the escape. A well-known and trusted anchorman referred to Glass as 'a young American *who says* "he was a hostage"'. This way of talking cast doubt on whether Glass even was a hostage, let alone whether he escaped! The decoupled expression 'he was a hostage' is embedded in the frame *he says* ('he was . . .'). By this means the truth was imperceptibly changed into a serious allegation. In fact, it turned out that the newsman himself had not doubted the truth, but that he had in a moment of confusion simply made a slip. Nevertheless, the ill-chosen words seemed to confirm the general aura of suspicion.

Both examples illustrate how ubiquitous our use of metarepresentations is in everyday life. Our beliefs about beliefs are often more important than the beliefs themselves, and these are more important than the facts when communication takes place. The examples also illustrate the potential fickleness of a coherent theory of mind. More concretely, they illustrate what it means to read between the lines, as opposed to taking utterances literally. Even able autistic individuals are known for their tendency towards literalness. An inability to read between the lines in situations such as this would lead precisely to the misunderstandings that are typical of Autism.

A failure in decoupling would be one example of how the ability to form and/or handle metarepresentations could be impaired. Such a failure would have serious consequences for development. It is conceivable that decoupling failure characterizes a particularly handicapped subgroup of autistic children. It could be that another subgroup, despite an intact decoupling mechanism, are still impaired in metarepresentational ability for other reasons. For instance, they may not be able to make use of this ability. Some may be able to apply it only in very restricted situations, when not too much information has to be pulled together. This would prevent them from ever being able to understand higher-order representations, for example, bluff and double bluff, but would let them succeed in attributing beliefs.

## Wing's Triad of Impairments Explained

If the mind of the autistic child were such that the basic decoupling mechanism were faulty, as Alan Leslie suggests, then several seemingly unrelated features of Autism would suddenly fit together like long-lost pieces in a jig-saw puzzle. Better than any other theory so far it can explain the three symptoms that constitute Wing's triad of impairments and which are seen in all autistic children.

Wing's triad refers to impaired social relationships, impaired communication, and impaired make-believe play.[9] Leslie has argued that theory of mind, which is crucial to normal social interaction and communication, as well as pretence have their origin in the same relatively late-maturing primitive mechanism. A very specific neurological fault could therefore be postulated affecting precisely this component of cognitive development. It is clear that the component also made its appearance late in evolution. Animals below our nearest relatives, the great apes, do not have the capacity to form metarepresentations. It is very doubtful even if the great apes have it.[10]

This theory would explain why the unequivocal diagnosis of Autism cannot be made before the second, or even third year of life (allowing for variation in speed of developmental progress). The critical behaviour for diagnosis does not normally show itself until that age and we now know why this is so.

Perhaps the most appealing aspect of the account is that it gives a specific reason why children have problems in developing a theory of mind. Lack of a theory of mind makes sense out of the whole host of seemingly unconnected behavioural symptoms which we have considered in the preceding chapters. What often appears as a language problem can be better understood as a problem in the semantics of mental states. Similarly, what appears as a problem in affective relationships can be understood as a consequence of the inability to realize fully what it means to have a mind and to think, know, believe and feel differently from others. What often appears as a problem in learning to become socially competent can be understood from exactly the same point of view: learning outwardly the forms of social rules is not sufficient – one needs the ability to read between the lines, and yes, to read other people's thoughts.

The lack of shared attention between autistic children and their mothers has been identified as one of the earliest and best discriminators of autistic from other mentally handicapped children, as we have seen in chapter 9. This feature, too, can be attributed to an inability to consider

others as having interests that might either be similar or different from
one's own. The behaviour arising from this failure in the very young
autistic child includes lack of showing and pointing out things of
interest. It also includes the able autistic person's endless monologues
about topics in which the partner shows no interest. Another striking
feature of autistic children, their poor use of eye contact, falls into place.
It can be explained as an inability to learn the 'language of the eyes', that
is, to learn to use and understand the signals associated with particular
mental states. Lack of theory of mind can account for both the avoidance
of social contact and for an inappropriate approach: both are consequences of not understanding other people in terms of what they think or
feel or want. Communication failure is an inevitable consequence of this
deficiency.

The explanation of Wing's triad as a consequence of one and the same
developmental fault clearly has much to commend it. However,
classically autistic children all show additional symptoms over and above
the triad of impairments. We must think here of two major features: the
peculiar pattern of intellectual abilities, and the repetitive phenomena of
stereotypies and rituals. For this reason we have all along been
considering a wider explanation of Autism.

In preceding chapters we have explored and explained the characteristic pattern of intellectual abilities of autistic children, as well as their
narrow and obsessive interests. The various phenomena manifest
themselves most flamboyantly in the *idiot savant*. They can be explained
as effects of central cognitive dysfunction. This dysfunction can be seen
as detachment, that is, a weak drive for central coherence of all
information. Information processing up to the point of interpretation by
a central system can be assumed to be normal in nuclear Autism. Such
was the conclusion from the evidence about perceptual problems. In
autistic children the various specific input processors do not show an
abnormal absence of cohesive effects. This absence is only shown at the
highest level of central thought. This level is also the level of
metarepresentation. Here we can look down on our own thoughts as a
space traveller may look back at earth. Mentalizing ability can be seen as
a cohesive interpretative device par excellence: it forces together complex
information from totally disparate sources into a pattern which has
*meaning*. The ability which allows us to know that we know may be the
key to the ability to make sense.

# 11

# A Literal Mind

## Knowing How One Knows

Milton is an intelligent autistic boy of 12 who took part in our experiments on reading. He read – fluently – selected passages of text and we asked various questions to test his text comprehension and general knowledge. After he had given a particularly good answer we asked quite accidentally, 'Oh, how did you know that?' His matter of fact reply was: 'By telepathy.' We repeated the question on several other occasions, and he always answered in the same way. He never said, 'I just read about it', or 'My teacher told me' or 'It's obvious isn't it'.

Milton had an explanation of how knowledge came to be in his head: it was put there by telepathy. How different this explanation is from an ordinary theory of mind that a bright 12-year-old might have! Nevertheless it suggests a glimmer of understanding that there are such things as thoughts. Alas, a glimmer is not enough.

The idea that a strong drive towards coherence of large amounts of information is characteristic of a normal mind, but not of an autistic mind, is helpful here. Milton did not pull together simultaneously information from his own past experience, from general world knowledge, from the text that he just read, nor from the intentions behind our questions. Instead he gave a stereotypic all-purpose answer. It is the sort of cause-and-effect explanation that would have been quite adequate for the question: 'How does the iron stick attract the pins?' – Answer: 'By magnetism.' Clearly for everyday purposes cause-and-effect understanding of the physical world is different from that of the mental world.

In one experiment, Josef Perner and colleagues investigated whether autistic children could understand what caused them to have a piece of knowledge.[1] What caused it was that they had seen something which somebody else had not seen. The experiment was of the utmost simplicity. Josef took a trinket from a whole box of things by lucky dip and put it in a cup. He then ostentatiously let the child look inside, making clear all the time that I (who sat at the other end of the table) was not allowed to look inside. He verified that this was understood by asking: 'Did you *see* what is in the cup?' and 'Did Uta *see* what was in the cup?' Now the critical questions were: 'Do you *know* what is in the cup?' and 'Does Uta *know*?' Astonishingly half of the autistic children that were tested failed. All were of a mental age above that at which normal children would easily pass such a simple test.

There are obvious implications of such a striking finding. In many autistic children we cannot take it for granted (as we would in a normal three-year-old) that they realize that 'to see is to know' and if someone has not seen something, he does not know. From this point of view we must expect that many autistic children will not necessarily tell an important fact. After all why should anybody else not know a fact as they know it? In the experiment a child quite happily said, 'Yes, Uta knows [what is in the cup]', when I had not seen the object and could not have known.

There is a further consequence of the failure to know where knowledge comes from. The child does not understand the difference between justified knowledge and a mere guess. For instance, in our experiment one child insisted there was a panda in the cup (even though he had not seen it and said he had not seen it). When he was shown what it actually was, a rose, he did not react with surprise. Could it be that he often experiences wrong expectations of this type?

It has often been said that the world is unpredictable to an autistic child. If we systematically apply the reasoning that led to the various experiments on mentalizing ability, then perhaps some of this world could be made more predictable for autistic children. As a first step we can be more precise about what they find unpredictable, namely what people do on the basis of their mental states; and what they find predictable, namely what people do as a direct consequence of physical events. The same autistic child who can understand very well why a customer pays the shopkeeper, or why a person jumps out of the way of a falling rock, may not understand why a polite guest declines a further offer of food when he is still hungry; why an employee who wishes to be promoted gives flowers to the boss's secretary; why a schoolgirl complains of a stomach ache whenever she has not done her homework; or why a toddler exaggerates his hurt by crying when his brother pushed him.

## Improbable Ideas

Telepathy is a strong concept. It reminds us that we have no sense organ for receiving thoughts directly, although it would be interesting if we had. We all go about our business with other people under the unshakeable assumption that people have thoughts. In order to understand other people and to predict their behaviour we normally do not need to invoke telepathy, but we are led by a much grander theory of how thoughts arise, and how thoughts influence behaviour. This theory is not a luxury. Predicting the behaviour of an enemy on the basis of the enemy's thoughts can be a matter of life or death. For instance, if I believe that he thinks I am hiding in the ditch, then I am *not* going to hide in the ditch, but in the hut. Furthermore, if the door of the hut creaks, I shall open it only while the dog is barking, so that the noise is masked and cannot be heard.

The inferences that are necessary to confound an enemy are computed on the basis of large amounts of information from different sources. This information must be pulled together. How is this possible? I have repeatedly argued that it is helpful to assume that when processing complex high-level information the human mind works as if propelled by a central cohesive force. Because of this central drive for coherence we know what is relevant and what is not. Relevant pieces of information can be pulled together with one overriding aim: to make sense. It is not so much fast and accurate responses to complex information that we have to explain, but above all, sensible responses, responses that take into account other people's needs to make sense.

To be able to mentalize does not mean to have fanciful ideas about what might be in the mind of somebody else, but to *know* for certain what one can surmise about another's thoughts and what one cannot surmise. Two anecdotes may illustrate this point.

The first anecdote is about an able autistic young man who despite suffering from Autism is very helpful with household chores and running errands. He often goes shopping and is trusted with money. One day, as his mother was mixing a fruit cake, she said to him: 'I haven't got any cloves. Would you please go out and get me some.' The son came back a while later with a carrier bag full of girlish clothes, including underwear, from a High Street boutique.

Clearly, the boy had misperceived the word 'cloves' as 'clothes', an understandable confusion, particularly as the word 'cloves' is much rarer than the word 'clothes'. However, what normal young man would assume his mother asked him casually to buy her clothes, just like that?

The hypothesis is so outlandish that it should have been rejected immediately. 'I *must* have misheard what she said' would be the expected response, followed by a request for clarification.

The second anecdote comes from Coleman and Gillberg's book.[2]

> A 10-year-old . . . autistic girl (full scale WISC IQ 100) . . . showed catastrophic anxiety when the nurse, about to do a simple blood test, said: 'Give me your hand; it won't hurt.' The girl calmed down immediately when another person said: 'Stretch out your index finger.' She had understood, at the first instruction, that she was to cut off her hand and give it to the nurse.

As in the previous anecdote, this story gives an example of an error that is at once understandable, yet totally outlandish from one's experience and from cultural conventions. Throughout this book there are examples of so-called literal comprehension. What this means, and why it occurs, are keys to the understanding of Autism.

In everyday life we cannot afford too many errors of literal interpretations; we seek interpretations that are coherent within a wider context that takes in social and cultural experiences. It is unlikely that the two autistic individuals in the anecdotes had so little life experience that they could not interpret the situations appropriately. Rather, they did not use experience in the same way as other children of the same background with the same IQ and age. It is interesting that the girl straight away abandoned her extraordinary interpretation of the nurse's request when an unambiguous instruction was given. This would not have been the case if she had a deep-seated suspicion of nurses. If only she had such a suspicion! It would make sense of her action in the normal way. For instance, it might fit into a coherent pattern of hospital phobia, and would not be simply a bizarre reaction.

One way to overcome fragmented literal interpretations in everyday communication is to put priority on our hypotheses about what other people might think, know, wish or believe. This is normally accomplished by a theory of mind. It has been a constant theme throughout this book that autistic children do not strive for coherence in their interpretation of input. This includes not striving for a psychological interpretation of people's behaviour.

Improbable behaviour is improbable because it does not belong to a coherent system of thought (or theory) about other people's intentions. The two autistic children behaved as if 'anything is possible'. From some point of view this is perfectly justified: it can reflect reality. 'Anything is possible' is what the roulette player *should* entertain as the correct theory when he considers whether to bet on black or red. But instead he adopts a theory from which he predicts whether red will turn up next. The gambler is captured by the erroneous belief that there are patterns in chance events and that he can outwit chance. This is a type of gambler's fallacy. Beliefs in patterns and meaning are justified, however, in many situations. These include social relationships and intentional communication. In these cases the gambler's fallacy is not a fallacy. It almost always works!

There is also, of course, a theorist's fallacy. A theory can lead to an inappropriate description of available information. Just like the gambler I cannot resist the belief that there are patterns. However, it would be remarkable if the relevant facts about Autism were a meaningless assortment produced by chance.

Many researchers would agree that Autism involves an information-processing dysfunction. I suggest that there is dysfunction in only one aspect of central processes, namely the drive for coherence. It cannot have escaped the reader that in order to propose my theory I myself have demonstrated the effect of a strong cohesive drive! This clear example of the recursiveness of human thoughts can be contrasted with Autism as an example of a non-recursive mind.


## Context and Communication

I have previously drawn a distinction between communication of bare messages and a particularly subtle kind of intentional communication. It is this subtle kind that makes humans special, as different from animals on the one hand as from intelligent machines on the other. We can be efficient transmitters of bare information and so can machines. We can socially and affectively relate to other people, and all higher animals can likewise relate to each other. But humans have something more. They have the possibility of sharing in a wide, wild inner world of relationships and meanings where constant gambles are being taken, and won, and lost. Autistic children, impervious as they are to such gambles, cannot fully participate in such a world. It may fascinate them, or terrify them, but it will not readily admit them as players.

One of Digby Tantam's patients was a highly intelligent autistic man who was obsessively interested in thrillers and toxicology books. He could never understand the psychology that the detective used to solve a case in the novels he read so avidly. In particular, he could never understand why someone should lie. So why would he read detective stories? And why toxicology books? Tantam's perceptive suggestion is as follows: 'Clearly, the fictional detective's ability to impute motive was a source of considerable interest to him. It frightened him that he was unable to do this. He reassured himself he could solve the crime without psychological insight, by a toxicological analysis of the body.'

Context is at once the most essential ingredient in full intentional communication, and the one feature that distinguishes it from bare message transmission. The hallmark of the latter is the piecemeal handling of information. In principle, there is nothing wrong with this. On the contrary, this mode of information processing guarantees stability: the same code always means the same thing, as in a computer. In everyday human communication this guarantee does not apply. Here, there is an *obligation* to use context. This means often having to say 'it depends'. The meaning of any utterance in word or gesture can only be properly understood by *not* treating it piecemeal, but placing it in context.

Dan Sperber and Deirdre Wilson have this to say about context in communication:

> The set of premises used in interpreting an utterance constitutes what is generally known as the *context*. A context is a psychological construct, a subset of the hearer's assumptions about the world. It is these assumptions, of course, rather than the actual state of the world, that affect the interpretation of an utterance. A context in this sense is not limited to information about the immediate physical environment or the immediately preceding utterances: expectations about the future, scientific hypotheses or religious beliefs, anecdotal memories, general cultural assumptions, beliefs about the mental state of the speaker, may all play a role in the interpretation.[3]

What do these ideas suggest for more effective communication with autistic people? One thing they suggest is that it would be useful to adopt a literal and behaviourist mode as a partner of an autistic person, both as listener and as speaker. Implications need to be spelled out for the autistic person, even if they seem redundant and self-evident in normal communication. For instance, it was necessary to tell a young autistic man not to stare at the girls in his office, because they might take offence. Likewise, information needs to be actively solicited since the autistic person may 'forget' to mention an important fact.

A lot of the effort involved in communication has to be shouldered by the non-autistic partner. The partner has to emphasize what is relevant and has to elaborate topics carefully. Hints or raised eyebrows are unlikely to act as sufficient cues. Taking a literal attitude means working with autistic people, not against them, to paraphrase Temple Grandin's words.

With these suggestions I merely spell out what the sensitive and gifted teacher and carer of autistic individuals does intuitively. However, it is not always safe to trust intuition. Our intuitions about our own and others' mental states are constantly active and dominate our personal relationships. It is very hard but necessary to suppress them when trying to understand autistic people. It is only too tempting to slide into such assumptions as 'this child rejects my feelings'; 'he smiled because he knew I was going to phone his mother'; 'she smashed the furniture to punish us for sending away her nanny'. Not one of these assumptions is tenable if a child is unable to mentalize.

### Treatments that Work

I was skimming over the new book titles displayed at a conference on Autism when I overheard a parent groan: 'Oh no – not *another* book on what to do with your autistic child!' At least that particular criticism cannot be levelled at the present monograph! Why are some parents exasperated at how-to-cope books? One reason is that ideas on therapy and remedial education are not easily expressed as practical advice. Books treating various methods of teaching and management please some people but antagonize others. Furthermore, because of the tremendous individual differences between autistic children and because of their inevitably changing needs during the course of development, specific advice is often beside the point. However, parents have reasons for disillusionment with therapy itself, not just the way it is described. There is no getting round the fact that so far the underlying condition of Autism has been untreatable.

Some general recommendations have proved to be valid for the education and management of autistic children. First of all, the children really do need love, just like everybody else. Wendy Brown of Broomhayes School in Devon chose exactly the right words that mark out the ideal caregiver: It is necessary 'to like the child *because* he's autistic and not *in spite* of it.' Regardless of age, and regardless of intellectual level, the provision of a structured environment seems to be desirable. That this is beneficial was established by Rutter and Bartak after a careful long-term comparison of different policies for treatment at several centres for autistic children.[4] A firm, calm and reassuring approach to teaching is good for any child. It is also recommended for the autistic child. Gifted teachers are a rare commodity, but if such a person takes on an autistic child the effect can be stunning. A great deal can be taught within the limits of the child's capacity: language, social know-how, academic skills, world knowledge, artistic techniques, domestic and health care, and specific job skills.[5]

From my own experience I have been deeply impressed by the skill and devotion of many parents, teachers and therapists who get results without believing in miracles. I can also understand how desperate parents can get caught by the advertising 'hypes' which are the scourge of rehabilitation. One must remember that this is after all a multi-million dollar business.

There is a long way to go until precise recommendations can be made that derive from a sound scientific basis. But this is only to be expected. We are not expecting a magic pill or secret short-cut to normality. Instead it is still a good idea to continue with the best methods of education and care for autistic children available. It is also necessary to view critically those treatments that are based on proclaimed scientific but unproven foundations and which can do a great deal of harm without helping the child at all. When effectiveness and success is guaranteed by testimonials, then it is clear that scientific evidence is lacking!

What does the theory proposed in this book have to offer for the care of autistic people? In answer to this question Margaret Dewey wrote back to me posing an analogous question: Is it helpful to know that dyslexic people have a specific cognitive disability? The theory is well founded but it does not immediately point to a treatment. By being put forward, however, it opens the mind to looking for new ways of teaching children who cannot learn by traditional methods. Experience may in time build up a body of successful techniques, to be tried on individual dyslexic children and modified according to their needs. It will be somewhat different for each child. This same will presumably apply in the case of autistic children. There are bound to be many different ways of applying the theory.

As an example of how she applied the idea that autistic children have difficulty in mentalizing, Margaret Dewey related the following incident:

> Donald came home from the autistic school, somewhat upset by a delayed start to the journey home. His parents sent him into the kitchen to get himself a drink. Soon his father followed to see whether Donald was all right. He arrived just in time to see Donald pouring milk down the kitchen drain. Of course, he reacted by shouting at Donald to stop, because the milk comes in gallon containers and is not cheap. He assumed this was some kind of weird expression of Donald's inner turmoil that day. Donald was greatly upset when reprimanded and immediately dropped to the floor and began to cry.

The interpretation based on the theory is that Donald did not like the taste of the milk as it was old and might have started to go bad. He might have decided to pour it down the drain as he had seen his parents do with bad milk. What he did not do is defend his action when his father told him to stop. This is exactly what one would expect from a child who does not realize that someone else does not necessarily have the same knowledge as himself. Therefore, the shouted order to stop was a totally unexpected reaction, a shocking turn of events which made no sense to him. His usually loving father should have praised him for throwing away bad milk! This new interpretation greatly helped the parents when comforting Donald.

What makes this interpretation a testable hypothesis is that on a similar occasion it would be possible to check at the critical moment exactly what Donald's belief was. The hypothesis is much more precise than the interpretation that Donald reacted badly to having had a bad day. It focuses on communication failure, and again it focuses only on one aspect of communication, namely the conveying of mental states (thoughts about something). It is here where practical problems arise and where sometimes they can be prevented.

What I hope the theory in this book will offer to those who are close to an autistic person is that it would give them a better understanding of the real handicap that is caused by Autism. This handicap is in its nature more similar to blindness or deafness than to, say, shyness. Imagine trying to bring up a blind child without realizing that it is blind. One might get quite impatient with the child bumping into things! A child cannot learn well from an impatient or angry teacher. Therefore it is important for all teachers, therapists, parents and friends to have some knowledge of the nature of the handicap.

Once a handicap is identified the next question is: Can it be compensated for? There are, for instance, many examples of dyslexic people compensating for their handicap and becoming good readers, despite it all. There are also examples of autistic people who learn what non-literal remarks mean; how to tell from body language if someone is lying; and what to do to make people friendly and helpful. One very bright autistic boy realized early on that he did not catch on to jokes, and it became an obsession with him to learn to get the point. After years of asking to have cartoons explained by his parents he became quite skilful at it, even if he seldom appreciated the joke. Obviously, mentally retarded autistic children could not be expected to compensate to the degree that is sometimes possible in special cases.

Some special cases may seem to the outsider not to be autistic at all. Nothing strange may be noticed in a structured encounter with such a person. It will, however, be possible to tell the difference between well-behaved autistic and normal people outside routine situations which conventional rules do not allow for. It is hard to judge how much effort it costs to achieve outwardly normal behaviour. Many would think even high costs are worth the results, others might choose a different option and, rather than aiming for compensatory learning, decide to make allowances for the handicap and request others to do so as well.

We all can make allowances for different kinds of handicap – think of ramps for wheelchairs, for example. However, we can become intolerant when we do not understand the nature of the handicap. Conversely, the more we understand, the better we can adjust. A totally blind person is more readily given assistance because it is possible to imagine what it is like not to be able to see at all. A person whose sight is impaired in special ways often receives little sympathy. People cannot imagine what such a partial disability is like. They feel bewildered when the person with the white stick starts reading a book.

An autistic person with many compensatory skills might likewise get less sympathy than the one who is totally mute and aloof. 'Surely, he can't be autistic – he makes eye contact and he speaks to me' is a familar remark. Similarly one hears, 'Surely, she can't be dyslexic, she reads a book!' The common point here is that appearances can be deceptive. Compensatory learning does occur, but this does not mean that the underlying handicap has vanished. Furthermore, just as blindness comes in degrees, Autism (and dyslexia) may come in degrees too.

When will there be a proper cure for Autism? Perhaps, when a full understanding of the aetiology is achieved, a means of prevention and treatment will be found. The remedy would have to be applied at the beginning of the chain of causal events that leads to Autism. One might speculate that a treatment could be found to undo the damage, permitting the child to start development afresh. It would be unreasonable to expect anything simpler.

A pertinent example here is the rare Lesch-Nyhan syndrome.[6] Symptoms consist of mental retardation, movement abnormalities, self-mutilation and gout. It seems an unlikely constellation, but a single specific cause has been pinpointed for all. This cause is deficiency in an enzyme (Hypoxanthine-guanine-phospho-ribosyl-transferase). Unfortunately, knowledge of the disorder has not yet led to successful treatment. One might think that supplying the missing enzyme would suffice, but this is not so. Treatment of individual symptoms is necessary even though they are secondary consequences of the underlying pathology. Perhaps the enzyme would act as a cure if it could be supplied at the right time, before birth.

From this example I draw the conclusion that it will be necessary to take account of the psychological symptoms of Autism over and above any hopes for biological cure.

## Sound and Unsound Theories of Autism

As with all disorders where the aetiology is largely unknown, weird and wonderful speculation will flourish. The riddle of the beautiful autistic child locked in his own world is an irresistible challenge to amateur psychologists. They are tempted to base their answers on a few facts and observations. Some make analogies to vaguely related phenomena from elsewhere – for instance, institutionalized infants, monkeys deprived of maternal care, children who refuse to talk, schizophrenic patients or seagulls in conflict. This is not the way to proceed. But how do we know which are sensible ways to proceed?

Any sensible theory of Autism must be compatible with what we know about normal child development and about abnormal development in mentally deficient chidren. For instance, the idea that children with a mental age of less than three should recognize subtle attitudes people have towards them is preposterous. Theories that do not take into account just how different the mind of an autistic child is from that of a normal adult or an animal cannot be taken seriously. In chapter 3, discussing myths of Autism, we came across a variety of them. Amongst the earliest attempts at explanation was the case of the blessed fools of Old Russia, where possession by the Holy Spirit served as a highly workable theory for many centuries. Another theory was advanced to explain the behaviour of the wild boy of Aveyron: total absence of the influences of society and culture. This particular explanation has survived a long time and is a precursor of the theory that Autism is caused by faulty mothering. Since such theories are basically unsound, why are they so popular? Ironically, it is the parents who often hope for environmental rather than intrinsic biological explanations.

> The fact that behavioral development is subject to at least temporary environmental depression is known both to the laity and the profession. Very naturally, therefore, parents of defective children eagerly look for extrinsic causes which might account for the observed retardation. The parents wishfully hope that these causes operate as an obstruction which can be removed by treatment, or which will spontaneously disappear and release the impeded potentialities of development.[7]

This is how Gesell and Amatruda described the problem in 1941, in their classic work on *Developmental Diagnosis*. Parental failure is not at all what parents have in mind when they hope to implicate environmental factors, but it often is prominent amongst such factors in traditional therapists' minds. While some still cling to the unsupported notion that maternal deprivation could be a cause of Autism, the reverse may actually be the case. Poor mother/child bonding, if it is to be associated with Autism at all, must be seen as an effect rather than a cause of Autism. In fact, the popularity of the notion probably stems from metaphorical elaboration of 'autistic aloneness' which, like other myths of Autism, is of symbolic rather than scientific value.

Theories that consider Autism as emotional maladjustment, or as a form of adult mental illness are obsolete. We now know that Autism is a type of mental handicap due to abnormalities of brain development. As Michael Rutter put it in 1983: 'The problem is one of an inherent inadequacy of the child's cognitive equipment rather than performance or function that has 'gone wrong' in equipment which is fundamentally sound in itself.'[8] In pure Autism, it is only mental functions, only some mental functions, and again only some aspects of these that are impaired. The physical appearance of the classic autistic child is normal, the ability to move around is normal, the ability to handle objects is normal. Moreover, in the purest cases, the ability to perceive the world through the senses is normal, and so are the capacities to form abstract concepts, categorize events, understand spatial relationships, know about cause and effect, and make logical inferences. Such is the riddle of Autism that the missing ingredient is so subtle that even in the problem areas of social interaction and communication a great deal of competence exists. This subtle and often elusive ingredient is what a good theory of Autism needs to identify and to explain.

Pure Autism is rare, as the population studies have proved. Autism in combination with other developmental disorders is much more common. It is for this reason that confusion about the essential underlying impairments was inevitable. Theorists can go astray here very easily. After all, there are many autistic children who do not have a normal appearance, cannot move well, are clumsy when handling objects, have problems with their sensory perception, do not speak or have considerable problems in abstract thinking. Many are totally cut off and cannot communicate at all. All of these impairments, striking, significant and handicapping as they are, had to be stripped away because they are not part of the core of Autism. They are therefore not part of a specific theory of Autism. What I have done is focus on the common denominator which underlies all features that are present in the most able as well as the most impaired autistic individuals.

To identify the core features we had to look below the surface of the symptoms. It was then that we could see the red thread that was running through the evidence. It is the inability to draw together information so as to derive coherent and meaningful ideas. There is a fault in the predisposition of the mind to make sense of the world. Just this particular fault in the mechanics of the mind can explain the essential features of Autism. The rest is secondary. If we lose sight of this fact, we lose sight of the overall pattern.

# Suggestions for Further Reading

The literature on Autism is vast. A bibliography spanning the 40 years from 1943 to 1983 listed over 1200 titles of articles and books. The last seven years have probably doubled this number. The references I selected for the interested reader to follow up has been guided by the principle that each reference can serve as a key to a host of further relevant references. This resulted in reviews, book chapters and later papers, being suggested in preference to original papers. The exceptions are those references that act as a documentation for work that I described in some detail and also for conclusions that were drawn on the basis of specific studies which have not usually been quoted in reviews.

For anyone who is keen to explore the topic of Autism in depth, the following publications provide excellent starting points.

The *Journal of Autism and Developmental Disorders*, published by Plenum Press, New York. It comes out four times a year and presents current scientific research. From 1970 to 1978 the name was *Journal of Autism and Childhood Schizophrenia*.

The recent *Handbook of Autism and Pervasive Developmental Disorders*, edited by Donald Cohen, Anne Donnellan and Rhea Paul (published by Wiley's, New York) is a useful compendium.

Eric Schopler and Gary Mesibov are editors of the series 'Current Issues in Autism', published by Plenum Press, New York, at the rate of about one volume every year.

A concise yet comprehensive review of the whole field of Autism research that is still worth consulting although published in 1981 is 'Infantile Autism reviewed: a decade of research', *Schizophrenia Bulletin*, 7, pp. 388–451, by Marian DeMyer with J. N. Hintgen and R. K. Jackson.

A volume edited by Michael Rutter and Eric Schopler (published 1978 by Plenum Press, New York) and entitled *Autism: A Reappraisal of Concepts and Treatment* contains a variety of research reviews which continue to be useful.

Lorna Wing's book: *Autistic Children: A Guide for Parents* is invaluable for anyone who has mainly practical questions in mind. The book was first published in 1980 by Constable, London, and has by now been translated into many different languages.

For those wishing to obtain more information on the effects of mental retardation, I would recommend the compassionate and knowledgeable chapter by Janet Carr, 'The severely retarded autistic child'. In: *Early Childhood Autism: Clinical, Educational and Social Aspects*, edited by Lorna Wing, 2nd Edition, 1976 (Oxford: Pergamon).

Information concerning the autistic child of normal intelligence can be obtained in Digby Tantam's booklet, '*A Mind of One's Own: A Guide to the Special Difficulties and Needs of the More Able Autistic Person for Parents, Professionals and Autistic People*,' published by the National Autistic Society, London, 1988.

*Autism and Asperger's Syndrome* (U.Frith (ed.), Cambridge: Cambridge University Press, 1991) will contain chapters by L. Wing, C. Gillberg, D. Tantam and M. Dewey as well as an annotated translation of Asperger's 1944 landmark paper.

*The Annotated Bibliography of Autism 1943–1983*, eds A. J. Tari, J. L. Clewes and S. J. Semple, which was published in 1985 by the Ontario Society for Autistic Children, Guelph is helpful as a survey and as a guide to literature searches.

# Notes

### Notes to chapter 1 (pp. 1–15)

1 L. Kanner, (1943) 'Autistic disturbances of affective contact', *Nervous Child*, 2, pp. 217–50.

2 H. Asperger, 'Die autistischen Psychopathen im Kindesalter', *Archiv für Psychiatrie und Nervenkrankheiten*, 117 (1944), pp. 76-136.

3 D. Tantam, (1988) 'Asperger's syndrome. Annotation', *Journal of Child Psychology and Psychiatry*, 29, pp. 245–55.

4 American Psychiatric Association (1987), *Diagnostic and Statistical Manual of Mental Disorders*, 3rd rev. edn (DSM-III-R) (Washington, DC: American Psychiatric Association).

5 World Health Organization (1987), *Mental Disorders: A Glossary and Guide to their Classification in Accordance with the 10th Revision of the International Classification of Diseases (ICD-10)* (Geneva: World Health Organization).

6 M. Rutter and E. Schopler (1987), 'Autism and pervasive developmental disorders: concepts and diagnostic issues', *Journal of Autism and Developmental Disorders*, 17, pp. 159–86.

7 M. Rutter and L. Hersov (eds) (1985), *Child and Adolescent Psychiatry: Modern Approaches*, 2nd edn (Oxford: Blackwell).

8 C. C. Park (1987), *The Siege: The First Eight Years of an Autistic Child*; 2nd edn, with an epilogue: 'Fifteen Years After' (Boston, Mass.: Atlantic-Little, Brown).

9 P. Everard (1980), *Involuntary Strangers* (London: John Clare).

10 A. Lovell (1978), *In a Summer Garment: The Experience of an Autistic Child* (London: Secker & Warburg). Published in paperback as *Simple Simon* (London: Lion Publishers, 1983).

11 E. Schopler and G. B. Mesibov (eds) (1983), *Autism in Adolescents and Adults* (New York: Plenum Press).

## Notes to chapter 2 (pp. 16–35)

1 H. Lane (1977), *The Wild Boy of Aveyron* (Cambridge, Mass.: Harvard University Press/London: Allen & Unwin; pb edn Granada, 1979).
2 A. Ritter von Feuerbach (1832), *Kaspar Hauser: An account of an individual kept in a dungeon separated from all communication with the world from early childhood to about the age of 17* (original publication; English trans. London: Simpkin & Marshall, 1833).
3 S. Curtiss (1977), *Genie: A Psychological Study of a Modern-day 'Wild Child'* (New York: Academic Press).
4 D. Skuse (1984), 'Extreme deprivation in early childhood. II. Theoretical issues and a comparative review.' *Journal of Clinical Psychology and Psychiatry*, 25, pp. 543–72.


## Notes to chapter 3 (pp. 36–50)

1 N. Challis and H. W. Dewey (1974), 'The blessed fools of Old Russia', *Jahrbücher für Geschichte Osteuropas*, NS 22, pp. 1–11.
2 Dom R. Hudleston, *The Little Flowers of St Francis of Assisi* (1st English trans., rev. and amended; London: Burns Oates, 1953).
3 J. Wyndham (1960), *The Midwich Cuckoos* (Harmondsworth: Penguin; 1st publ. 1957).
4 E. T. A. Hoffmann (*c.* 1814), *The Best Tales of Hoffmann* (Stories 1st publ.; English trans. New York: Dover, 1967).
5 P. K. Dick (1972), *Do Androids Dream of Electric Sheep?* (London: Panther).
6 J. Weizenbaum (1976), *Computer Power and Human Reason: From Judgement to Calculation* (San Francisco: Freeman & Co.).


## Notes to chapter 4 (pp. 51–67)

1 V. Lotter (1966), 'Epidemiology of autistic conditions in young children: I. Prevalence', *Social Psychiatry*, 1, pp. 124–37.
2 V. Lotter (1967), 'Epidemiology of autistic conditions in young children: II. Some characteristics of the parents and children', *Social Psychiatry*, 1, pp. 163–73.
3 S. E. Bryson, B. S. Clark and I. M. Smith (1988), 'First report of a Canadian epidemiological study of autistic syndromes'. *Journal of Child Psychology and Psychiatry*, 29, pp. 433–45.
4 C. Lord, E. Schopler and D. Revicki (1982), 'Sex differences in autism', *Journal of Autism and Developmental Disorders*, 12, pp. 317–30.
5 L. Wing (1981), 'Sex ratios in early childhood autism and related conditions', *Psychiatry Research*, 5, pp. 129–37.
6 E. Newson, M. Dawson and P. Everard (1984), 'The natural history of able

autistic people: their management in social context. Summary of the report to the DHSS in four parts', *Communication*, 18, pp. 1–4, and 19, pp. 1–2.

7  M. Rutter and L. Lockyer (1967), 'A five to fifteen year follow-up study of infantile psychosis: I. Description of sample', *British Journal of Psychiatry* 113, pp. 1169–82.

8  B. J. Freeman, E. R. Ritvo, R. Needleman and A. Yokota (1985), 'The stability of cognitive and linguistic parameters in autism: a five-year prospective study', *Journal of the American Academy of Child Psychiatry*, 24, pp. 459–64.

9  H. C. Steinhausen, D. Gobel, M. Breinlinger and B. Wohlleben (1986), 'A community survey of infantile autism', *Journal of the American Academy of Child Psychiatry*, 25, pp. 186–9.

10 G. I. Goldstein and D. F. Lancy (1985), 'Cognitive development in autistic children', in L. S. Siegel and F. J. Morrison (eds), *Cognitive Development in Atypical Children: Progress in Cognitive Development Research* (New York: Springer).

11 E. Schopler, C. E. Andrews and K. Strupp (1979), 'Do autistic children come from middle class parents?', *Journal of Autism and Developmental Disorders*, 9, pp. 139–52.

12 L. Wing (1980), 'Childhood autism and social class: a question of selection?', *British Journal of Psychiatry*, 137, pp. 410–17.

13 C. Gillberg (1984), 'Infantile autism and other childhood psychoses in a Swedish region: epidemiological aspects', *Journal of Child Psychology and Psychiatry*, 25, pp. 35–43.

14 W. H. Green, M. Campbell, A. S. Hardesty, D. M. Grega, M. Padron-Gayol, J. Shell and L. Erlenmeyer-Kimling (1984), 'A comparison of schizophrenic and autistic children', *Journal of the American Academy of Child Psychiatry*, 23, pp. 399–409.

15 S. Wolff, S. Narayan and B. Moyes (1988), 'Personality characteristics of parents of autistic children', *Journal of Child Psychology and Psychiatry*, 29, 143–53.

16 L. Wing and J. Gould (1979), 'Severe impairments of social interaction and associated abnormalities in children: epidemiology and classification', *Journal of Autism and Developmental Disorders*, 9, pp. 11–30.

17 L. Wing and A. J. Attwood (1987), 'Syndromes of autism and atypical development', in D. J. Cohen, A. Donnellan and R. Paul (eds), *Handbook of Autism and Pervasive Developmental Disorders* (New York: Wiley).

18 American Psychiatric Association (1987), *Diagnostic and Statistical Manual of Mental Disorders*, 3rd rev. edn (DSM-III-R) (Washington, DC: American Psychiatric Association).

19 L. Wing (1988), 'The continuum of autistic characteristics', in E. Schopler and G. B. Mesibov (eds), *Diagnosis and Assessment* (New York: Plenum Press).

20 I. Kolvin et al. (1971), 'Studies in the childhood psychoses I to VI', *British Journal of Psychiatry*, 118, pp. 381–419.

21 Green et al. (see n. 14).

22 L. Petty, E. M. Ornitz, J. D. Michelman and E. G. Zimmerman (1984), 'Autistic children who become schizophrenic', *Archives of General Psychiatry*, 41, pp. 129–35.

23 E. M. Ornitz, D. Guthrie and A. H. Farley (1977), 'The early development of autistic children', *Journal of Autism and Childhood Schizophrenia*, 7, pp. 207–30.

24 Newson et al. (see n. 6).

25 H. Knobloch and B. Pasamanick (1975), 'Some etiologic and prognostic factors in early infantile autism and psychosis', *Pediatrics*, 55, pp. 182–91.

## Notes to chapter 5 (pp 68–81)

1 A. M. Thompson, (1986), 'Adam – a severely deprived Colombian orphan: a case report', *Journal of Child Psychology and Psychiatry*, 27, pp. 689–95.

2 C. Gillberg and S. Steffenburg (1987), 'Outcome and prognostic factors in infantile autism and similar conditions: a population-based study of 46 cases followed through puberty', *Journal of Autism and Developmental Disorders*, 17, pp. 273–87.

3 M. Coleman and C. Gillberg (1985), *The Biology of the Autistic Syndromes* (New York: Praeger).

4 E. Schopler and G. B. Mesibov (eds) (1987), *Neurobiological Issues in Autism* (New York: Plenum Press).

5 L. Wing (ed.) (1988), *Aspects of Autism: Biological Research*. (London: Gaskell, Royal College of Psychiatrists).

6 M. L. Bauman and T. L. Kemper (1985), 'Histoanatomic observations of the brain in early infantile autism', *Neurology*, 35, pp. 866–74.

7 H. A. Walker (1978), 'A dermatoglyphic study of autistic patients', *Journal of Autism and Childhood Schizophrenia*, 7, pp. 11–21.

8 H. V. Soper, P. Satz, D. L. Orsini, R. R. Henry, J. C. Zvi and M. Schulman (1986), 'Handedness patterns in autism suggest subtypes', *Journal of Autism and Developmental Disorders*, 16, pp. 155–66.

9 G. R. Delong (1978), 'A neuropsychologic interpretation of infantile autism', in M. Rutter and E. Schopler (eds), *Autism: A Reappraisal of Concepts and Treatment* (New York: Plenum Press).

10 D. Fein, M. Humes, E. Kaplan, D. Lucci and L. Waterhouse (1984), 'The question of left hemisphere dysfunction in infantile autism', *Psychological Bulletin*, 95, pp. 258–81.

11 E. Courchesne, R. Yeung-Courchesne, G. A. Press, J. R. Hesselink and T. L. Jernigan (1988), 'Hypoplasia of cerebeller lobules VI and VII in autism', *New England Journal of Medicine*, 318, pp. 1349–54.

12 G. M. Anderson and Y. Hoshino (1987), 'Neurochemical studies of autism', in D. J. Cohen, A. Donnellan and R. Paul (eds), *Handbook of Autism and Pervasive Developmental Disorders* (New York: Wiley).

13 A. L. James and R. J. Barry (1980), 'A review of psychophysiology in early onset psychosis', *Schizophrenia Bulletin*, 6, pp. 506–25.

14 A. R. Damasio and R. G. Maurer (1978), 'A neurological model for childhood autism', *Archives of Neurology*, 35, pp. 777–86.
15 B. E. Hetzler and J. L. Griffin (1981), 'Infantile autism and the temporal lobe of the brain', *Journal of Autism and Developmental Disorders*, 11, pp. 317–30.
16 R. Ridley and H. F. Baker (1983), 'Is there a relationship between social isolation, cognitive inflexibility, and behavioural stereotypy? An analysis of the effects of amphetamine in the marmoset', in K. A. Miczek (ed.), *Ethopharmacology: Primate Models of Neuropsychiatric Disorders* (New York: Liss).
17 J. M. Rumsey and S. D. Hamburger (1988), 'Neuropsychological findings in high-functioning men with infantile autism, residual state', *Journal of Clinical and Experimental Neuropsychology*, 10, pp. 201–21.
18 D. Fein, B. Pennington, P. Markovitz, M. Braverman and L. Waterhouse (1986), 'Toward a neuropsychological model of infantile autism: are the social deficits primary?', *Journal of American Academic Childhood Psychiatry*, 25, pp. 198–212.
19 S. Folstein and M. Rutter (1977), 'Infantile autism: a genetic study of 21 twin pairs', *Journal of Child Psychology and Psychiatry*, 18, pp. 297–321.
20 G. S. Fish, I. L. Cohen, E. G. Wolf, W. T. Brown, E. C. Jenkins and A. Gross (1986), 'Autism and the fragile-X syndrome', *American Journal of Psychiatry*, 143, pp. 71–3.
21 I. Kolvin, C. Ounsted and M. Roth (1971), 'Studies in the childhood psychoses. V. Cerebral dysfunction and childhood psychoses.' *British Journal of Psychiatry*, 118, pp. 407–14.
22 M. Konstantareas (1986), 'Early developmental backgrounds of autistic and mentally retarded children. Future research directions', *Psychiatric Clinics of North America*, 9, pp. 671–88.
23 E. G. Stubbs (1988), 'The viral-autoimmune hypothesis. Does intrauterine cytomegalovirus plus antibodies contribute to autism?' in L. Wing (ed.) *Aspects of Autism: Biological Research*. (London: Gaskell, Royal College of Psychiatrists).
24 L. Wing (1979), 'Mentally retarded children in Camberwell (London)', in H. Hafner (ed.), *Estimating Needs for Mental Health Care* (Berlin: Springer).
25 C. Gillberg, L. Anderson, S. Steffenburg and B. Borjesson (1987), 'Infantile autism in children of immigrant parents. A population-based study in Göteborg, Sweden', *British Journal of Psychiatry*, 150, pp. 856–8.

### Notes to chapter 6 (pp. 82–102)

1 A. Gesell and C. S. Amatruda (1974), *Developmental Diagnosis – Normal and Abnormal Development*, 3rd rev. edn (New York: Harper & Row; 1st edn, 1941).
2 L. Kanner (1971), 'Follow-up study of eleven autistic children originally reported in 1943', *Journal of Autism and Childhood Schizophrenia*, 1, pp. 119–45.

3 L. Lockyer and M. Rutter (1970), 'A five to fifteen year follow-up study of infantile psychosis: IV. Patterns of cognitive ability', *British Journal of Social and Clinical Psychology*, 9, pp. 152–63.

4 L. Waterhouse and D. Fein (1984), 'Developmental trends in cognitive skills for children diagnosed as autistic and schizophrenic', *Child Development*, 55, pp. 236–48.

5 L. Selfe (1977), *Nadia: A Case of Extraordinary Drawing Ability in an Autistic Child* (London: Academic Press).

6 S. Wiltshire (1987), *Drawings: Selected and with an Introduction by Sir Hugh Casson* (London: Dent).

7 N. O'Connor and B. Hermelin (1988), 'Low intelligence and special abilities. Annotation', *Journal of Child Psychology and Psychiatry*, 29, pp. 391–6.

8 R. F. Asarnow, P. E. Tanguay, L. Bott and B. J. Freeman (1987), 'Patterns of intellectual functioning in non-retarded autistic and schizophrenic children', *Journal of Child Psychology and Psychiatry*, 28, pp. 273–80.

9 M. Ohta (1987), 'Cognitive disorders of infantile autism: a study employing the WISC, spatial relationship conceptualization and gesture imitations', *Journal of Autism and Developmental Disorders*, 17, pp. 45–62.

10 T. N. Carraher, D. W. Carraher and A. D. Schliemann (1985), 'Mathematics in the street and schools', *British Journal of Developmental Psychology*, 3, pp. 21–9.

11 M. Donaldson (1978), *Children's Minds* (Glasgow: Fontana/Collins).

12 B. Hermelin and N. O'Connor (1970), *Psychological Experiments with Autistic Children* (Oxford: Pergamon).

13 U. Frith (1970), 'Studies in pattern detection in normal and autistic children: I. Immediate recall of auditory sequences', *Journal of Abnormal Psychology*, 76, pp. 413–20.

14 U. Aurnhammer-Frith (1969), 'Emphasis and meaning in recall in normal and autistic children', *Language and Speech*, 12, pp. 29–38.

15 U. Frith (1970), 'Studies in pattern detection in normal and autistic children: II. Reproduction and production of color sequences', *Journal of Experimental Child Psychology*, 10, pp. 120–35.

16 A. Shah and U. Frith (1983), 'An islet of ability in autistic children: a research note', *Journal of Child Psychology and Psychiatry*, 24: 4, pp. 613–20.

17 R. Kolinsky, J. Morais and A. Content (1987), 'Finding parts within figures: a developmental study'. *Perception*, 16, pp. 399–407.

18 H. A. Witkin and D. R. Goodenough (1981), '*Cognitive Styles: Essence and Origins.*' (New York: International University Press).

### Notes to chapter 7 (pp. 103–17)

1 J. R. Bemporad (1979), 'Adult recollections of a formerly autistic child', *Journal of Autism and Developmental Disorders*, 9, pp. 179–98.

2 U. Frith and S. Baron-Cohen, 'Perception in autistic children', in D. J. Cohen, A. Donnellan and R. Paul (eds) (1987), *Handbook of Autism and Pervasive Developmental Disorders* (New York: Wiley).

3 J. L. Borges (1956), 'Funes the Memorious'; English trans. in *Fictions* (New York: New Directions, 1962).

4 E. Schopler (1965), 'Early infantile autism and receptor processes', *Archives of General Psychiatry*, 13, p. 327.

5 B. Hermelin and N. O'Connor (1970), *Psychological Experiments with Autistic Children* (Oxford: Pergamon).

6 J. A. Ungerer and M. Sigman (1987), 'Categorization of skills and receptive language development in autistic children', *Journal of Autism and Developmental Disorders*, 17, pp. 3–16.

7 O. I. Lovaas, R. L. Koegel and L. Schreibman (1979), 'Stimulus over-selectivity in autism: a review of research', Psychological Bulletin, 86, pp. 1236–54.

8 S. J. Weeks and R. P. Hobson (1987), 'The salience of facial expression for autistic children', *Journal of Child Psychology and Psychiatry*, 28, pp. 137–52.

9 D. Park and P. Youderian (1974), 'Light and number: ordering principles in the world of an autistic child', *Journal of Autism and Childhood Schizophrenia*, 4, pp. 313–23.

10 T. Grandin and M. Scariano (1986), *Emergence Labelled Autistic* (Tunbridge Wells, Kent: Costello).

11 U. Frith and B. Hermelin (1969), 'The role of visual and motor cues for normal, subnormal and autistic children', *Journal of Child Psychology and Psychiatry*, 10, pp. 153–63.

12 G. Perec (1978), trans. D. Bellos, *Life, a User's Manual* (London: Collins, 1987; original publ. Paris: Hachette).

13 C. D. Frith and D. J. Done (in press), 'Stereotyped Behaviour in Madness and in Health', in S. F. Cooper and C. T. Dourish (eds), *The Neurobiology of Behavioural Stereotypy* (Oxford: Oxford University Press).

14 G. Berkson and R. K. Davenport, Jr (1962), 'Stereotyped movements of mental defectives: I. Initial survey', *American Journal of Mental Deficiency*, 66, pp. 849–52.

15 G. Murphy (1985), 'Self-injurious behaviour in the mentally handicapped: an update', *Association of Child Psychology and Psychiatry Newsletter*, 7, pp. 2–11.

16 J. Asendorpf (1980), 'Nichtreaktive Stressmessung: Bewegungsstereotypien als Aktivierungsindikatoren', *Zeitschrift für experimentelle und angewandte Psychologie*, 27, pp. 44–58.

17 R. Ridley and H. F. Baker (1983), 'Is there a relationship between social isolation, cognitive inflexibility and behavioural stereotypy? An analysis of the effects of amphetamine in the marmoset', in K. A. Miczek (ed.), *Ethopharmacology: Primate Models of Neuropsychiatric Disorders* (New York: Liss).

18 U. Frith (1972), 'Cognitive mechanisms in autism: experiments with color and tone sequence production', *Journal of Autism and Childhood Schizophrenia*, 2, pp. 160–73.

19 J. Boucher (1977), 'Alternation and sequencing behaviour, and response to novelty in autistic children', *Journal of Child Psychology and Psychiatry*, 18, pp. 67–72.

## Notes to chapter 8 (pp. 118–35)

1 R. Paul (1987), 'Communication', in D. J. Cohen, A. Donnellan and R. Paul (eds), *Handbook of Autism and Pervasive Development Disorders* (New York: Wiley).
2 E. Schopler and G. Mesibov (eds) (1985), *Communication Problems in Autism* (New York: Plenum Press).
3 W. H. Fay and A. L. Schuler (1980), *Emerging Language in Autistic Children* (Baltimore: University Park Press/London: Arnold).
4 S. Baron-Cohen (1988), 'Social and pragmatic deficits in autism: cognitive or affective?' *Journal of Autism and Developmental Disorders*, 18, pp. 379–402.
5 H. Tager-Flusberg (in press), 'A psycholinguistic perspective on language development in the autistic child', in G. Dawson (ed.), *Autism: New Directions on Diagnosis, Nature and Treatment* (New York: Guildford Press).
6 L. Bartak, M. Rutter and A. Cox (1975), 'A comparative study of infantile autism and specific developmental receptive language disorders: I. The children', *British Journal of Psychiatry*, 126, pp. 127–45.
7 D. Cantwell, L. Baker, and M. Rutter (1978), 'A comparative study of infantile autism and specific developmental receptive language disorders. IV. analysis of syntax and language function.' *Journal of Child Psychology and Psychiatry*, 19, pp. 351–62.
8 A. Schuler and B. M. Prizant (1985), 'Echolalia', in E. Schopler and G. B. Mesibov (eds), *Communication Problems in Autism* (New York: Plenum Press).
9 L. Kanner (1946), 'Irrelevant and metaphorical language in early infantile autism', *American Journal of Psychiatry*, 103, pp. 242–6.
10 L. Bartak and M. Rutter (1974), 'The use of personal pronouns by autistic children', *Journal of Autism and Childhood Schizophrenia*, 4, pp. 217–22.
11 A. Karmiloff-Smith (1985), 'Language and cognitive processes from a developmental perspective', *Language and Cognitive Processes*, 1, pp. 61–85.
12 M. Snowling and U. Frith (1986), 'Comprehension in "hyperlexic" readers', *Journal of Experimental Child Psychology*, 42, pp. 392–415.
13 T. Grandin and M. Scariano (1986), *Emergence Labelled Autistic* (Tunbridge Wells, Kent: Costello).
14 F. Curcio and J. Paccia (1987), 'Conversations with autistic children: contingent relationships between features of adult and children's response adequacy.' *Journal of Autism and Developmental Disorders*, 17, pp. 81–93.
15 C. A. M. Baltaxe (1977), 'Pragmatic deficits in the language of autistic adolescents', *Journal of Pediatric Psychology*, 2, pp. 176–80.
16 C. A. M. Baltaxe and J. Q. Simmons (1985), 'Prosodic development in normal and autistic children', in Schopler and Mesibov (eds), *Communication Problems in Autism* (New York: Plenum Press).
17 D. Sperber and D. Wilson (1986), *Relevance, Communication and Cognition* (Oxford: Blackwell).
18 Jerzy Kosinski (1980), *Being There* (London: Black Swan).

## Notes to chapter 9 (pp. 136–55)

1 F. R. Volkmar, S. S. Sparrow, D. Goudereau, D. V. Cicchetti, R. Paul and D. J. Cohen (1987), 'Social deficits in autism: an operational approach using the Vineland Adaptive Behavior Scales', *Journal of the American Academy of Child Psychiatry*, 26, 156–61.

2 B. Hermelin and N. O'Connor (1970), *Psychological Experiments with Autistic Children* (Oxford: Pergamon).

3 M. Rutter (1983), 'Cognitive deficits in the pathogenesis of autism.' (p. 526) *Journal of Child Psychology and Psychiatry*, 24, pp. 513–31.

4 H. Knobloch and B. Pasamanick (1975), 'Some etiologic and prognostic factors in early infantile autism and psychosis', *Pediatrics*, 55, pp. 182–91.

5 M. Sigman and J. A. Ungerer (1984), 'Attachment behaviors in autistic children', *Journal of Autism and Developmental Disorders*, 14, pp. 231–44.

6 M. Sigman, P. Mundy, T. Sherman and J. Ungerer (1986), 'Social interactions of autistic, mentally retarded, and normal children and their caregivers', *Journal of Child Psychology and Psychiatry*, 27, pp. 647–56.

7 P. Mundy, M. Sigman, J. Ungerer and T. Sherman (1986), 'Defining the social deficit of autism: the contribution of non-verbal communication measures', *Journal of Child Psychology and Psychiatry*, 27, pp. 657–69.

8 K. A. Loveland and S. H. Landry (1986), 'Joint attention and language in autism and developmental language delay', *Journal of Autism and Developmental Disorders*, 16, pp. 335–49.

9 F. Curcio (1978), 'Sensorimotor functioning and communication in mute autistic children', *Journal of Autism and Childhood Schizophrenia*, 8, pp. 281–92.

10 R. P. Hobson (1986a), 'The autistic child's appraisal of expressions of emotion', *Journal of Child Psychology and Psychiatry*, 27, pp. 321–42.

11 R. P. Hobson (1986b), 'The autistic child's appraisal of emotion: a further study', *Journal of Child Psychology and Psychiatry*, 27, pp. 671–80.

12 D. M. Ricks and L. Wing (1976), 'Language, communication and the use of symbols in normal and autistic children', in L. Wing (ed.), *Early Childhood Autism: Clinical, Educational and Social Aspects*, 2nd edn (Oxford: Pergamon).

13 A. H. Attwood, U. Frith and B. Hermelin (1988), 'The understanding and use of interpersonal gestures by autistic and Down's syndrome children', *Journal of Autism and Developmental Disorders*, 18, pp. 241–57.

14 J. W. Astington, P. L. Harris and D. R. Olson (eds) (1988), *Developing Theories of Mind* (Cambridge: Cambridge University Press).

15 D. Premack and G. Woodruff (1978), 'Does the chimpanzee have a theory of mind?', *Behavioural and Brain Sciences*, 4, pp. 515–26.

16 H. Wimmer and J. Perner (1983), 'Beliefs about beliefs: representation and constraining function of wrong beliefs in young children's understanding of deception', *Cognition*, 13, pp. 103–28.

## Notes to chapter 10 (pp. 156–74)

1 B. Nicolson and C. Wright (1974), *Georges de la Tour* (London: Phaidon).
2 H. Wimmer and J. Perner, (see chapter 9, note 16)
3 S. Baron-Cohen, A. M. Leslie and U. Frith (1985), 'Does the autistic child have a "theory of mind"?', *Cognition*, 21, pp. 37–46.
4 A. M. Leslie and U. Frith (1988), 'Autistic children's understanding of seeing, knowing and believing', *British Journal of Developmental Psychology*, 4, pp. 315–24.
5 J. Perner, U. Frith, A. M. Leslie and S. R. Leekam (in press), 'Exploration of the autistic child's theory of mind: knowledge, belief and communication', *Child Development*.
6 S. Baron-Cohen, A. M. Leslie and U. Frith (1986), 'Mechanical, behavioural and intentional understanding of picture stories in autistic children', *British Journal of Developmental Psychology*, 4, pp. 113–25.
7 T. Landolfi (1961), *Gogol's Wife and Other Stories* (English trans. New York: New Directions).
8 A. M. Leslie (1987), 'Pretense and representation: the origins of "theory of mind"', *Psychological Review*, 94, pp. 412–26.
9 L. Wing (1981), 'Language, social and cognitive impairments in autism and severe mental retardation', *Journal of Autism and Developmental Disorders*, 11, pp. 31–44.
10 D. Premack (1986), *Gavagai! Or the Future History of the Animal Language Controversy* (Cambridge, Mass.: MIT Press).

## Notes to chapter 11 (pp. 175–87)

1 J. Perner, U. Frith, A. M. Leslie and S. Leekam (in press), 'Exploration of the autistic child's theory of mind: knowledge, belief and communication', *Child Development*.
2 M. Coleman and C. Gillberg (1985), *The Biology of Autistic Syndromes* (New York: Praeger).
3 D. Sperber and D. Wilson (1986), *Relevance, Communication and Cognition* (Oxford: Blackwell), p. 15.
4 M. Rutter and L. Bartak (1973), 'Special education treatment of autistic children: a comparative study: I. Follow-up findings and implications for services', *Journal of Child Psychology and Psychiatry*, 14, pp. 241–70.
5 P. Howlin and M. Rutter (with M. Berger, R. Hemsley, L. Hersov and W. Yule) (1987), *Treatment of Autistic Children* (Chichester: Wiley).
6 W. L. Nyhan (1978), 'The Lesch-Nyhan syndrome', *Developmental Medicine and Child Neurology*, 20, pp. 376–8.
7 A. Gesell and C. S. Amatruda (1974), *Developmental Diagnosis – Normal and Abnormal Development*, 3rd rev. edn (New York: Harper & Row; 1st edn, 1941).
8 M. Rutter (1983), 'Cognitive deficits in the pathogenesis of autism', *Journal of Child Psychology and Psychiatry*, 24, pp. 513–31.

# Index